MotoGP
Season Review 2005

OFFICIAL TIMEKEEPER

MotoGP

WORLD CHAMPIONSHIP

MotoGP
Season Review 2005
Julian Ryder

Published in November 2005

A catalogue record for this book is available from the British Library

ISBN 1 84425 233 7

Library of Congress catalog card no. 2005926145

Haynes Publishing, Sparkford, Yeovil,
Somerset BA22 7JJ, UK
Tel: +44 (0) 1963 442030
Fax: +44 (0) 1963 440001
E-mail: sales@haynes.co.uk
Website: www.haynes.co.uk

Haynes North America, Inc.,
861 Lawrence Drive, Newbury Park,
California 91320, USA

Printed and bound by J.H.Haynes & Co Ltd,
Sparkford, Yeovil, Somerset BA22 7JJ, UK

This product is officially licensed by Dorna SL, owners of the MotoGP trademark (© Dorna 2005)

Managing Editor Louise McIntyre
Design Lee Parsons, Richard Parsons
Sub-editor Kay Edge
Advertising Sales David Dew (Motocom)
Photography Covers, The Season, Riders' Rider of the Year portraits, and race action by Andrew Northcott/AJRN Sports Photography. Portraits of Mick Doohan and MotoGP riders in The Season in Focus by Mark Wernham. Pages 11 (main), 20, 63, 64/65, 130, 131 (bottom), 133 (top), 134 (top) and 168/169 by Milagro

Author's Acknowledgements

Thanks to:

In the paddock Jerry Burgess and his crew, Mike Trimby and all IRTA staff, Randy Mamola, David Dew, Stuart Shenton, Chuck Aksland, Jurgen Fuchs, Peter Clifford, Yoko Togashi, Ian Wheeler, Ali Forth, Mac Mackay, Phaedra Haramis, Chaz Davies, James Ellison, Shakey Byrne, and especially Mick Doohan for writing the Foreword

In the press room Andrew Northcott for the stunning action pictures in this book, Mark Wernham for much of the portraiture, Neil Spalding, Nick Harris, Eva Jirsenska, Dr Martin Raines, Toby Moody and my other colleagues at Eurosport; and in affectionate memory of Maurice Bula

CONTENTS
MotoGP 2005

Natural born winner.

2005 MotoGP
WORLD CHAMP7ON

New MOTUL 300V Factory Line range
High performance and reliable.

Designed and developed in conjonction with some of the world's top factory racing teams, our new 300V Factory Line range incorporates all our latest technological innovations.

TEAM SPONSOR
YAMAHA
FACTORY RACING
MOTO GP 2005

MOTUL

fluid force

FOREWORD
MICK DOOHAN

If Valentino Rossi stays fit and motivated there's every chance he will break Giacomo Agostini's records and become the greatest rider in the history of 500cc or MotoGP road racing.

Valentino dominated MotoGP again in 2005, claiming a fifth successive championship title and winning 11 races. He's won an incredible 53 races in just six years in the class and switching from Honda to Yamaha has made no difference to his performances.

It's possible Valentino is already the best rider ever, especially when you factor in his 125cc and 250cc World Championship titles earlier in his career.

Statistics don't mean everything, but they don't lie either, and if Valentino can maintain his current strike-rate and better Agostini's records then it will confirm his position through sheer weight of results. Ago won eight championships and 68 Grand Prix races, the most of any rider since the premier road racing category began in 1949. Valentino and I are second equal in championships, both winning five. In terms of race wins I'm second on 54, one more than Valentino, but I'd expect him to go past me early next season.

The thing that sets Valentino apart from his current rivals is his consistency. He finished on the podium 16 times from 17 races in 2005, with Marco Melandri next best with seven. Consistency is what wins championships, as well as talent and determination. Valentino excels in all these areas – he's always a factor regardless of the track conditions, weather, or any other variables which come into play.

There are some other reasons behind Valentino's success. His father Graziano raced Grand Prix bikes so Valentino grew up in the paddock and that gave him a good grounding in the sport and how everything works.

Valentino works hard and thinks about every aspect of his racing. He's also fortunate to have linked up with Jerry Burgess, who previously helped me win my championships. The continuity from this type of relationship creates a stable working environment.

Other riders who switch teams usually have to develop new working relationships, but when Valentino went from Honda to Yamaha he took Jerry and some of his crew with him, and that's been a factor for sure.

In the second half of the 2005 season we saw Melandri and Nicky Hayden come on strong. They are young and improving, and if they keep getting consistently quicker then they may be the biggest challenge Valentino faces in trying to break Agostini's records. They both won their first MotoGP race in 2005, in what was their third year in the class. Both have now proved they can win, and one of the exciting things about 2006 will be to see whether they can take it to Valentino on a race-by-race basis.

There's plenty to look forward to.

MICK DOOHAN
WORLD CHAMPION 1994, '95, '96, '97 & '98

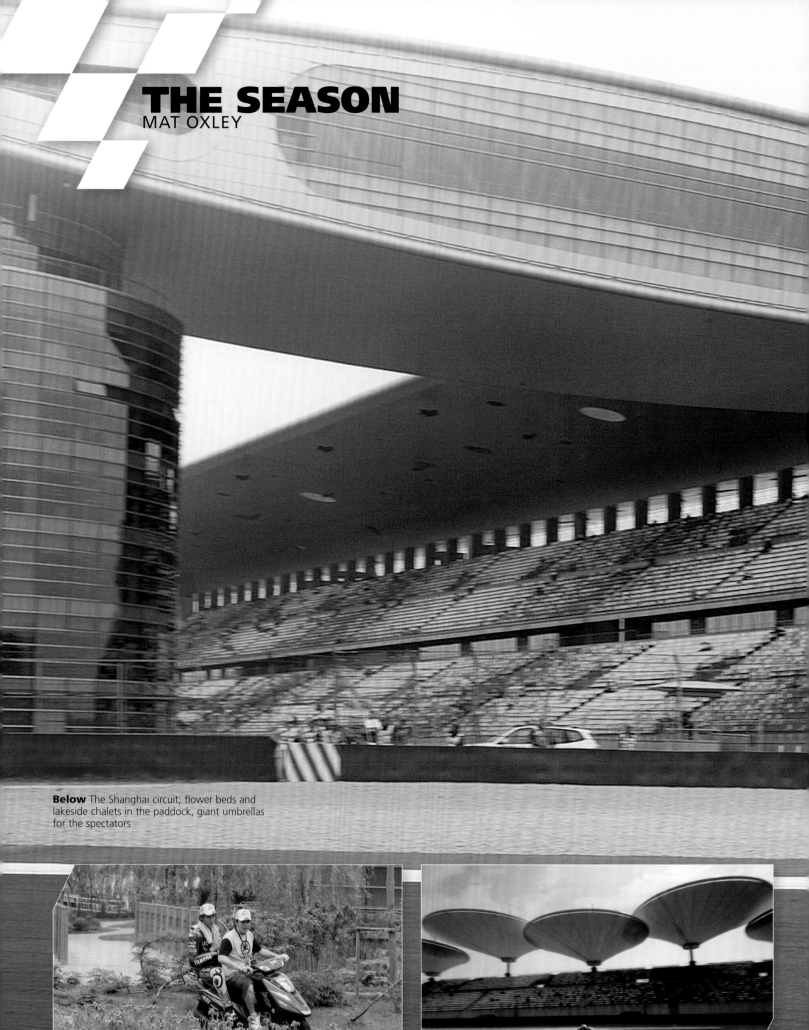

THE SEASON
MAT OXLEY

Below The Shanghai circuit; flower beds and lakeside chalets in the paddock, giant umbrellas for the spectators

A YEAR OF LIVING DANGEROUSLY

New countries, new tracks, new winners: MotoGP 2005 had everything. Thankfully it also remained true to its roots and gave us racing that'll be talked about for decades

In troubled times, motorcycle racing can provide a cosy little world in which to lose oneself, for brief moments of self-indulgence at least. As bike-mad Hollywood legend Steve McQueen once said: 'Every time I start thinking of the world as all bad, I see people out having a good time on motorcycles, makes me take another look.'

Of course, MotoGP isn't a cosy little world. It isn't just a bunch of people mucking about on motorcycles, it's the fastest, loudest, scariest two-wheel contest known to humanity, with riders performing the kind of superhuman feats of skill and daring that make F1 cars seem little more than a terrifyingly expensive version of a PlayStation game – a steering wheel, a few buttons and an invoice for several hundred million dollars.

The reason that MotoGP continues to attract more and more fans is simple – in a world awash with over-hyped, overly contrived sporting events it's something very real, it's what motorsport should be all about: competitors riding the fine line between glory and disaster, using

eat, breathe, live MotoGP?

You've bought the book, now relive the very best of the action on DVD and VHS.

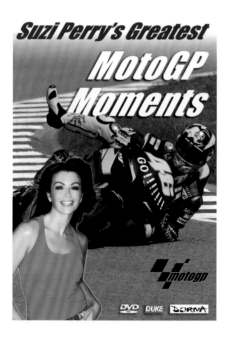

MotoGP Review 2005
Relive an awesome, high-octane season of racing as MotoGP Review 2005 brings you all the exciting highlights from the practices and races, and an on-board lap from every circuit. See the thrills and spills of the races as no spectator can, via on-bike and trackside cameras in this sensational season review. A must-have for any fan, old or new!
DVD £19.99 180+mins No.1737
VHS £16.99 180mins No.1738

MotoGP 250/125 Review 2005
This official review of the 125 and 250cc classes will have you on the edge of your seat as it brings all the exhilarating action from the 2005 season to life. The programme includes the sensational highlights from each and every one of the rounds plus interviews with the eventual 2005 champions.
DVD £19.99 180+mins No.1739

Suzi Perry's
Greatest MotoGP Moments
In this Official MotoGP production, TV presenter Suzi Perry brings you the most exhilarating moments of MotoGP World Championship action from the past three seasons. Featuring Rossi, Gibernau, Chili, Checa, Capirossi, Biaggi, Hayden, Melandri, Barros, Edwards and others. Enjoy the spectacular slides and falls, the championship-deciding manoeuvres, ecstatic celebrations and behind-the-scenes private moments. Share some weird and wacky moments too!
DVD £16.99 60+mins No.1760

technique and technology to bend the laws of physics just as far as they'll go, taking big risks for big rewards. It's the original extreme sport, and that's extreme with an E, not an X. If Ernest Hemingway were alive today, his celebrated opinion of the sporting world would have been slightly different from the original; something like this, perhaps: 'There are only three sports: bullfighting, motorcycle racing and mountaineering; all the rest are merely games.'

No, MotoGP isn't for the timid. Which is why its biggest stars of 2005 were lion-hearted men like Valentino Rossi, Loris Capirossi, Nicky Hayden and Marco Melandri, all four personifying the motorcycle racing ideal – shockingly fast and aggressive on the track, sweet and charming off it (well mostly, anyway). We're lucky that the grid is still populated by such people, young men with no airs and graces, even though they're finally joining the ranks of the super-rich. During 2005 Rossi became the first MotoGP racer to be ranked in the Forbes rich list, his 2004 earnings estimated at €24 million, and his celebrity rating just below former US president Bill Clinton. And yet Rossi still isn't a celebrity in the current sense of the word – thankfully he has resisted getting sucked into the oily morass of the celeb circuit and he doesn't make a habit of going out with supermodels (or even pretending to).

An alternative candidate for man of the year, though, would have to be Capirossi, if only because his success was so much less expected than Rossi's. The little Italian with the big heart showed his strength when Bridgestone tyres came good in the latter stages of the season. No-one is more entertaining to watch on a motorcycle than Capirossi. While Rossi's style is pure

poetry, faultlessly neat but frighteningly fast, like a modern-day Eddie Lawson, Capirossi and his Marlboro Ducati resemble a monkey strapped to a rocket, Loris's little body hunched over the big Duke, all stunning lean angles and big handfuls of throttle. Remarkably, this was Capirossi's 16th season of GP racing. In other words, the 32-year-old Italian has spent exactly half his life on biking's world stage, and he's still the same straight-down-the-line bloke he was at the end of his debut 1990 GP campaign, when an Italian restaurant on Phillip Island created the Capirossi pizza in honour of his 125 world title.

Above Who's that with Colin Edwards? Matt LeBlanc and Brad Pitt schmoozing at Laguna Seca

Below He came, he saw, he didn't quite conquer. Next year, maybe

Left Laguna Seca's iconic Corkscrew was a highlight of Grand Prix motorcycling's return to the USA

Of course, Rossi's achievements in 2005 were greater than Capirossi's – superhuman, legendary and ground-breaking. During the course of last season it became obvious that his success with Yamaha wasn't just about winning races. His input into the factory's YZR-M1 project changed the balance of power in MotoGP, because Yamaha's in-line four finally became a better motorcycle than Honda's V5. Just two years ago no-one would have believed that was possible.

Furthermore, Rossi's departure from Honda has apparently thrown the racing arm of the world's biggest motorcycle manufacturer into some state of confusion. Honda's hegemony wavered for the first time since GPs went four-stroke, the factory experiencing its most difficult season in more than a decade of premier-class racing. Honda won just four races in 2005, its least successful performance since 1993, when HRC number one Mick Doohan was still struggling with a rotten leg, and Suzuki's Kevin Schwantz and Yamaha's Wayne Rainey were doing all the winning. Not only that, at Motegi in September Honda endured its first Japanese GP defeat in five years, and at Sepang its first-ever MotoGP race result without a rider on the podium; the last time that happened in the premier class was at the Sachsenring in 2001.

Conversely Ducati enjoyed its best-ever run in MotoGP. Capirossi's back-to-back wins at Motegi and Sepang were hugely significant, not just because they were Ducati's and Bridgestone's first-ever consecutive premier-class victories, but because they were the first successive wins achieved by a non-Japanese manufacturer since MV Agusta's fire-engine red 500s ruled in the early 1970s. It's reassuring that a brave little factory in northern Italy can still take on and defeat the might of the Japanese, even at the highest level.

Honda's main worry, it seemed, was getting the RCV into corners properly. In MotoGP going slow is the new going fast, because when most tracks have the throttle fully open for 15 per cent of the time and closed for 40 per cent, it's easy to understand why effective engine braking is at least as important as good horsepower. In other words, Ducati and Yamaha have surpassed Honda with their engine-braking software. Even Kawasaki and Suzuki improved their bikes during 2005, although the front rank remained as elusive as ever to the greens and the blues.

Equally elusive for them was title sponsorship, with both Kawasaki and Suzuki running in their own colours for the third consecutive season. This is a bit of a mystery.

On average, men think about
the GSX-R1000 every 3 seconds.

GSX-R1000

Call 0845 850 8800 or visit www.suzuki.co.uk

SUZUKI
Ride the winds of change

Above MotoGP is just as popular as ever in its heartland, as Sete's fans demonstrate in Catalunya

Below The best surprise of the year, the new Istanbul Park track, is a nice place to work in and a fabulous track to race on

of sponsors, keen to take advantage of a sport that is relentlessly building TV viewing figures and crowd figures? And if the factory teams are having a tough time, what about the smaller outfits like Team Roberts and WCM? You can't have guys up at the front without others racing behind them – the slower crews are a crucial part of MotoGP's long-term success.

Even though the sponsors haven't yet woken up to it, MotoGP's burgeoning popularity is visible to the eye at places like Donington, where the once-empty lawns now throng with fans, only 60 per cent or so wearing Rossi caps and T-shirts. Even at Sepang this year, where the grandstands had remained resolutely empty since the track hosted its first GP in 1999, there was barely a seat left in the house. What does all this mean? It means that bike racing has gone mainstream. These days it's not just bikers and speed freaks who make pilgrimages to motorcycle GPs, it's (how should this be put?) normal people as well – everyday punters who might go to a football match one weekend, an F1 race the next. In reaching them, MotoGP has succeeded in doing what no other class of motorcycle road racing has managed.

And the sport continues to cross fresh horizons, like the championship's new venues in China and Turkey, where bike racing followed closely in F1's slipstream. Both events were popular with the MotoGP paddock, for different reasons, Shanghai for its awe-inspiring infrastructure, Istanbul for its rousing rollercoaster of a racetrack which reminded everyone that new circuits don't need to be slow and boring. True, the crowds did stay away from both events, but hopefully these two nations will eventually be seduced by MotoGP's rorty

True, neither factory has covered itself in glory in MotoGP, and big-money sponsorship beyond tobacco has continued to be hard to find, even for the more successful teams. Four or five years ago the reasons were obvious – bike racing still hadn't built the kind of mainstream fan base that would impress multinationals into writing cheques with a proper number of noughts on them. But all that has changed over the past few seasons. Rossi's irresistible smile and the overwhelming roar of four-stroke motors have taken bike racing to a whole new audience, now reaching parts of the world it never used to reach. There's no doubt that Dorna has done a good job here, but where are the queues

charms. Laguna Seca's return to the GP calendar after a decade's absence was met with far greater enthusiasm, the Americans falling for MotoGP like they'd never fallen for the 500s. Hardly surprising, really: two-strokes were never going to make sense to a nation whose motorcycle heritage is based around Harleys.

But if we gained two new racetracks and regained an old one, we did also lose one. The epic Assen circuit is currently undergoing modifications – a whole section of the track is being dug up to make way for an entertainment mall and car park – that will emasculate its unique character. From now on, therefore, Assen will be much like any other modern identikit track, which is a real tragedy for race fans with any respect for history.

The sport's expanding crowds certainly disprove one old theory, that bike racing fans only come to the tracks for one thing – to see spectacular crashes. In the premier class it seems that highsides hardly ever happen anymore, thanks to ever-improving four-stroke technology. Back in the bad ol' days of 500s, weekends were littered with the wreckage of highside tumbles – trashed fairings, smashed bones and long queues at the Clinica Mobile. Can you remember the last time you saw Rossi or any of his rivals jump on the gas too hard and get catapulted over the handlebars? No, neither can we, although perhaps it was Alex Hofmann who gassed up his Kwacker during a MotoGP demo on the streets of Estoril back in April. In what was certainly the most embarrassing MotoGP incident of 2005, the keen young German was spat off his green bike like a Ninja gone wrong, suffering a broken wrist. Traction control wasn't designed to look after show-offs at 15mph...

Of course, current MotoGP technology will soon be out of date. Even though Honda, Kawasaki and maybe some other factories will have all-new bikes for 2006, the 990s will be consigned to the dustbins of history at the end of next year, to be replaced by 800s. The 2005 season heralded the first efforts to rein in the 250 horsepower 990cc monsters, but everyone already knew that reducing fuel capacity by approximately 10 per cent would do little to quell the fiery beasts. Lap and race records tumbled pretty much everywhere in 2004, hence the more drastic solution of cutting engine capacity by around 20 per cent from 2007. Only time will tell if the doomsayers' prophecies that these bikes will be more highly stressed – and therefore more difficult to control and more expensive to maintain – are proven correct.

One thing is certain, though: the first four seasons of MotoGP have been something of a golden age. We've been able to watch in genuine awe as arguably the greatest motorcycle racer of all time has tamed what are undoubtedly the most insane racing motorcycles ever created. As Rossi says: 'Maybe we're lucky to be racing these bikes, because soon they'll become legend.'

The demise of the 990s may also coincide with Rossi's exit, if he's finally won over by F1's charms. No doubt about it, Valentino's departure will leave a yawning chasm in the sport. Ever since he switched to the big bikes in 2000, the Italian has been MotoGP's guiding light, and although there are some bright new faces in the class there's no-one with such talent or charisma. It shouldn't come as a surprise: like football's Pele or boxing's Muhammad Ali, someone like Rossi only comes along once in every two decades. Very soon we will need to move on, excited by faces of the future, not reflecting too much upon the glories of the past.

Sadly, some teams and sponsors seem too scared to invest in new talent, so the MotoGP grid has grown older with each passing year. Indeed, the average age of premier-class racers has been gradually edging upward for years. In 1985, when Fast Freddie Spencer took the title, the average age of the top few premier-class racers was 27; by 1995, when Mick Doohan was king, it was 28. During 2005 it was 29, despite Rossi's relative youth. There are probably three main reasons for this. One: safer tracks and better riding gear mean longer careers. Two: sponsors have an increasingly crucial say in who gets the top rides, and big, faceless corporations like big, familiar faces. Three: ever more complex technology requires more experienced riders.

It's up to the factories to make sure that they bring new faces into MotoGP: they're the ones who should be talent-spotting. It's no use running away from the future – hiring safe, experienced racers who will turn in some kind of a performance – rather than taking inspired risks with brave new talent that will really excite us. And finally the factory bosses do seem to have woken up to this fact, so now MotoGP does have a young future to look forward to. There's Dani Pedrosa, Chris Vermeulen, Randy de Puniet and Casey Stoner lining up to take on established MotoGP youngsters like Melandri, Hayden, John Hopkins and Toni Elias. Judging by the last couple of 2005 GPs, Rossi won't have such an easy ride in 2006...

Below How many more times will he take the chequered flag before he decides to move on?

MotoGP KINGS, AGAIN!

Michelin's 25th premier-class World Champion Valentino Rossi knows a bit about motorcycle tyre performance, so when the Italian describes Michelin's latest MotoGP tyres thus "it's like magic, you give a lot of gas but the tyre doesn't spin!" you'd better believe him.

Despite increased competition from its major rivals during 2005, Michelin continued to dominate bike racing's fastest and most technically challenging race series. The renowned French tyre brand won all but two of the season's 17 premier-class GPs and took the top five places in the final points standings.

Of course, 2005 wasn't just about Rossi. Bike racing's biggest star may have ruled for the fifth year in a row but MotoGP's new generation scored its first MotoGP victories, with Nicky Hayden (Repsol Honda Team RC211V-Michelin) and Marco Melandri (Telefonica Movistar Honda RC211V-Michelin) taking their debut wins.

The racing was faster than ever before, records falling at every race. And while the factories continued to build faster, better-handling MotoGP bikes, Michelin was there to help riders transfer that increased performance to the tarmac. The biggest advance during 2005 was the company's revised construction rear tyre which gave a larger footprint for extra grip, while maintaining light steering. The tyre ruled in all conditions – dry, damp and soaking wet.

"As always Michelin make a very good tyre," says Rossi. "This year we worked especially hard on traction because it is important that you have enough traction to use all the power. Now it is sometimes possible to make the fastest lap on the last lap, which means the tyres work incredible!"

Working with Rossi and his fellow MotoGP heroes is why Michelin goes racing. The company uses their feedback to create better high-performance street tyres like the Power Race, Pilot Sport and Pilot Power. And to enjoy the thrill of winning races, of course!

www.michelinsport.com

MICHELIN'S ROLL CALL OF PREMIER-CLASS WORLD CHAMPIONS

1976	Barry Sheene	(Texaco Heron Team Suzuki RG500-Michelin)
1977	Barry Sheene	(Texaco Heron Team Suzuki RG500-Michelin)
1981	Marco Lucchinelli	(Nava Olio Fiat Suzuki RG500-Michelin)
1982	Franco Uncini	(Gallina Suzuki RG500-Michelin)
1983	Freddie Spencer	(Honda NS500-Michelin)
1985	Freddie Spencer	(Rothmans Honda NSR500-Michelin)
1986	Eddie Lawson	(Marlboro Yamaha YZR500-Michelin)
1987	Wayne Gardner	(Rothmans Honda NSR500-Michelin)
1988	Eddie Lawson	(Marlboro Yamaha YZR500-Michelin)
1989	Eddie Lawson	(Rothmans Honda NSR500-Michelin)
1990	Wayne Rainey	(Marlboro Team Roberts Yamaha YZR500-Michelin)
1992	Wayne Rainey	(Marlboro Team Roberts Yamaha YZR500-Michelin)
1993	Kevin Schwantz	(Lucky Strike Suzuki RGV500-Michelin)
1994	Mick Doohan	(Honda NSR500-Michelin)
1995	Mick Doohan	(Repsol Honda NSR500-Michelin)
1996	Mick Doohan	(Repsol Honda NSR500-Michelin)
1997	Mick Doohan	(Repsol Honda NSR500-Michelin)
1998	Mick Doohan	(Repsol Honda NSR500-Michelin)
1999	Alex Crivillé	(Repsol Honda NSR500-Michelin)
2000	Kenny Roberts	(Telefonica Movistar Suzuki RGV500-Michelin)
2001	Valentino Rossi	(Nastro Azzurro Honda NSR500-Michelin)
2002	Valentino Rossi	(Repsol Honda RC211V-Michelin)
2003	Valentino Rossi	(Repsol Honda RC211V-Michelin)
2004	Valentino Rossi	(Gauloises Fortuna Yamaha YZR-M1-Michelin)
2005	Valentino Rossi	(Gauloises Yamaha YZR-M1-Michelin)

TECHNOLOGICAL PARTNER TEAM CAMEL HONDA

RIDERS' RIDER OF THE YEAR

OF THE

2005

If you want to know who's the best rider of the year,
you ask the riders themselves. That's what we did.
Every rider who rode in more than one MotoGP race
was asked to nominate his top six riders of the year
in order. Riders were asked not to vote for themselves
or, in the case of the Checas, their brother. Voting
was secret. The scrutineers then allocated six points
for a first place down to one point for sixth.
The results are over the page.

The result was never in doubt. Just like last year, Valentino Rossi was the runaway winner of the Riders' Rider of the Year 2005.

But this year Valentino increased his score by 14 points from precisely the same number of voters. Twenty-four of the voters judged him to be the best; last year it was 21. But the big difference was in the spread of votes; in a major change from last year's pattern, only two other riders received first-place votes (and remember that one of them must have been from Valentino as he couldn't vote for himself). Marco Melandri received one nomination but Loris Capirossi received three, enough to put the Ducati rider into second place in the poll. Loris was the overwhelming choice for second place with 11 of his fellow racers judging him next best after Rossi. Five put Marco second, and three had Valentino as runner-up. No-one put Rossi any lower than second.

Four other riders received second-place votes: Sete Gibernau had four, John Hopkins two, and Max Biaggi and Colin Edwards one each. Edwards and Hopkins also received a third-place nomination each, along with Alex Barros, while Shinya Nakano got three third places and, as last year, is higher in our poll than in the World Championship itself.

If you're looking for the man whose peers rate him highly despite a disappointing season, it has to be John Hopkins. Last year he was eighth in the Riders' Rider of the Year, eight places higher than his final championship position. This year he's eighth again and six places higher than his final MotoGP placing. Nicky Hayden didn't

1st
VALENTINO ROSSI
159 POINTS

3rd
MARCO
MELANDRI
81 POINTS

2nd
LORIS
CAPIROSSI
97 POINTS

5th
COLIN
EDWARDS
31 POINTS

4th
NICKY
HAYDEN
45 POINTS

Shell
ADVANCE
MOTORCYCLE OILS

MORE LIFE FOR BIKES

ENGINES LAST LONGER WITH NEW SHELL ADVANCE

www.shell.com/advance

6th
SETE
GIBERNAU
29 POINTS

7th
SHINYA
NAKANO
28 POINTS

8th
JOHN
HOPKINS
24 POINTS

9th
MAX
BIAGGI
23 POINTS

10th
ALEX
BARROS
17 POINTS

AS VOTED FOR BY

Nobuatsu Aoki
Alex Barros
Franco Battaini
Troy Bayliss
Max Biaggi
Shane Byrne
Loris Capirossi
Carlos Checa
David Checa
Colin Edwards
Toni Elias
James Ellison
Sete Gibernau
Jurgen van den Goorbergh
Nicky Hayden
Alex Hofmann
John Hopkins
Olivier Jacque
Marco Melandri
Shinya Nakano
Kenny Roberts
Roberto Rolfo
Valentino Rossi
Makoto Tamada
Tohru Ukawa
Chris Vermeulen
Ruben Xaus

get any first or second place votes, but 11 voters had him either third or fourth, which put him clear in fourth place overall, well ahead of a group of five covered by only eight votes and led by Colin Edwards. After Alex Barros in tenth place, nobody received a points score in double figures, but there were still one or two interesting results. A replacement rider was mentioned for the first time; three respondents nominated Olivier Jacque, and it wasn't just a case of solidarity among ex-250 racers. One works rider had James Ellison on his list, and Toni Elias attracted a couple of mentions.

Looking back at last year's results, the biggest improver is Marco Melandri, who didn't even make the top ten in 2004. Put that alongside Nicky Hayden's result, up from tenth to fourth, and you can see the poll is accurately reflecting the rise of these two young guns. Similarly, the Riders' Rider of the Year poll is accurate if you want to check whose star is on the wane. Sete Gibernau drops from a solid second place in 2004 with 93 votes to sixth place with just 29. Last year Max Biaggi was third with 83 points, now he's ninth with just 23. Makoto Tamada drops out of the top ten to make way for the mercurial Marco Melandri, the only change in personnel in the Riders' Rider of the Year top ten.

The first two years of Riders' Rider of the Year have seen convincing victories for Valentino Rossi. He has scored well over 100 points in both years; no-one else has got into three figures. No-one is betting against him making it a hat-trick in 2006.

BRK.

FBT

RIDE-BY-WIRE COMES OF AGE

Electronic throttles on MotoGP bikes have come a long way in a very short time. When the class started in 2002 all the bikes used conventional cable-controlled throttles – exactly the same as you'll find on any street bike.

BASIC PROBLEMS: BASIC TRICKS

The initial concern of the designers of MotoGP's first generation of bikes was to find a way of controlling the damaging effects of engine braking. In normal use, as a motorcycle enters a corner and as the rider shuts the throttle, the rear wheel starts to drive the engine rather than the engine doing the driving. Some of the grip potential of the tyre is being used merely to turn over a shutdown motor, and to complicate the issue the chain tries to move the swingarm around and unsettles the rear suspension. The problem was worse in MotoGP than in Superbike because all the riders were used to two-strokes, and on two-strokes there simply wasn't the same level of engine braking that the new 990cc four-strokes were generating.

The first layer of defence was a slipper clutch, exactly as used on Superbikes. The 'back torque limiter' is a mechanical clutch that automatically disengages when the rear wheel tries to drive the crankshaft. It was soon discovered that, with the higher outputs and increased compression of the MotoGP bikes, the slipper clutches were getting quite hot and bothered by the amount of work they were required to do. At

Left Under the nose fairing of the Yamaha M1

Below Heat-sensitive paint on an M1 slipper clutch

RACING BATTLAX

Bridgestone's development in the white heat of MotoGP competition has continued during 2005 and scaled even greater heights. Most recently, Loris Capirossi secured three consecutive pole positions in Japan, Malaysia and Qatar and converted the first two into historic victories for his Ducati team.

Other highlights of the 2005 season included Olivier Jacque's astonishing second place in the wet as MotoGP visited China for the very first time and a runner-up place for Suzuki's Kenny Roberts in the extraordinary conditions at Donington Park. And Capirossi's Ducati team-mate, Carlos Checa, contributed to Bridgestone's stunning year with two visits to the podium in Malaysia and Australia proving that whatever the conditions, Bridgestone continues to move forward.

Bridgestone's new partners for 2005 have enjoyed their success thanks partly to Bridgestone's ongoing development work and an unwavering determination to succeed. We will maintain that determination for 2006 and beyond, ensuring that wet or dry, road or track, you too can feel the benefits of our success.
www.bridgestone-eu.com

Rider : Loris Capirossi Team : Ducati Marlboro Team Series : MotoGP Machine : Ducati Desmosedici GP5 Tyres : Bridgestone Battlax Racing slick

BT-002 PRO
SUPERSPORT / SUPERSTOCK

SLICK
125 TO MOTOGP

RAIN
125 TO MOTOGP

this point development seemed to move in different directions. Some factories, notably Yamaha and Suzuki, tried electronically operated 'active' clutches which did not rely on a simple mechanical set-up but were activated by a computer-controlled motor. The rest of the factories fitted 'throttle kickers' designed to raise the tickover revs of an engine so that when the rider shuts the throttle some fuel and air are still let into the engine. This increases tickover and reduces the amount of engine braking with which the clutch has to deal.

BASIC PROBLEMS: ADVENTUROUS IDEAS

Over at Aprilia, however, things were decidedly more adventurous. Their engine had been designed with a lot of help from Cosworth, and Aprilia knew that they would need some form of electronic throttle system to produce a powerband and style of delivery which would be acceptable to the rider. They chose not to use Cosworth's system and decided to develop their own. This was the first true fly-by-wire system on a MotoGP bike, with all the throttle butterflies controlled electronically the whole time. Aprilia's main difficulty was that their basic engine design was particularly challenging when it came to throttle response. The ride-by-wire system could be tuned to change the response the rider got from any given degree of throttle movement, but Aprilia found it impossible to control the very lightweight crankshaft's desire to rev up extremely quickly using electronics. When combined with some quite experimental chassis design decisions, Aprilia were right up against it from the start.

ELECTRONIC THROTTLES: EMBRYONIC SOLUTIONS

One of the difficulties with tracing the emergence of this particular piece of electronic wizardry is that the technology has a direct application to road bikes. A properly developed ride-by-wire system will give a factory the ability to modify an engine's throttle responses either for maximum economy on the road or for the best possible emissions control. In the world we live in such a technology has a very high commercial value, sufficient in some ways to make the cost of MotoGP quite acceptable.

The first time there was any evidence that something was changing was Barros's sensational ride on the RC211V in Japan towards the end of 2002. Alex stepped from his two-stroke Honda on to a four-stroke and proceeded to beat Rossi in a straight race. Barros's bike looked really stable going into corners whereas Rossi's machine was jumping and sliding all over the place. In one of the sessions the Brazilian crashed and a large brown box with a substantial number of cables emerging from it could be seen through the smashed fairing. To this day Honda will not confirm what the unit was, but it seems most likely that it was the factory's first foray into ride-by-wire throttles.

During the second year of MotoGP in 2003 Honda admitted to using a secondary throttle system. This was

Above Aprilia's early ride-by-wire hardware

Below The 2003 Aprilia with fuel injectors clearly visible

Top The last of the carburettor Yamahas – Abe's bike from the 2003 IRTA tests

Above Yamaha starts to get really serious; Checa's bike with flat-slide throttle valves being prepared at Brno in 2003

a computer-controlled air bleed allowing air and fuel mixture into the inlet tract when the computer systems on the bike detected excessive engine braking. Kawasaki, in their first year of MotoGP competition, had a small stepper motor driven from their ECU to increase tickover, while Yamaha had a revised set of throttles that made the bike sound like it had morphed into a flatulent CB500 twin at the end of straights. At the time Yamaha wouldn't say what they were doing but we now know that they were tuning in a kicker system on a guillotine-style (flat-slide) fuel-injection system.

Ducati's first season of MotoGP competition was also in 2003. Over the course of that year most of the Ducati's parts were seen and analysed, but one piece remained permanently under cover or behind the fairing: a small stepper motor mounted up on the dash which essentially increased the tickover level as and when the engine-control computer decided it was required. It's difficult to confirm, but the motor itself looked remarkably similar to a standard Yamaha EXUP power-valve actuation motor given a new role in life.

Suzuki's 2003 bike was almost fully automatic and, judging by the team's pit-lane reaction when the bikes were first unpacked, most of the features were also unexpected. It took a year of ups and downs (literally) before the system was simplified for 2004. In that year, though, a lot was learned. We heard many riders' criticisms about throttles that would not react accurately to rider input, leading to comparisons with video games and in some cases the system was blamed for collisions caused by an increase in speed when the rider had just shut the throttle.

THROTTLES WITH DELICACY

The first two years of the formula taught everyone that the first priority in MotoGP was a well-sorted engine and chassis and a good connection from the rider's hand to what was happening at the tyre. Only once those basics were in place could engine output start to increase and systems be introduced to deal with that additional power.

Aprilia announced a retrenchment with a new heavyweight crankshaft and a linear-response ride-by-wire system. This calmed the engine down sufficiently for it to be a good starting point for further development. At about the same time Ducati, and then Kawasaki, discovered Weber Marelli's missing-spark traction-control system. It was quite normal practice to measure both front- and rear-wheel speeds, with any major deviation between the two values being attributed to throttle-induced wheelspin. The old two-stroke method of controlling excess spin was particularly quick and effective: simply retarding the ignition would reduce both power and the tendency to spin; most four-strokes had this from day one. Weber Marelli went a stage further for the four-strokes by cutting sparks from selected cylinders on the Ducati, thus reducing power even further. By mid-season it was not uncommon to hear the bike coming out of a corner generating a noise not dissimilar to a burst of machine-gun fire. The Kawasakis were suffering severe traction problems, and by the end of the year were using the same system. It seemed to kick in at almost every corner.

We now know that Yamaha had swapped from a flat-slide fuel-injection system to a butterfly system, along with the other changes for Rossi in early 2004. This was combined with an irregular firing order that endowed the M1 with an improbable level of grip. During the course of the year Honda admitted to using a throttle system that gave riders different throttle openings in different gear ratios. In first gear it was suggested that a full 90° of throttle movement at the handlebar would only result in 45° at the throttle butterfly, 60° in second and 75–80° in third. The important thing was that, as the throttle reacted to the slightest movement of the rider's hand, rider feel was very important. Since then Kyoichi Yoshii, who took over as Chief Engineer of the Motor Sports Development Group in late 2004, has confirmed that the system operated in all six gears pretty much from day one.

Yamaha were staying very quiet at this time. They had clearly made an advance, and there were many (still unsubstantiated) rumours of a connection with Toyota's Formula 1 team (Toyota and Yamaha have a cross shareholding). Yamaha were clearly changing something, for their bikes behaved very strangely at Le Mans: suddenly they all became difficult to start and Rossi stalled on the line. The only comment was that the fuelling system had now become fully Weber Marelli, replacing the previous system which used parts from three different manufacturers. At Suzuki a great deal of automation was being removed so that the riders were back in control of the bike; but the throttle stayed. Ducati were also clearly aware that while their throttle system might help control wheelspin they needed to have a motor that helped produce grip as well as the Yamaha. Ducati's major effort went into providing a good basic engine, a 'twin-pulse' system that was usable, rather than developing a throttle system designed to control the uncontrollable.

So where were we? By the end of 2004 the rules were pretty much defined. If an engine made enough power to be competitive wheelspin and engine braking needed to be controlled using electronics to modify the throttle positions to give the desired effect. However, the motor had to be at least vaguely correct before electronics would be able to control it sufficiently. Those bikes with very light crankshafts ended up with substantially more weight while those with regular firing orders were redesigned for irregular power delivery. For 2005 a new fuel restriction came into force, two litres down on the previous limit, at 22 litres. That was going to be difficult on a bike with a high-revving 990cc engine which had to go the full distance in a GP; improving the fuel consumption so that each bike would finish the race became a major new factor in everybody's preparations.

THROTTLES THAT MAKE THE UNRIDEABLE RIDEABLE

Electronic systems in 2004 had included wasted-spark traction control. This effectively takes an engine that makes too much power and deliberately misfires a cylinder or two in order to reduce power dramatically when excessive wheelspin is detected. That waste of fuel became very difficult to deal with under the 22-litre limit in 2005. Fuel consumption was the focus in all teams' efforts, but the most spectacular results came from Ducati. They debuted not only an electronic throttle system but a computer-controlled automatic clutch as well. This was designed to disengage fully on the

entrance to a corner and then re-engage smoothly as the bike accelerated back out again.

The systems were trialled in the weeks leading up to the season but only made it onto Capirossi's and Checa's bikes at the final tests before the start of the racing year. It was clear from the start that the riders were not particularly keen, but they persevered. The system got as far as final qualifying at the first Grand Prix in Spain, then an accident causing Capirossi to break a bone in his foot signalled the end and the system was removed. Ducati soldiered on, fine-tuning their electronic throttle system, while they waited for Bridgestone to develop a family of tyres that would suit their chassis and also provide stable grip for the duration of a GP. Just as electronic throttles were initially dismissed as unnecessary fripperies, it seems quite likely that the automatic clutch will be back sooner rather than later.

While all this was going on Yamaha's 2005 M1 acquired an uprated engine-control computer to help it deal more accurately and quickly with the demands being placed upon it. All the systems work from the basic premise that the engines can make too much power pretty much all the time; it's a question of managing that power and delivering it smoothly and accurately and without any lag.

Yamaha's system uses a pair of throttle butterflies controlled by the rider – he has a 495cc twin if you like – and an electric motor operates the other two, the second 495cc twin. By having one pair of throttles directly under the rider's control all the sensitivity needed to deal with the limited amount of grip available on a MotoGP bike is retained. The second pair smoothes the

Below Yamaha operates two throttle butterflies by cable and two by electric motor, controlled by Weber Marelli's most powerful processor, the Marvel 6

power delivery using very accurate engine data, held in the computer, of the engine's performance at any particular rev and throttle opening. Using the pairs of throttles independently, Yamaha constructed a group of settings which delivers a consistent supply of torque to the rear wheel. An example would be the point at which the engine suddenly hits its powerband: the rider would be holding constant throttle on his pair of butterflies but the automatic pair would be shutting down at a rate designed to keep the 'as delivered to the rear wheel' torque constant – exactly what the rider's hand is asking for. Colin Edwards, who has more experience than most of the differing systems, conceded that the bike would be completely unrideable without the throttle system: 'You can dial in the throttles to give you exactly what torque you want for any corner.' Once they have a good basic setting the rider and his crew chief have to fine-tune it for any given circuit. This throttle has allowed the Yamaha to be tuned for more and more top-end power.

Over at Kawasaki the arrival of Ichiro Yoda from Yamaha caused a few changes. The first task was to get an irregular firing order, which transformed the grip levels of the ZX-RR. The second was to obtain an electronic throttle system; Kawasaki's was developed by Danilo Casonato, their Italian electronics engineer, and is similar to Yamaha's but has three butterflies controlled by the rider and one by a computer linked to the engine management system. Also like the Yamaha, it uses Weber Marelli-developed software as the base. Casonato said, 'What matters is the zone. There is a certain group of settings where a rider is comfortable – we can change the butterflies, the ignition advance, or miss ignition on the

cylinder, all these things can be adjusted to get the bike into the most effective zone to be competitive on the track and it's up to the rider and his crew chief to perfect that zone.' One crew chief was even more frank: 'When I first saw the readings I thought this is crazy, this is all bullshit, you can have a situation where the rider shuts his throttle just as the computer is opening its throttle, but it works, the rider can't feel it and the whole bike worked better.'

Kawasaki first fitted their system to Olivier Jacque's bike in Shanghai. After just two practice sessions it was obvious that it was a quantum leap forward, and Nakano's bike was similarly equipped. It certainly didn't hurt Jacque's performance in the race, although a mechanical malfunction in the system appears to have stopped Nakano. The combination of improved grip and improved throttle control made the Kawasaki pretty competitive for a while. Senior Kawasaki engineers were sent over to look at the project and conceded that they needed to learn from it but that, in their view, it would be four to five years before it could be production-ready and would appear on one of their street bikes.

We now have full-blown torque by wire. All riders feel the torque of an engine through the seat of their pants, but while they are used to feeling it they can ride faster if the supply of torque is linear. The perfect world is where a rider turns the throttle 25 per cent and gets 25 per cent more torque. It assumes that there is always more power available than can be used, but that's usually about right with a 990cc MotoGP engine.

Below Fuelling used to be tuned by a mechanic with decades of experience and a box full of needles and jets; now it's an engineer with a laptop

moment of truth

Racing doesn't only depend on how fast you go but also how quickly you slow down. Every corner demands a unique response in how, when and where you brake. And at these moments, the engineering decisions you've made will decide whether it's going to be a hot lap or not.

But if you've fitted AP Racing brakes, you'll know your rider has the confidence to brake deeper at every corner – from start to finish.

That's because AP Racing have spent over 40 years honing their art to perfection – supplying brakes to over 100 GP winners and numerous championships in the process.

And that's simply the truth.

For a catalogue detailing the AP Racing range brakes, clutches, actuation products and ancillaries call our technical sales team or visit our website.

AP RACING
WHELER ROAD
COVENTRY
CV3 4LB
ENGLAND
TEL +44 (0)24 7663 9595
FAX +44 (0)24 7663 9559
EMAIL: sales@apracing.co.uk

AP RACING

the science of friction

AP-MTC/B-1

THE TYRE WAR

Michelin have been top dog in MotoGP for the whole of the 990cc formula, with Honda and Yamaha using their products exclusively. Dunlop, previously strong contenders, rule the smaller 125 and 250 classes but have found MotoGP tough. Bridgestone have been quietly building their challenge for a few years, taking the series extremely seriously, and last year suddenly became very competitive at several circuits. Unfortunately at Mugello in 2004 one of Bridgestone's tyres exploded underneath Shinya Nakano and the Kawasaki spat him down the track right in front of the pits. Makoto Tamada, then the race leader, suffered similar difficulties but managed to pull off before the tyre deflated. Bridgestone bounced back to win in Rio, courtesy of Tamada. What was apparent was that the Bridgestones and Michelins suited different tracks: instead of simply competing against Michelin at all circuits, Bridgestone would either be right off the pace or capable of winning.

For 2005 Bridgestone found a new soul-mate in Ducati. The strategy of differentiation suited Ducati: on different tyres they would either be blisteringly competitive or in with the pack. Early in testing for 2005 we suddenly heard of some stupendous lap times set by Ducatis on Bridgestones in Malaysia. It's apparent now that the tyres must have been qualifiers: during the first half of the year Bridgestone certainly didn't understand the Ducati chassis, but were quite competitive on the Kawasakis and Suzukis. By Brno, however, Bridgestone had learned what the Ducati needed and were on a track where they have historically gone well. More to the point, the tyres not only gripped but their performance was stable throughout the race – always an important point when judging the quality of a racing tyre.

By Motegi Bridgestone were on a roll. Loris Capirossi not only got on pole position but also won the race, and then followed up with a similar performance in Malaysia a week later. Bridgestone's strategy has been to take on Michelin everywhere, but in their deal with Ducati they accepted that when a circuit suited Bridgestone tyres the Ducati would be perfectly capable of taking on the Yamahas and Hondas for the win.

One of the fundamentals for tyre design is comprehensive knowledge of each circuit and the demands that each individual circuit makes for good grip. Over a period of years each tyre company builds up a record of the type of tarmac at each circuit and the way it wears; each year before the Grand Prix they take a view of how the track will have matured over the previous year and tyres are constructed that take into account everything they know. One of Michelin's strengths has been the depth of their database; and until now it has served them well.

Each of the factories supported by Bridgestone has a separate test team; the more circuits they test at, the more likely they are to have the data that's needed to be competitive. It's easy to predict that if you have a Japan-based test team with the Japanese Superbike champion as your test rider doing lap after lap after lap of the Motegi circuit, you should get a very effective tyre for that circuit. It goes without saying that you also need a good bike; Ducati wouldn't have won if they hadn't put an awful lot of the problems of their 2004 Desmosedici firmly behind them.

The accuracy of the data that Bridgestone has for the Motegi and Sepang circuits is shown by Michelin's response. For 2006 Michelin

Top Rossi's race tyre just before the off – a sight visible for the few seconds between the tyre warmer coming off and Valentino setting off down pit lane

Above The leading generals in the tyre war: Bridgestone's motorcycle racing manager Hiroshi Yamada and Michelin's chief of motorcycle competition Nicolas Goubert

may also decide to field test teams, which will inevitably lead to an increase in tyre budgets.

Over in British Superbike, Michelin were also in a fight: Dunlop were using the lessons learnt on the D'Antin Ducati, together with their exceptional knowledge of British tracks, to give Michelin a hard time. Unashamedly using full MotoGP specifications, Dunlop's superior database gave them a sufficient edge to even win at Donington, the one circuit where Michelin might be expected to have at least equal experience.

But there is still more to the tyre war. Getting the right compounds is tricky: each tyre company has its own suppliers, providers of all those small chemical packages that, when combined in the right way and with the right construction, create a tyre that works on every surface and on every bike, and retains its properties throughout a race. The suppliers for all three tyre companies will be looking for additives with specific properties, and all these suppliers will be contracted direct to each company and won't be sharing any secrets elsewhere.

The tyre war, then, isn't just a matter of the tyre companies going head to head. It's a war between their entire supply chains; a war co-ordinated by the racing departments based on the latest and best intelligence. Just like a real war.

THE BIKES
2005 MotoGP MACHINERY

Two V5s, three straight fours, three V4s. Two steel frames, six aluminium beam chassis. Three different tyre manufacturers. One winner

YAMAHA
YZR-M1

Right Calipers staying on fork legs with wheel out suggest the system was designed when it was thought the new wet-weather regulations would specify changing wheels rather than bikes

Far right Why the cut-out in the brake lever? Because telemetry said the brakes were being applied by the wind at speed on long straights...

Yamaha built a completely new motorcycle for 2005. It was still called the M1 and was still an across-the-frame in-line four using four valves per cylinder. This year's bike, though, shows many changes from last year's. The totally new chassis (the 'arched Deltabox' of last year is gone) is narrower at the front engine mounts and revised to take both the shorter, narrower engine and the longer swingarm. These modifications allow the Yamaha to turn more quickly and yet stay more stable, with the chassis reacting less aggressively to forces generated when 250bhp is being transmitted down the drive chain.

The new engine still has the crank rotating backwards, but it has revised gear-driven camshafts. Yamaha have built a train of gears up the back of the cylinder block from the balancer shaft. Using gears means that Yamaha can use higher revs, and by putting the gear train behind the block it means that the engine can be as narrow as possible. The in-line four layout gives Yamaha much more freedom in gearbox design and they have taken advantage of this to set the clutch quite high at the rear of the cylinders using a vertically stacked gearbox and so producing a very short engine. This makes the 2005 M1 motor one of the smallest 1000cc fours ever built.

Initial testing was successful, but once the season started it was apparent that there were some set-up details that did not allow the bike to work as well as was hoped. It was easy to see substantial changes being made in front ride height, with the bike being lifted up on the forks to find a balance that worked better for Rossi. During the course of these set-up changes Valentino had a near-crash in the final pre-season tests and then a crash in practice at Jerez. Yamaha used their two top runners as a team to try and find a good set-up, with Colin Edwards experimenting to find the right direction and Rossi concentrating on the racing.

Yamaha use a Weber Marelli engine management system that has two butterflies controlled directly by the rider and two by a computer-controlled servo motor. By having two independently operated butterfly sets Yamaha can deliver exactly the power they want to ease the rider's job, offer more effective traction control and deliver better fuel economy.

Far left Even an M1 uses some oil

Left One of the things Yamaha have spent considerable time on this year is tidying up their wiring loom

HONDA
RC211V

Right New two-into-one exhaust would suggest a higher rev ceiling than in '04

Far right Factory bikes reverted to 2003 rear suspension layout

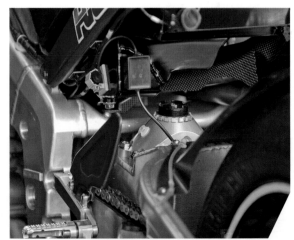

The RC211 is the oldest and most effective design of motorcycle in the MotoGP championship. Constantly developed since its launch, the V5 now produces some 260bhp at the crankshaft. This year, however, Honda have been marking time while they develop a new bike for 2006. The customer bikes are all very similar to last year's works bikes, and include a Pro-Link rear suspension system that is mounted upside-down (compared to the original design) in a much stronger swingarm. The customer chassis is not adjustable at the headstock or the swingarm pivot.

The works bikes, however, used a combination of parts. The Honda chassis are the first for years to have adjustable headstocks and swingarms, and they are the old 2003 design. During the course of 2005 the works riders have all had at least one chassis with re-welded swingarm pivots, and for the Sachsenring both Biaggi and Gibernau received revised frames with steeper headstock angles. During the Brno test Honda had a revised swingarm for both Biaggi and Gibernau to use in their current bikes, the design appearing to combine the strength of the 2004 swingarm with the original 2003 rear suspension layout. Melandri was given a new chassis at Motegi, effectively a works chassis like the one used by Nicky Hayden but without the adjustable steering head.

The new bike – seen for the first time at the Brno test – has a revised, shorter engine, a lighter chassis and a longer swingarm. It is effectively a completely new motorcycle, although looking at it you can see the similarities to the older design. Having missed a substantial part of the Brno test while some safety issues were dealt with, the bike was not seen again this year, but it shows just how serious Honda are about getting the MotoGP title back for the championship's final year as a 990cc series in 2006.

Far left See the machining behind the sprocket? It's only seen on works engines. Is it just extra attention to detail or does it signify some major difference between customer and factory motors?

Left Nicky Hayden's dirt-track heritage means he prefers a big rear disc brake; compare it with the rotor on Biaggi's bike in the main picture

DUCATI
DESMOSEDICI

Right Like Yamaha, Ducati redesigned their caliper mounts for quick wheel changes under flag-to-flag wet-weather racing rules

Far right The auto clutch never raced but its switches weren't removed

Ducati had a disastrous year in 2004, when they took too big a step in their chassis and engine redesign. For 2005 they have corrected those problems and have been developing the bike steadily while waiting for Bridgestone to get the tyres right. By the time we got to Brno the Bridgestone gamble was looking a very high-risk strategy. Their performance in the second half of the year has justified that gamble, however, and it is to Ducati's credit that once competitive tyres were available the Desmosedici was ready.

One issue that has clearly concerned them, though, is fuel consumption. At the final MotoGP tests before the start of the year they debuted an automatic clutch system. This was designed to replace the slipper clutch and also to allow the engine to save fuel for a hundred or so metres before each corner by nearly freewheeling. The system proved difficult to set up and was dropped once Capirossi hurt his foot in a crash.

Despite not having the use of the auto clutch, Ducati have completed all the races without running out of fuel, thanks in the main to big advances in engine management. They used the latest Weber Marelli fuel injection, but some of the credit should also go to the specially designed Shell fuels and lubricants they use. Unlike Yamaha, who have two throttle valves operated by the rider, the Ducati system has all four throttles motorised.

Ducati's engine is a Desmodromic V4 with 90° between the cylinders and a firing order called 'twin-pulse' by the factory. This appears to fire all four cylinders during the course of one revolution, leaving a second revolution with no power pulses to allow the tyre to get its grip back on the track surface. The Ducati twin-pulse engine is producing approximately 260bhp, and has just about caught up in power terms with the screamer engine that they stopped using in June 2004. The difference is that the twin-pulse motor produces usable power.

Far left An extra thousand rpm on the tachometer compared to last year

Left Capirossi started the season with an outrigger bearing on the swingarm pivot. It disappeared when the Bridgestones started working

KAWASAKI
NINJA ZX-RR

56

Right Kawasaki's frame is light, stiff and effective

Far right Wires everywhere; Kawasaki haven't yet got their wiring as tidy as some people

Kawasaki surprised everybody last year with their tiny SRT/Kawasaki-designed bike. It has a minimalist aluminium beam chassis with engine mounts that extend to the top of the crankcases and a combined seat/tank/airbox unit that bolts on above it, and which is unique in pit lane. The design means that the Kawasaki doesn't have a separate weighty fuel tank: its airbox back is integrated with the fuel-tank design and it's easy to access the fuel-injection system through a flap on the top of the tank.

Last year the engine was the same normal in-line four with the standard firing order as used in 2003. While the bike was a lot better and more agile with the new chassis, Kawasaki could never get the grip they needed going into and out of corners. For 2005 they have tried new firing orders for the engine. The first new motor fired pairs of cylinders simultaneously, making a big difference to grip and traction. Kawasaki have now developed a 'B3' variant that fires only two pistons together, allowing the other two to fire in the conventional fashion. This softens the impact on the crankshaft and gearbox but does not appear to slow the bike in any way.

Kawasaki have also developed a full ride-by-wire Weber Marelli system which debuted in Shanghai. The combination of a whole year's experience with the chassis, improved grip and traction from the new firing order, better throttle and traction control plus increasingly competitive Bridgestone tyres should have meant that Kawasaki would be quite a threat in the latter half of the year. The one missing component was bulk power, and efforts were made to develop more. Despite new engine parts being tested they seemed to be rather unreliable, however, with the bike reverting to the smoky behaviour seen a few times in 2004.

Over the course of the season Kawasaki have tried several different exhaust systems to maximise the benefit of their pure big-bang style of engine. The most successful appears to be the original four-into-four individual pipe system without muffling, but during the year several Akrapovic designs have been tried which link the pipes in different ways.

Far left Shinya obviously has two fuel maps to choose from

Left Kawasaki went through several exhaust designs, starting with the four-into-one in the main picture and this four-into-two-into-four that appeared briefly at Donington, before settling on four separate pipes

SUZUKI
GSV-R

Right Both riders tried this thinner air intake early in the year

Far right One of Hopkins' many fuel tank variations

Suzuki had a frustrating season. At the start of the year they boosted their engine considerably with at least another thousand rpm and a substantial increase in horsepower. Unfortunately all the other factories did something similar, except that they also concentrated effort on boosting their bikes' out-of-the-corner potential – and this is where the Suzuki suffers. The GSV-R currently uses an in-house engine management system built with assistance from Mitsubishi, but its traction control is not as effective as the systems used by other teams.

Suzuki have had an interesting year with their Bridgestone tyres. Where outright power is a secondary consideration, the Suzuki has proved really competitive. The wet-weather Bridgestones are at least as good as the equivalent Michelins, letting Kenny Roberts lead the Chinese Grand Prix for a brief period and score a superb second place at Donington. John Hopkins has found he can use the Bridgestone qualifying tyres to great effect as well, with several excellent qualifying performances. In races, though, it is as if Bridgestone's new-found competitiveness hasn't spread to the tyres used by Suzuki.

Over the course of the year the team has experimented with several different exhaust systems, throttle body and airbox designs. Monitoring the changes in the airbox volume has been fairly easy as the team has had to expand the rear of the fuel tank to keep the standard 22-litre capacity. Every time they created a bigger hole at the front of the tank to increase the size of the airbox, the size of the lump added to the back of the fuel tank has increased.

Far left Colour-coded springs indicate how Suzuki fine-tune their slipper clutch with different spring rates

Left Suzuki use their own dedicated flash-load computer for programming their engine management

This was supposed to be the year of the V6, an engine and bike designed wholly in the Czech Republic by ambitious mini-bike firm Blata. The bike was due by mid-season, but this got pulled back to the Czech race at Brno. It still didn't show and all we have seen are a few newspaper photos of a part-finished prototype. The project was started at a time when it was thought that, at worst, the 990cc limit would be reduced to 900cc. It would be technically feasible, if the engine were designed correctly from the start, to shrink the capacity that much and still be able to use the bike. The announcement at Mugello this year that the class would change to 800cc for 2007, however, has destroyed any hope of using a 990cc engine as a basis for the 2007 formula. The logic of continuing the project when only one year's use can be had out of the bikes must be marginal at best.

WCM have continued to use the old in-line four-valve fours originally built in mid-2003. They employ Harris chassis with team-built engines using parts sourced from the old-design R-1 and GSX-R 1000 engines melded together in special castings. The bikes themselves have been going a lot faster this year. Much of this is down to major improvements made by Dunlop in the course of the first half of the 2005 season, but also to the very impressive James Ellison: a few chassis changes have allowed him to ride the bike as he wishes. Technically, however, the WCM is unchanged from two years ago, except for a different type of slipper clutch and a longer swingarm.

The team has got to decide very shortly whether to make new spares to keep their four-cylinder machines going through to the end of the 990cc formula, or try to find engines from another source.

Above right WCM's riders only had one bike each and spares availability was also an issue. They also had the last genuine throttle cables in pit lane

Right In response to rider James Ellison's requests, the bike got a lengthened swingarm

TEAM ROBERTS
PROTON KR

Although withdrawn at Brno, the Roberts Proton KTM project has been technically very interesting. KTM originally built a superbly specified four-cylinder race engine, but once it became apparent how much it was going to cost to compete in MotoGP, the project was stopped. At about the same time, Kenny Roberts's operation ceased developing its own motors and began looking for an engine. It seemed a marriage of convenience to combine the two. Unfortunately the project still lacked the critical funding required to be competitive, and the resulting pressures led to its demise.

KTM's motor was a 990cc 75 degree V4. It's capable of high revs and is equipped with pneumatic valves. Power is produced in a wide seamless band. From the experience this year, however, it's apparent that it was going to require some further work to be competitive. The major development within MotoGP in the past two years has been a tremendous increase in mid-range grunt and the ability to then use it through electronic controls. The KTM had missed out on this development, but several new exhausts and a clutch constructed in-house have been tested. Also, new cams were on their way when the project folded.

In the same way, we have seen the Roberts Proton chassis on four-strokes for three years, the current version being a logical development of the John Barnard-designed chassis from last year, but we've never got to see these chassis wrapped around engines that make competitive amounts of power. There's no doubt that Roberts's team of engineers are creative and clear thinking. While it's a shame that the KTM project failed, it would make a very interesting technical addition to the grid if Roberts could obtain a competitive motor to build into his chassis for 2006.

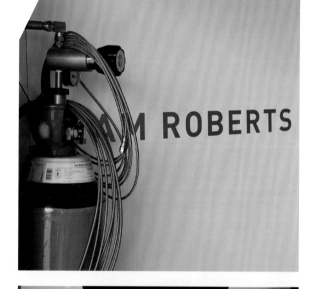

Above right Compressed air cylinder for pressurising the on-board reservoir for the pneumatic valve system

Right Take a good look down the KR Proton's big air intake and you can see the fuel injectors

MORIWAKI
MD211VF DREAM FIGHTER

Mamoru Moriwaki's dream continued this year with two wild-card entries for the best 'shop project' in the world. Using a team made up of his tuning shop employees, Moriwaki came back with two Honda RC211V-engined specials.

When the garage door went up in Shanghai a cursory glance revealed a new fairing and seat but apparently not much else. However, in reality, this year's bikes are almost completely new with revised frames looking as if they hold the engine slightly higher in the chassis, plus much stronger, more heavily braced swingarms. The resulting set-up had the bike sitting lower on the forks which, together with the newer, shorter nose fairing, would suggest that the previous models were being affected by crosswinds and lift.

The bikes that appeared at Motegi were different again, with a new chassis using thicker-wall tubing. The engines appeared to be the early-model V5s Moriwaki used last year, with the same Mk1 exhaust systems. The components are second to none, however, with TT25 Ohlins forks, Nissin brakes and this year, for the first time, Michelin tyres – and all with factory technicians in attendance.

Above right Like Ducati, Moriwaki use a tubular steel frame

Right Honda clearly approved of the project – they sent their chief test rider to ride it in China

THE RIDERS
2005

THE SEASON IN FOCUS

Every rider's season summed up in words and numbers, from Valentino Rossi to the wild cards whose races lasted less than a lap

The following nine pages detail the results of every rider who raced in MotoGP in 2005. They're arranged in final championship order with a data panel under each entry for the regular team riders. Wild-card and injury-replacement riders are dealt with on pages 59 and 61.

The data strips have two numbers or a single number and a code letter or letters under each race. The first number is the rider's qualifying position, the second his finishing position. The letter 'i' means a rider was absent through injury, 'f' instead of a number in the

results means a fall, and 'dnf' means 'did not finish' – usually due to a mechanical problem. You will also find 'ns' for 'non-starter' in several riders' Sachsenring results; this means they didn't take part in the restarted race. The rider's points total for the season appears at the end of the strip. For further details check each race report's data pages or go to page 200 for a tabulated version of the results of all 17 races in the 2005 MotoGP World Championship.

www.dainese.com

Carmi e Ubertis Milano

DAINESE

NO·PAIN·MORE·GAIN

VALENTINO ROSSI   **7**   WORLD CHAMPION

The simbol of victory. The symbol of protection.

DAINESE.
Inspired by humans.

VALENTINO ROSSI 1

NATIONALITY Italian
DATE OF BIRTH 16 February 1979
TEAM Gauloises Yamaha Team
2005 SEASON 11 wins, 5 pole positions, 6 fastest laps

Anyone who thought that Valentino's motivation would be lacking after the miracles of 2004 was disabused of that notion in the very first race of the year. His last-lap pass on Sete Gibernau ensured the only man to trouble him for the previous two years was never a threat in 2005.

Rossi's fifth consecutive premier class title put him alongside Giacomo Agostini and Mick Doohan, previously the only men to have won that number of crowns or more. Add in his 125 and 250cc crowns and he's equal with the total won by Phil Read and John Surtees. Only Ago (15), Angel Nieto (13), Mike Hailwood and Carlo Ubbiali (nine each) have won more. Only Rossi and Ago have won the premier class on both a two-stroke and a four-stroke, and only Rossi and Eddie Lawson have won back-to-back titles on different makes of bike. Rossi has won more races consecutively and more races in a season than any other Yamaha rider. The records go on and on, but one goal did elude him. He didn't beat Doohan's record for wins in a year. Still, there's always 2006.

SPA	POR	CHN	FRA	ITA	CAT	NED	USA	GBR	GER	CZE	JPN	MAL	QAT	AUS	TUR	VAL	POINTS
1-1	4-2	6-1	1-1	1-1	3-1	1-1	2-3	1-1	4-1	4-1	11-f	7-2	3-1	2-1	4-2	15-3	367

MARCO MELANDRI 2

NATIONALITY Italian
DATE OF BIRTH 7 August 1982
TEAM Movistar Honda MotoGP
2005 SEASON 2 wins, 3 fastest laps

Finishing the year second overall when you have had three non-scoring races due to crashes shouldn't be possible, but that's what Marco did thanks to the four end-of-season races. In Qatar he pushed Rossi all the way, in Australia he was just beaten for third but set his first ever fastest lap, and then came the back-to-back wins in Turkey and Valencia. That sequence took him from fifth overall to a convincing second in the series. He set the fastest lap in each of the last three races. When he starts setting pole positions as well he's going to be dangerous.

He started the year well, unlike his fellow young gun Nicky Hayden, never finishing below fourth in the first seven events and giving Rossi a scare at Assen. Next came Laguna Seca and Donington; Marco decided that both were dangerous and promptly proved his point by crashing – three times in the States. It took him a while to regain his form, but from Motegi onwards he was using a works chassis which cured the problems he was having with tyre degradation.

SPA	POR	CHN	FRA	ITA	CAT	NED	USA	GBR	GER	CZE	JPN	MAL	QAT	AUS	TUR	VAL	POINTS
3-3	5-4	2-3	3-4	7-4	2-3	3-2	11-f	3-f	5-7	5-6	3-f	9-5	5-2	8-4	2-1	2-1	220

ATTILA&CO

GAS THANKS ITS PARTNER: **HONDA**

CLOTHING FOR THE HUMAN RACE

GAS, OFFICIAL SPONSOR OF THE REPSOL HONDA TEAM.

GAS
Keep it simple.

NICKY HAYDEN 3

NATIONALITY American
DATE OF BIRTH 30 July 1981
TEAM Repsol Honda Team
2005 SEASON 1 win, 3 poles, 2 fastest laps

A season of firsts for the young Kentucky rider; first pole position, first win and first fastest lap in MotoGP. Just as importantly, he ended the season with a run of four consecutive rostrums. Although his win at Laguna Seca was a thing of beauty, it was one of those rare ocassions when track knowledge (and maybe familiarity with the roadside furniture) is vital. You could easily argue that Phillip Island, where he pushed Rossi every inch of the way, was a better showing or that the duel with Melandri in Valencia proved more.

This was Nicky's third year on the factory Honda and the pressure was well and truly on for him to achieve on a regular basis. The year started in the worst possible way when he crashed out of a safe third position at Jerez, then he finished second and ninth in the next two races. Starting the season slowly had been his problem at the start of the 2004 season, and it's something his team will be looking out for in 2006.

At the end of 2005, though, he looked every inch the future of Honda's MotoGP hopes.

SPA	POR	CHN	FRA	ITA	CAT	NED	USA	GBR	GER	CZE	JPN	MAL	QAT	AUS	TUR	VAL	POINTS
4-f	9-7	5-9	5-6	4-6	5-5	5-4	1-1	5-f	1-3	2-5	6-7	6-4	8-3	1-2	3-3	3-2	206

COLIN EDWARDS 4

NATIONALITY American
DATE OF BIRTH 27 February 1974
TEAM Gauloises Yamaha Team
2005 SEASON 3 rostrums, 1 fastest lap

Colin did exactly what he was recruited to do and, perhaps, what only he could do. His consistency – he was the only man to score points in every race and he never finished outside the top ten – backed up Rossi perfectly. It enabled Yamaha to win the Constructors' title they so wanted in their golden jubilee year, and also helped the Gauloises Yamaha squad retain the Teams' title. Job done. The fact that he also gets on well with Valentino personally helped as well. Colin conducted The Doctor on a tour of Las Vegas after Laguna Seca; enquire after

the sordid details and he says he can tell you but he'll have to kill you afterwards.

Towards the end of the season Colin started trying to move his riding style away from its Superbike roots. After some fruitless practice sessions he adopted Rossi's settings and consciously tried to ride the Yamaha M1 as if it were a 250.

Colin was part of the entertaining struggle for second in the Championship but not getting a rostrum finish after Laguna Seca meant he lost touch with Melandri and Hayden.

SPA	POR	CHN	FRA	ITA	CAT	NED	USA	GBR	GER	CZE	JPN	MAL	QAT	AUS	TUR	VAL	POINTS
15-9	7-6	13-8	2-3	12-9	7-7	6-3	5-2	6-4	7-8	9-7	13-6	10-10	4-4	5-6	5-7	6-8	179

MAX BIAGGI

5

NATIONALITY Italian
DATE OF BIRTH 26 June 1971
TEAM Repsol Honda Team
2005 SEASON 4 rostrums, 1 fastest lap

For the first season in his MotoGP and 500cc career, Max Biaggi didn't win a race. That on its own would be bad enough, but to get what he always proclaimed he wanted – a full factory Honda – and then fail to deliver was nothing short of disastrous for him. And yet despite the impression that he was having a terrible season, he was second in the Championship over four races from Brno to Losail. How did he manage to do that?

From the first race, Max was complaining about front-end chatter, and he wasn't imagining it: sometimes you could even see his front wheel bouncing on TV pictures. However, there was no way he would or could change his 250-derived riding style with its high corner speeds and extreme lean angles. 'Smooth is always fast,' says Max.

However, his dreadful end to the season, especially the disaster of Istanbul where he was beaten by Honda replacement rider Chris Vermeulen, sealed his fate. Conspiracy theories multiplied but HRC had no compunction in replacing Biaggi with 250 star Dani Pedrosa for 2006.

SPA	POR	CHN	FRA	ITA	CAT	NED	USA	GBR	GER	CZE	JPN	MAL	QAT	AUS	TUR	VAL	POINTS
16-7	8-3	14-5	8-5	3-2	4-6	9-6	7-4	8-f	6-4	10-3	5-2	12-6	13-dnf	6-f	12-12	5-6	173

LORIS CAPIROSSI

6

NATIONALITY Italian
DATE OF BIRTH 4 April 1973
TEAM Ducati Marlboro Team
2005 SEASON 2 wins, 3 poles, 1 fastest lap

Ducati's over-winter conversion to Bridgestone tyres meant the first half of Loris's season had only one highlight; the rostrum at Mugello. But from Brno onwards, as the bike and tyres started to work together, he was his old self. In the space of four races he set pole three times in a row, scored back-to-back victories, got another rostrum and set a fastest lap. It was by far the Ducati factory's best run in GPs and it surely would have been even better but for that horrible crash in the first practice session in Australia. A monumentally quick highside at Doohan's, Phillip Island's first corner, put Loris in hospital with bleeding in a lung. He described it as the worst crash of his career. Three weeks later he was back riding at Valencia, looking pale and drawn but determined to defend his sixth place in the Championship.

Without that crash it could so easily have been second he was shooting for; after Malaysia he was up to third in the points table and very much the man in form. Pretty amazing seeing as he was as low as 12th after Shanghai and only eighth after Brno.

SPA	POR	CHN	FRA	ITA	CAT	NED	USA	GBR	GER	CZE	JPN	MAL	QAT	AUS	TUR	VAL	POINTS
6-13	6-9	3-12	10-7	6-3	6-12	7-10	14-10	11-6	8-9	3-2	1-1	1-1	1-10	i	i	7-7	157

SETE GIBERNAU

7

NATIONALITY Spanish
DATE OF BIRTH 15 December 1972
TEAM Movistar Honda MotoGP
2005 SEASON 4 rostrums, 5 poles, 1 fastest lap

You wouldn't wish Sete Gibernau's luck on your worst enemy. The Curse of Qatar with which Rossi hexed him in 2004 was still operating at maximum efficiency in 2005. Sete crashed while leading in Portugal and Great Britain, ran off track while leading in Germany, Qatar and Turkey, ran out of petrol in the Czech Republic and had his bike stop in Valencia. Add in a couple more crashes that were his own doing and you have a picture of misery. And that's before you factor in that brutal pass that Rossi put on him on the very last corner of the very first race.

But there was no doubting his mastery of the qualifying tyre. Even when practice went badly, Sete could make the situation look better. He started from the front row 14 times in 17 races and sat on pole five times – the same number as Rossi. Sete won the BMW Award for best aggregate qualifier by well over three seconds.

For two years Sete Gibernau was the only man to consistently give Rossi a race. Maybe it's impossible to maintain that intensity for three years.

SPA	POR	CHN	FRA	ITA	CAT	NED	USA	GBR	GER	CZE	JPN	MAL	QAT	AUS	TUR	VAL	POINTS
2-2	2-f	1-4	4-2	2-f	1-2	2-5	13-5	2-f	2-2	1-dnf	7-f	2-f	2-5	3-5	1-4	1-dnf	150

ALEX BARROS

8

NATIONALITY Brazilian
DATE OF BIRTH 18 October 1970
TEAM Honda Pons
2005 SEASON 1 win, 1 pole, 2 fastest laps

Only four men beat Rossi all year, and the first of them was Alex Barros. That victory in Portugal, the second round, sent him to China running second in the Championship. When it rained for race day, Rossi named him as one of the two men he feared most. Sure enough, Alex set the fastest lap of the race but only after he'd come in for a ride-through penalty that put him out of contention for the top ten, never mind a rostrum.

His only other rostrum also came in the rain, in that memorable Donington race. In

the last part of the season he made a habit of qualifying badly and then fighting his way to a respectable result. His last front-row start was in Germany; he then ran into serious problems with feel at the front of his bike, and after the British race he only scored two more top-five finishes.

Injuries from two heavy race crashes, in France and Australia, certainly didn't help his cause, but a season that started so well ended disappointingly. MotoGP's most experienced rider may not be back for the 2006 season.

SPA	POR	CHN	FRA	ITA	CAT	NED	USA	GBR	GER	CZE	JPN	MAL	QAT	AUS	TUR	VAL	POINTS
8-4	1-1	11-11	11-f	13-7	9-4	8-7	3-f	4-3	3-5	7-4	10-f	11-8	14-9	12-f	8-9	8-5	147

CARLOS CHECA

9

NATIONALITY Spanish
DATE OF BIRTH 15 October 1972
TEAM Ducati Marlboro Team
2005 SEASON 2 rostrums

When the Ducati team's Bridgestone tyres came good in the middle of the year, so did Carlos. However, a crash-happy start to the season meant he was never going to finish high up the Championship. In China he was fast in warm-up and had Bridgestone's excellent rain tyres for the race, but crashed spectacularly and aquaplaned up the pit entrance road on his back. At the Sachsenring his crash in qualifying – a highside on the fastest part of the track – was probably the fastest of the year. He marched to the barrier, leant on it, took a deep breath, went back to the pits for his other bike – and improved his lap time.

It's impossible not to like and admire the guy. Nevertheless, despite being part of Ducati's best-ever GP result in Malaysia and scoring a crafty third place in Australia, Carlos lost his job at the end of the year. It's hard not to believe that he was only one good result away from keeping his job, but it's also likely that he will return in 2006 with another competitive ride. And despite what the cynics say, not just because of his passport.

SPA	POR	CHN	FRA	ITA	CAT	NED	USA	GBR	GER	CZE	JPN	MAL	QAT	AUS	TUR	VAL	POINTS
12-10	3-5	7-f	9-f	8-5	8-11	13-9	8-f	13-5	11-f	6-8	9-4	8-3	6-6	4-3	9-5	4-4	138

SHINYA NAKANO

10

NATIONALITY Japanese
DATE OF BIRTH 10 October 1977
TEAM Kawasaki Racing Team
2005 SEASON No rostrums, poles or fastest laps

It's difficult to know what to make of Shinya's season. Like all the other Bridgestone users, he suffered badly at Catalunya and Qatar from problems with his tyres, but the Kawasaki's lack of grunt also hamstrung the team at power tracks like Brno. The most worrying aspect of his season was that his best run of results came in the first few races.

There was also a serious amount of bad luck when circumstances should have conspired to give him a chance of a rostrum finish, as happened at Motegi in 2004. But in China

water in new fly-by-wire electrics meant he sat and watched while temporary team-mate Olivier Jacque took Kawasaki's best-ever result, and in Malaysia he was skittled early on when a good result looked not just possible but probable.

However, as our Riders' Rider of the Year poll demonstrates, Shinya is still held in high regard by his competitors. He has re-signed for Kawasaki for 2006 and the factory has promised a completely new bike. If it isn't as competitive as he's been told, Shinya will do a lot of complaining.

SPA	POR	CHN	FRA	ITA	CAT	NED	USA	GBR	GER	CZE	JPN	MAL	QAT	AUS	TUR	VAL	POINTS
5-5	10-8	10-dnf	6-8	9-10	12-9	4-8	10-9	12-f	12-6	11-12	14-f	4-f	7-7	10-7	10-10	9-11	98

MAKOTO TAMADA   11

NATIONALITY Japanese
DATE OF BIRTH 4 November 1976
TEAM JIR Konica Minolta Honda

He was expected to give Rossi a hard time this year, but Makoto never came to terms with his new Michelin tyres. Lack of confidence in the front, especially early in races, was a recurring theme. There was also the not insignificant matter of the wrist injury he suffered in practice for the second race of the year, Portugal. That kept him out of three races and he needed further operations after he came back for Mugello. At least he got on the rostrum at home in Japan, but he was a distant third and aided by the Rossi/Melandri crash; a far cry from the dominating victory there 12 months previously. The Japanese race was a metaphor for his whole season – satisfactory but well below expectations. The question being asked at the end of the year was, will Tamada be back on Bridgestones in 2006?

SPA	POR	CHN	FRA	ITA	CAT	NED	USA	GBR	GER	CZE	JPN	MAL	QAT	AUS	TUR	VAL	POINTS
7-8	i	i	i	10-8	10-dnf	11-14	9-7	9-7	15-10	12-10	4-3	15-12	10-dnf	9-8	7-8	10-9	91

TONI ELIAS   12

NATIONALITY Spanish
DATE OF BIRTH 26 March 1983
TEAM Fortuna Yamaha Team

His storming end to the season tends to obscure the fact that Toni was looking seriously impressive before he suffered multiple fractures in a testing crash after the French GP. At Shanghai he was running in third place before he was called in for a ride-through penalty. He missed the three races after France and came back, still far from fit, at Laguna – not the place you want to ride with a bad wrist. Once he'd had the metalwork removed from his arm, he went from strength to strength. His end-of-season run from Qatar onwards was wonderful to watch. His fighting sixth place in Istanbul, where he passed the same group of riders twice, was one of the highlights of the first Turkish GP. No wonder Honda were so pleased to recruit him for 2006. Elias and Melandri? That's a team that'll be hard to beat.

SPA	POR	CHN	FRA	ITA	CAT	NED	USA	GBR	GER	CZE	JPN	MAL	QAT	AUS	TUR	VAL	POINTS
13-12	15-14	8-14	12-9	i	i	i	17-13	17-9	17-12	15-14	17-9	14-11	9-8	7-9	6-6	13-10	74

KENNY ROBERTS   13

NATIONALITY American
DATE OF BIRTH 25 July 1973
TEAM Team Suzuki MotoGP

The World Champion of 2000 finally said goodbye to Suzuki after a season that most observers considered lacklustre. However, post-Brno Kenny was looking more competitive and was starting to out-qualify his team-mate and beat him in races. The trouble was that, to put it charitably, he appeared to have problems with his motivation when a rostrum finish wasn't on the cards. On the two occasions when it was, China and Great Britain, Kenny broke down while leading and finished second. The Donington Park ride was a reminder of how and why he became a World Champion. Despite the factory's loyalty, it was too little too late. He was at home nursing the broken wrist he suffered in the first practice session for the Australian GP when the news came through that Suzuki wouldn't be renewing his contract.

SPA	POR	CHN	FRA	ITA	CAT	NED	USA	GBR	GER	CZE	JPN	MAL	QAT	AUS	TUR	VAL	POINTS
14-dnf	14-12	9-dnf	14-13	11-15	13-15	15-16	12-14	16-2	9-11	17-11	8-8	5-7	11-11	i	i	i	63

JOHN HOPKINS   14

NATIONALITY American
DATE OF BIRTH 22 May 1983
TEAM Team Suzuki MotoGP

There's no doubt that John Hopkins was often over-riding the Suzuki in the search for either a front-row start or a top-six finish. He equalled his career best qualifying of second place at Motegi and got his best ever race finish there with fifth. The following week he backed it up with another front-row start – the first time in his career he'd started successive races from the front row. However, when he was in with a chance of the rostrum or a good finish he had a tendency to make mistakes. In Portugal he crashed when it started raining, in China he ran off track, and at Donington he did the same thing when his visor misted. There's no doubt that John is an extremely talented rider and he's young, so there's time for him to mature. Suzuki have shown their faith in him by signing John to a new two-year contract.

SPA	POR	CHN	FRA	ITA	CAT	NED	USA	GBR	GER	CZE	JPN	MAL	QAT	AUS	TUR	VAL	POINTS
11-14	11-f	4-7	7-16	5-11	11-dnf	12-13	6-8	10-11	10-ns	8-13	2-5	3-9	12-17	11-10	14-15	11-13	63

TROY BAYLISS 15

NATIONALITY Australian
DATE OF BIRTH 30 March 1969
TEAM Honda Pons

The ex-World Superbike Champ's riding style and the Honda RCV never came to an agreement. Troy knew from winter testing that he had problems and they never went away: a brace of sixth places was the best he could do, and his best qualifying position was fourth at Laguna Seca, the one track that seemed to repay his physical style. He didn't make another second-row start. His season ended prematurely when he suffered a very nasty broken arm training on a motocross bike at home the week before the Japanese GP. By then it was obvious that he would have difficulty getting a ride in MotoGP for 2006, but Troy was welcomed back with open arms by the Ducati World Superbike team for which he had so much success. And the factory haven't forgotten his fearless riding in 2003, Ducati's first year in MotoGP.

SPA	POR	CHN	FRA	ITA	CAT	NED	USA	GBR	GER	CZE	JPN	MAL	QAT	AUS	TUR	VAL	POINTS
9-6	13-11	12-f	15-10	17-13	15-8	14-11	4-6	7-f	16-ns	13-9	i	i	i	i	i	i	54

RUBEN XAUS 16

NATIONALITY Spanish
DATE OF BIRTH 18 February 1978
TEAM Fortuna Yamaha Team

Definitely a candidate for the man who suffered most in the season. The 2004 MotoGP Rookie of the Year was the first crasher of 2005 and he carried on crashing, although he usually confined it to practice and qualifying rather than the race. Ruben's main problem appeared to be an inability to adjust to the Yamaha M1 after years on Ducatis. Most people think an across-the-frame four-cylinder motorcycle is the norm – not Ruben. Well before the end of the year it looked as if he had opted to see his time out as painlessly as possible. His talk of taking it easy early on, not taking too many risks, and getting a few points sounded so wrong coming from a man with his rostrum-or-straw-bales attitude to motorcycle racing. Being put in the shade by younger team-mate Toni Elias cannot have helped either.

SPA	POR	CHN	FRA	ITA	CAT	NED	USA	GBR	GER	CZE	JPN	MAL	QAT	AUS	TUR	VAL	POINTS
17-18	12-10	16-10	16-12	15-14	16-10	16-12	16-11	14-f	18-13	20-18	19-10	16-15	16-14	15-12	16-14	17-15	52

ROBERTO ROLFO 18

NATIONALITY Italian
DATE OF BIRTH 23 March 1980
TEAM Team D'Antin – Pramac

Fresh up from the 250s and the lone D'Antin runner, Roby showed tenacity and flashes of inspiration aboard the year-old Ducati. In Catalunya and Qatar he got into the first corner in eighth place. It was a measure of the progress of both the rider and his Dunlop tyres that while he immediately sank back through the field in Catalunya, in Qatar his lap times didn't slip until a couple of laps from the flag. At Laguna Seca he also had a great ride that was curtailed a lap from the flag when he ran out of fuel due to excessive wheelspin. Both of his two crashes were down to other riders. A total of nine points-scoring rides in your first year in MotoGP is not a bad record, especially given the resources available to him and his team. It may well have been enough to get him a ride on a factory satellite squad in 2006.

SPA	POR	CHN	FRA	ITA	CAT	NED	USA	GBR	GER	CZE	JPN	MAL	QAT	AUS	TUR	VAL	POINTS
18-15	16-13	17-16	18-15	19-17	17-14	18-18	18-dnf	19-10	20-14	19-17	16-f	17-13	15-12	16-13	17-16	18-f	25

ALEX HOFMANN 19

NATIONALITY German
DATE OF BIRTH 25 May 1980
TEAM Kawasaki Racing Team

Two crashes ripped the heart out of Alex's season and ultimately cost him his job. The first was definitely the most bizarre crash of the year; it happened at about 5mph during a publicity stunt on Estoril seafront before the Portuguese GP, and resulted in a badly broken wrist. His crash in Japan while trying to pass Rolfo resulted in two plates and 16 screws in his foot and ankle. In all, he missed seven races through injury and rode while unfit in several more. His 29 races for Kawasaki, first as a wild card and for the past two years as a full-time team member, resulted in a best finish of eighth in the wet at Donington this year. Alex's record is undoubtedly made to look worse than it really is by the fact his team-mate has been Shinya Nakano – not the easiest racer in the world to be compared with.

SPA	POR	CHN	FRA	ITA	CAT	NED	USA	GBR	GER	CZE	JPN	MAL	QAT	AUS	TUR	VAL	POINTS
10-11	i	i	i	14-12	14-17	10-dnf	15-12	15-8	13-ns	14-15	12-f	i	i	i	i	12-14	24

FRANCO BATTAINI 22

NATIONALITY Italian
DATE OF BIRTH 22 July 1972
TEAM Blata WCM

Ater eight years in 250cc Grands Prix, all of them spent on Aprilias, Franco joined the smallest team in MotoGP for 2005. It was a hard year and his sit-back 250 riding style sometimes simply didn't work: at Laguna Seca, for instance, he couldn't get any feel or confidence in the front end. It took him until the tenth round, the German GP, to score his first point. Two more points-scoring rides followed, with a best of 11th in the crash-strewn Japanese GP. Although Franco may not have enjoyed the best of seasons, he never threw in the towel. If he was disappointed by the non-appearance of the Blata V6 or the fact his team-mate was attracting lots of positive comment, he didn't show it. If he cannot get a good ride in 2006 he could compete in triathlon at a very high level.

SPA	POR	CHN	FRA	ITA	CAT	NED	USA	GBR	GER	CZE	JPN	MAL	QAT	AUS	TUR	VAL	POINTS
19-17	19-dnf	20-f	21-17	21-18	21-19	21-20	21-17	21-f	22-15	21-20	20-11	19-16	19-16	18-15	19-17	21-16	7

JAMES ELLISON 23

NATIONALITY British
DATE OF BIRTH 19 September 1980
TEAM Blata WCM

In his first full season of MotoGP the Cumbrian impressed everyone: his team, the media, other riders. His qualifying performances in Germany and the Czech Republic were particularly impressive, as were his rides in China and the USA. In any case he was usually to be found racing with Rolfo and Xaus – and Byrne when he was with Team KR. The WCM team were seriously impressed with his abilities. They hadn't intended to develop their V4 any further but Ellison's insistence that a lengthened swingarm and chassis would allow him to ride the bike as he wanted provoked them to make a new chassis. James was immediately more competitive. Unfortunately, an accident tyre testing at Brno (when he went over three seconds quicker than he'd been in the race) resulted in an elbow injury that severely hampered the second half of his season.

SPA	POR	CHN	FRA	ITA	CAT	NED	USA	GBR	GER	CZE	JPN	MAL	QAT	AUS	TUR	VAL	POINTS
21-16	17-15	21-13	20-f	20-dnf	20-18	20-19	20-16	20-f	19-ns	18-19	ns	20-dnf	18-15	17-14	18-18	19-dnf	7

WILD CARDS & REPLACEMENT RIDERS

MotoGP regulations stipulate that when a team's regular rider is injured he can be replaced. It's also possible for wild-card entries to be nominated race-by-race by Dorna (MotoGP rights holders), IRTA (the teams' organisation), and the FIM (the sport's governing body) and its local affiliates. These are the men who couldn't give up the day job this time round.

OLIVIER JACQUE 17

Six replacement rides for Alex Hofmann plus one wild card meant Olivier had a busier season than he expected. The first one saw him take a magnificent second place in China and land himself a job as Kawasaki's test rider. It was his best result in MotoGP and the best by a wild card or replacement since Akira Ryo in 2002 at Suzuka – the very first MotoGP race.

JURGEN vd GOORBERGH 20

The ever-cheerful Dutchman replaced Makoto Tamada at the Chinese and French GPs. Like Olivier Jacque, he took full advantage of the soaking new Shanghai track to remind everyone of his talent. Despite having no time to test, he finished sixth in his first ride on a MotoGP four-stroke. The Konica Minolta team wouldn't get a better result until Tamada's third at Motegi.

a rider is only as good as
their team

Hein Gericke

EVERYTHING from HELMETS & race LEATHERS, to PERFORMANCE parts, security & TOURING equipment backed up with EXPERT advice & PROFESSIONAL service

HEIN GERICKE is the No.1 TEAM on the high street.

hotline: 0800 165 165

CHRIS VERMEULEN 21

The young Aussie took two rides as replacement in the Camel Honda team for Troy Bayliss; Australia and Turkey. HRC wanted him to go back to World Superbike before moving to MotoGP, so Suzuki stepped in and signed him for the 2006 season and beyond.

SHANE BYRNE 24

Started the season as Team KR's regular rider but found himself unemployed when the team and engine supplier KTM fell out. Thrown a lifeline by Camel Honda when Troy Bayliss was injured and had points-scoring rides in Malaysia and Qatar.

RYUICHI KIYONARI 25

The British Superbike Championship runner-up got his reward for the Suzuka 8 Hours victory when he replaced the injured Troy Bayliss at Camel Honda for the last race of the year. He last rode an RCV211V in 2003 when he took over after the death of Daijiro Kato.

DAVID CHECA 26

Carlos's little brother stood in for Toni Elias at Fortuna Yamaha when the regular rider was hurt testing after the French GP. Rode in Italy, Catalunya and Holland, scoring points in the second and third races. Won the Le Mans 24 Hours for Yamaha earlier in the year.

TOHRU UKAWA 27

Honda's test rider and a former MotoGP winner, Tohru was loaned out to the Moriwaki team for a wild-card ride in China. As he'd won 250 GPs in the wet, conditions should have suited him but he could only manage 15th in the bike's first race on Michelins.

NOBUATSU AOKI

Suzuki's test rider only got to do two GPs – Brno as a wild card and Valencia as a replacement for the absent Kenny Roberts. He finished in the Czech Republic without scoring but was going well and in front of his team-mate when the bike stopped in Valencia.

SHINICHI ITO

Ito split his year between winning the Japanese Superbike Championship on a Honda and being Bridgestone's MotoGP test rider on a Ducati. He replaced Capirossi at Istanbul but jumped the start, didn't come in for the penalty and was black-flagged.

NAOKI MATSUDO

The ex-Japanese 250 Champion and GP rostrum man rode for Moriwaki in the All-Japan Championship in 2005, so it was natural that he got a wild-card ride at Twin-Ring Motegi on the Honda V5-powered Dream Fighter. Unfortunately, his race lasted less than a lap.

JEREMY McWILLIAMS

MotoGP's oldest inhabitant returned for one ride amid much controversy. Team Roberts put him on their own bike in Brno after the split with engine suppliers KTM. It was a short-lived race, but it was good to be reminded that the Ulsterman is still fast.

KURTIS ROBERTS

Having endured a tough season in the AMA Superbike Championship on the Erion Honda, Kurtis returned to MotoGP to ride his father's bike in the last race of the year at Valencia. It didn't do much to cheer him up; he qualified next to last and retired in the race.

C5005 MotoGP 1 Set

C5006 MotoGP 3 Set

MotoGP 1 SCALEXTRIC

motogp
www.scalextricmotogp.com world championship rossi v hayden

MotoGP 3 SCALEXTRIC

motogp
www.scalextricmotogp.com world championship biaggi v gibernau

Race for Real with the 2005 Scalextric MotoGP range

C6020 Yamaha Go !!!!!!! - Valentino Rossi | C6023 Ducati 2005 - Carlos Checa | C6022 Honda Repsol 2005 - Max Biaggi | C6021 Honda Movistar 2005 - Sete Giberna

THE RACES
MotoGP 2005

THE SHAPE OF THINGS TO COME

Anyone who thought Valentino Rossi might lack a little motivation this season had their doubts well and truly answered by one of the greatest last laps of recent years

Was the Italian acting when he thumped his Yamaha's petrol tank in apparent anger after failing to win the BMW car at the pre-season test? Was he really telling the truth when he said that it would be a little more difficult to find the motivation to defend his title? Would this really be his last year in MotoGP? By the end of the first race of 2005 it appeared that the answers to all those questions were no, no and no.

Valentino Rossi brutally put down an attempt by Sete Gibernau to take an early championship lead on home ground, sending the local fans' hero into the gravel trap

on the very last corner with a move that was, to put it mildly, controversial. It came at the end of a final lap in which the lead changed four times.

The pattern of the 2004 season looked to be carrying on as Gibernau and Rossi pulled clear of the competition. Only Nicky Hayden could go with them, and when he lost the front end going into the last corner seven laps from the flag the leading duo were the best part of 20 seconds clear of third-place man Marco Melandri.

In a preview of the tactic we would come to know

Opposite Marco Melandri got on the rostrum in his first MotoGP race for Honda

Above The first corner of the year and the pattern of the race is already established

Below Nicky Hayden was in a safe third place when he crashed and ruined the start of his season

well as the season went on, Rossi shadowed Gibernau for much of the race before pouncing three laps from the finish. It looked like the end of what had been a tense but unspectacular contest, Valentino almost instantly pulling out a half-second lead while Sete looked to have no answer. He did, however, have persistence. Half way round the last lap Sete's pressure told and Valentino outbraked himself at the corner at the end of the back straight. Gibernau forced his Honda through on the inside and they touched on the exit as he showed Rossi the edge of the track. It took the World Champion just a couple of corners to come back. Somehow he magicked enough speed out of his Yamaha as they exited the big double right-hander in the stadium section to get past his rival going into the first of the pair of 100mph rights that lead up to the final corner. Rossi came alongside with his front wheel in the air, dived through and then nearly lost the front end. That fractional loss of momentum gave Sete the chance to get back in front. One corner left. The Spanish rider took the normal line, swinging across to the right of the track for the horseshoe left that ends the lap; Valentino saw a gap and dived straight up the inside. When two bikes come together in this manner it is always the man on the outside who suffers: Gibernau's Honda ricocheted off the Yamaha and into the gravel trap. He paddled it out and crossed the line eight seconds adrift of Rossi but in second place; which was, everyone agreed, the least he deserved.

The crowd was not amused and produced a new sound for MotoGP, booing aimed at Valentino Rossi. The Italian was first back to parc fermé where he

indulged in the usual backslapping with his mechanics, friends and management people. Gibernau stalked about with his helmet on for a while before giving Rossi what he hoped was a withering stare as he brushed past him. That started Valentino's mate Uccio off on the Italian equivalent of 'Who are you looking at?' which

Sete's factotum Edu seemed quite prepared to answer until a Dorna manager told them both to shut up.

The party then had to move to the rostrum via a narrow staircase. Sete led the way but stopped half way up to clutch a little theatrically at his left shoulder. This was too much for Valentino to resist: he looked down the lens of the TV camera, gestured at Gibernau and smirked. He later said he couldn't understand how an incident that happened at such low speed could have hurt Sete. In fact, on-board video replays showed that Rossi's front brake lever had speared Gibernau in the left shoulder, a shoulder that has undergone three operations after multiple dislocations. However, old hands reckoned that if he were going to play the injury card he should have gone to the medical centre immediately and missed the rostrum. It took the Spanish rider a while to accept Valentino's hand, when it was proffered but that didn't alter the crowd's opinion: 'Rossi, Rossi, hijo de puta!' [son of a whore] they screamed in unison. Sete refused to talk about the last lap, pointedly repeating that he was happy with everything he had done throughout the weekend.

All of which rather overshadowed the magnificent achievement of Marco Melandri, who'd made it to the rostrum after his first race on a Honda RCV211V. It was also the first time he'd been on the MotoGP podium at Jerez. Loyally, he stood by his team-mate rather than his fellow countryman in the debate over the incident, saying he didn't like Rossi's attitude on the rostrum. Elsewhere there was little joy for Honda. Nicky Hayden seemed a certainty for the final podium place until he crashed, and although the other Repsol rider, Max Biaggi, followed up a quite awful qualifying with a brave

race he could only finish seventh. Camel Honda men Barros and Bayliss raced better than they qualified, while the rider many tipped to give Rossi a hard time, Makoto Tamada, had a lacklustre weekend.

Both Ducati riders were handicapped by injury, so it was Shinya Nakano in his debut on the Kawasaki big-bang motor who was the first Bridgestone runner home in an impressive fifth place. Suzuki did not have a good time either: John Hopkins found his bike was seriously affected by the strong gusts of wind that both upset the bike and brought considerable amounts of dust onto the track. Thankfully the rain held off all weekend so there was no chance of seeing how the new flag-to-flag regulations would work, although it was finally decided that riders would be able to change machines and not have to change wheels. Neither did the other major regulation change have a noticeable effect. Reducing the fuel tank capacity by two litres didn't result in anyone failing to make it to the flag, and it didn't slow them down either – Rossi's race time was a minute quicker than the last dry race, in 2003.

Anyone who thought the World Champion would ease off a little as he pondered what to do after his Yamaha contract runs out at the end of the season had to think again. Valentino showed just how strong his will to win still is, and just how far he was prepared to go in pursuit of victory. And there were also hints that he was thinking of staying with bikes for at least one more year.

More immediately, it was impossible to imagine a better opening to the season. As BBC anchorman John Inverdale, not a noted motorsports fan, said: 'What wouldn't Formula 1 give for race finishes like that?'

Opposite It took a while before Sete Gibernau shook the proffered hand...

Below Valentino started the year as he meant to go on – winning

SLUSH BOX DELUXE

Above Carlos Checa,
injured but riding – without
the semi-automatic gearbox

Ducati continued their pre-season experiment with a semi-automatic gearbox right up until race day. The system made the bike sound like it was silently freewheeling into corners, but as soon as the throttle was opened it reverted to sounding like a normal bike. Seasoned paddock people were instantly reminded of the old plug chop technique used to test carburation: full throttle followed by total silence. What was happening?

The best guess is that as soon as the brakes were applied electronics disengaged the clutch then gradually re-engaged it as the brakes were released. However, there was no sign or sound of downshifting and the bike appeared to 'know' what gear it should be in coming out of the corner. Electronic corner counting or GPS mapping could both make that happen, but the real question is, why would Ducati want it to

happen? The answer has to be fuel economy, perhaps a 5–8 per cent improvement.

However, the riders reported that the result was a total lack of feel, as anyone who has missed a gear on a motorcycle and found a false neutral or gone into a corner with the clutch lever pulled in could tell you. Loris Capirossi said this was the first thing about which he'd had a serious disagreement with the factory, but as a loyal employee he'd do what he was told. His Saturday morning crash plus Carlos Checa's rib-cracking get-off in the pre-season Barcelona tests brought matters to a head. It was decided not to race with the system, the official reason being that the practice starts after Sunday morning warm-up had been found to cause more chain stretch than was acceptable. The man from Ducati's chain supplier was very quick to point out that whatever the problem was, it wasn't down to his product!

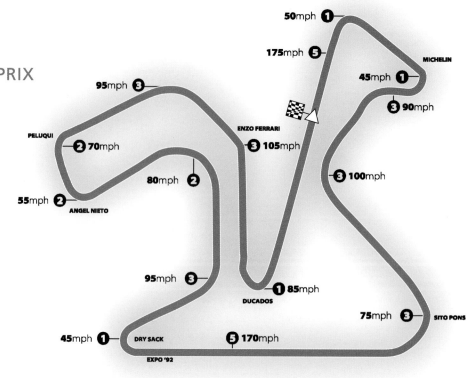

JEREZ
SPANISH GRAND PRIX

ROUND 1

RACE RESULTS

RACE DATE April 10th
CIRCUIT LENGTH 2.748 miles
NO. OF LAPS 27
RACE DISTANCE 74.196 miles
WEATHER Dry, 15°C
TRACK TEMPERATURE 32°C
WINNER Valentino Rossi
FASTEST LAP 1m 40.596s, 98.136mph, Valentino Rossi (record)
PREVIOUS LAP RECORD 1m 42.788s, 96.260mph, Valentino Rossi , 2004

Track map labels:
- 50mph 1
- 175mph 5
- MICHELIN
- 45mph 1
- 95mph 3
- 3 90mph
- PELUQUI
- ENZO FERRARI
- 2 70mph
- 3 105mph
- 3 100mph
- 80mph 2
- 55mph 2
- ANGEL NIETO
- 95mph 3
- 1 85mph
- DUCADOS
- 75mph 3
- SITO PONS
- 45mph 1
- DRY SACK
- 5 170mph
- EXPO '92

QUALIFYING

	Rider	Nationality	Team	Qualifying	Pole +	Gap
1	Rossi	ITA	Gauloises Yamaha Team	1m 39.419s		
2	Gibernau	SPA	Movistar Honda MotoGP	1m 39.915s	0.496s	0.496s
3	Melandri	ITA	Movistar Honda MotoGP	1m 40.179s	0.760s	0.264s
4	Hayden	USA	Repsol Honda Team	1m 40.465s	1.046s	0.286s
5	Nakano	JPN	Kawasaki Racing Team	1m 40.542s	1.123s	0.077s
6	Capirossi	ITA	Ducati Marlboro Team	1m 40.648s	1.229s	0.106s
7	Tamada	JPN	JIR Konica Minolta Honda	1m 40.707s	1.288s	0.059s
8	Barros	BRA	Camel Honda	1m 40.720s	1.301s	0.013s
9	Bayliss	AUS	Camel Honda	1m 40.774s	1.355s	0.054s
10	Hofmann	GER	Kawasaki Racing Team	1m 40.812s	1.393s	0.038s
11	Hopkins	USA	Team Suzuki MotoGP	1m 40.825s	1.406s	0.013s
12	Checa C.	SPA	Ducati Marlboro Team	1m 40.948s	1.529s	0.123s
13	Elias	SPA	Fortuna Yamaha Team	1m 41.029s	1.610s	0.081s
14	Roberts	USA	Team Suzuki MotoGP	1m 41.058s	1.639s	0.029s
15	Edwards	USA	Gauloises Yamaha Team	1m 41.176s	1.757s	0.118s
16	Biaggi	ITA	Repsol Honda Team	1m 41.233s	1.814s	0.057s
17	Xaus	SPA	Fortuna Yamaha Team	1m 42.286s	2.867s	1.053s
18	Rolfo	ITA	Team D'Antin – Pramac	1m 43.523s	4.104s	1.237s
19	Battaini	ITA	Blata WCM	1m 44.576s	5.157s	1.053s
20	Byrne	GBR	Team Roberts	1m 44.728s	5.309s	0.152s
21	Ellison	GBR	Blata WCM	1m 44.833s	5.414s	0.105s

FINISHERS

1 VALENTINO ROSSI One of the great last laps of all time, culminating in that brutal pass, meant the rest were playing catch-up right from the start. This win made Rossi the first man since Agostini to win the opening race in five consecutive seasons and the first Yamaha rider since Lawson in 1986 to win four races in a row.

2 SETE GIBERNAU Did everything right all weekend until the last three laps. Did he really let Rossi through for a look at his pace? Did he leave the door open at the last corner? All he would say was that he was happy with everything he did.

3 MARCO MELANDRI A brilliant beginning to his time with Honda – a front-row start and a rostrum finish – but you almost feel sorry for him because nobody seemed to take any notice after the leading duo's last-lap coming-together.

4 ALEX BARROS A brilliant fight back to a very respectable finish after making a mess of the start thanks to selecting the wrong engine management programme. Alex didn't know whether to be delighted or seriously upset.

5 SHINYA NAKANO A great race and a very encouraging first outing for the new big-bang Kawasaki engine. The fact he was able to back up his fifth place

in qualifying (not a surprise, thanks to Bridgestone's qualifiers) was especially impressive.

6 TROY BAYLISS The Aussie thought his result 'not bad for a first go' and, given his lack of confidence in winter testing, it was easy to agree with him. He was less than two seconds adrift of team-mate Barros.

7 MAX BIAGGI After the purgatory of qualifying Max rode an inspired race, but that didn't stop HRC making some threatening noises about his form, or perceived lack of it.

8 MAKOTO TAMADA Many pundits thought Tamada would be the man to challenge Rossi this season, but the

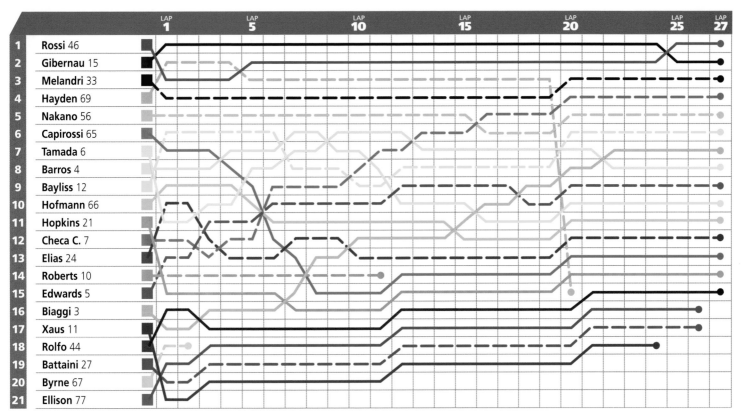

		LAP 1	LAP 5	LAP 10	LAP 15	LAP 20	LAP 25	LAP 27
1	Rossi 46							
2	Gibernau 15							
3	Melandri 33							
4	Hayden 69							
5	Nakano 56							
6	Capirossi 65							
7	Tamada 6							
8	Barros 4							
9	Bayliss 12							
10	Hofmann 66							
11	Hopkins 21							
12	Checa C. 7							
13	Elias 24							
14	Roberts 10							
15	Edwards 5							
16	Biaggi 3							
17	Xaus 11							
18	Rolfo 44							
19	Battaini 27							
20	Byrne 67							
21	Ellison 77							

RACE

	Rider	Motorcycle	Race Time	Time +	Fastest Lap	Average Speed
1	Rossi	Yamaha	45m 43.156s		1m 40.596s	176.912mph
2	Gibernau	Honda	45m 51.787s	8.631s	1m 40.897s	178.652mph
3	Melandri	Honda	46m 01.616s	18.460s	1m 41.043s	177.533mph
4	Barros	Honda	46m 10.094s	26.938s	1m 41.603s	176.291mph
5	Nakano	Kawasaki	46m 10.815s	27.659s	1m 41.467s	172.749mph
6	Bayliss	Honda	46m 11.665s	28.509s	1m 41.828s	174.986mph
7	Biaggi	Honda	46m 13.774s	30.618s	1m 41.525s	173.681mph
8	Tamada	Honda	46m 20.043s	36.887s	1m 41.723s	170.387mph
9	Edwards	Yamaha	46m 20.764s	37.608s	1m 41.596s	174.426mph
10	Checa C.	Ducati	46m 22.834s	39.678s	1m 41.851s	170.263mph
11	Hofmann	Kawasaki	46m 25.439s	42.283s	1m 42.275s	171.506mph
12	Elias	Yamaha	46m 38.613s	55.457s	1m 42.246s	174.986mph
13	Capirossi	Ducati	46m 45.528s	1m 02.372s	1m 42.189s	174.426mph
14	Hopkins	Suzuki	47m 02.502s	1m 19.346s	1m 42.606s	172.252mph
15	Rolfo	Ducati	47m 16.763s	1m 33.607s	1m 44.011s	171.568mph
16	Ellison	Blata	46m 22.019s	1 Lap	1m 45.575s	164.919mph
17	Battaini	Blata	46m 42.560s	1 Lap	1m 46.243s	165.478mph
18	Xaus	Yamaha	46m 04.511s	3 Laps	1m 45.691s	166.721mph
	Hayden	Honda	34m 52.000s	7 Laps	1m 40.892s	177.906mph
	Roberts	Suzuki	19m 04.036s	16 Laps	1m 42.458s	166.783mph
	Byrne	Proton KR	3m 42.196s	25 Laps	1m 46.018s	165.230mph

CHAMPIONSHIP

	Rider	Team	Points
1	Rossi	Gauloises Yamaha Team	25
2	Gibernau	Movistar Honda MotoGP	20
3	Melandri	Movistar Honda MotoGP	16
4	Barros	Camel Honda	13
5	Nakano	Kawasaki Racing Team	11
6	Bayliss	Camel Honda	10
7	Biaggi	Repsol Honda Team	9
8	Tamada	JIR Konica Minolta Honda	8
9	Edwards	Gauloises Yamaha Team	7
10	Checa C.	Ducati Marlboro Team	6
11	Hofmann	Kawasaki Racing Team	5
12	Elias	Fortuna Yamaha Team	4
13	Capirossi	Ducati Marlboro Team	3
14	Hopkins	Team Suzuki MotoGP	2
15	Rolfo	Team D'Antin – Pramac	1

Japanese rider had a largely anonymous weekend and was the lowest finisher of the Honda men.

9 COLIN EDWARDS Struggled with the useability of his bike all weekend but raced a lot better than he qualified for a respectable finish.

10 CARLOS CHECA The shoulder he'd dislocated at the Barcelona tests handicapped him and then there was the matter of the new engine braking system with which the team persisted right up until the race. Not a good weekend.

11 ALEX HOFMANN A good, competitive weekend. Alex was as quick as team-mate Nakano in some

qualifying sessions, and wasn't that far behind Checa's Ducati in the race.

12 TONI ELIAS Seriously impressive in qualifying but his lack of experience showed during the race; still, hardly a bad result for a first MotoGP race.

13 LORIS CAPIROSSI A practice crash cracked a small bone in his left ankle, and it was far from clear whether he would be able to race or not; but race he did, although far from fit. The effects of the injury would be felt for several races to come.

14 JOHN HOPKINS After a promising qualifying John went for tyres that proved too soft and the Suzuki did not cope at all well with the strong winds.

15 ROBERTO ROLFO A point in your first MotoGP race is no mean achievement, especially on a bike as difficult to get to know as the '04 Ducati, and on Dunlops. Rider and team were quietly pleased.

16 JAMES ELLISON A trouble-free ride but without the reward of a point, although he did have the satisfaction of beating team-mate Battaini.

17 FRANCO BATTAINI Happy to get the bike home but not at all amused to be beaten by his team-mate. Had to content himself with an impressive qualifying performance.

18 RUBEN XAUS Fell on lap one, came in for repairs, then went out again only to get a ride-through penalty for speeding in pit lane. Not an ideal afternoon.

NON-FINISHERS

NICKY HAYDEN Right there with the top two when he crashed seven laps from the flag. In a change from his previous persona he later stated that he 'refused to apologise for racing with those guys'.

KENNY ROBERTS For once 'electrical fault' as the reason for a dnf was true. It was a pressure-sensing switch in

the quickshifter that failed and started telling lies to the engine management software.

SHANE BYRNE After a blown motor in qualifying another engine went sick after just two laps. It had developed a misfire in morning warm-up and it very quickly became terminal in the race.

ESTORIL
PORTUGUESE GRAND PRIX

ROUND 2

SLIPSLIDING AWAY

Alex Barros had the perfect weekend, Sete Gibernau didn't and Valentino Rossi just extended his lead in the points table

Eight laps into the race it started to spit with rain. Race Direction instructed marshals to put out the white flags, meaning that the new rain regulations were now in force. Sete Gibernau is supposed to win when it rains, and for much of the race it looked as if he was going to. Only Alex Barros, who had been fastest in every session, including qualifying and warm-up, was able to go with him on the tricky track. Despite the damp patches the two Honda men pulled clear at fractionally under lap-record pace, leaving Rossi to fend off the attentions of Max Biaggi for third. It looked like the pattern of the race was set. Barros closed the gap to under a second only to have Gibernau respond and get his lead back up to over a second and a half; then the rain really started to come down.

Actually it only really arrived at the first two corners and, as fate would have it, the first man on the scene was Gibernau: he slid off at Turn 1 and damaged his bike enough to prevent him restarting. Sete felt himself very much a victim of circumstances, saying there was no warning and it was impossible to avoid crashing. Here was an opportunity

lost. If he'd stayed on his wheels and won the Spanish rider would have gone to the top of the points table, but he left Portugal fifth in the championship – a whole race win's worth of points behind Rossi after just two rounds. Suffering this injury to his title chances just a week after the insult of Jerez would test the mental strength of any rider. To his credit, Sete maintained the same sense of slightly offended dignity he'd shown the week before. The new rain rules, he maintained, were not perfect and it was necessary to keep working on the problem.

Valentino Rossi, the subject of some criticism for his attitude after the Jerez race, also uttered all the right words. At the first opportunity he said that, having seen the video, he now realised how Gibernau had been injured in their coming-together and knew that his shoulder had been hurt several times before. 'I am sorry if Sete is not 100 per cent fit for the race,' he said, pointedly not apologising for the move itself. The injured party himself extracted the maximum from the situation, first letting it be known that there were doubts whether he would be able to race, and then turning up late. The Jerez incident prompted FIM President Francesco Zerbi to write one of his flowery letters to both parties. When Gibernau's team-manager Fausto Gresini published it with his own pithy reply – which could be summarised as 'Why are you warning both riders when my man did nothing wrong?' – a vitriolic response was forthcoming and signed 'with much bitterness'. Cue much head-shaking from non-Italian journalists in the press room.

If Sete's left shoulder wasn't hurting as much as he claimed on Friday it certainly was on Saturday after

he highsided and landed heavily on it. He was not the only one to suffer; the left-hander at the end of the back straight also claimed Bayliss, Tamada and Elias in similar manner. Makoto Tamada was the worst off, with what looked like a broken scaphoid. On the strength of his form in 2004 the Japanese rider had been touted by many as a potential challenger to Rossi, but that prediction looked dead in the water after just two races.

Opposite Max Biaggi on the way to his first rostrum of the year

Above Rossi absorbs information from his data technician Matteo Flamigni

Below Gibernau's RCV spits flame on the overrun

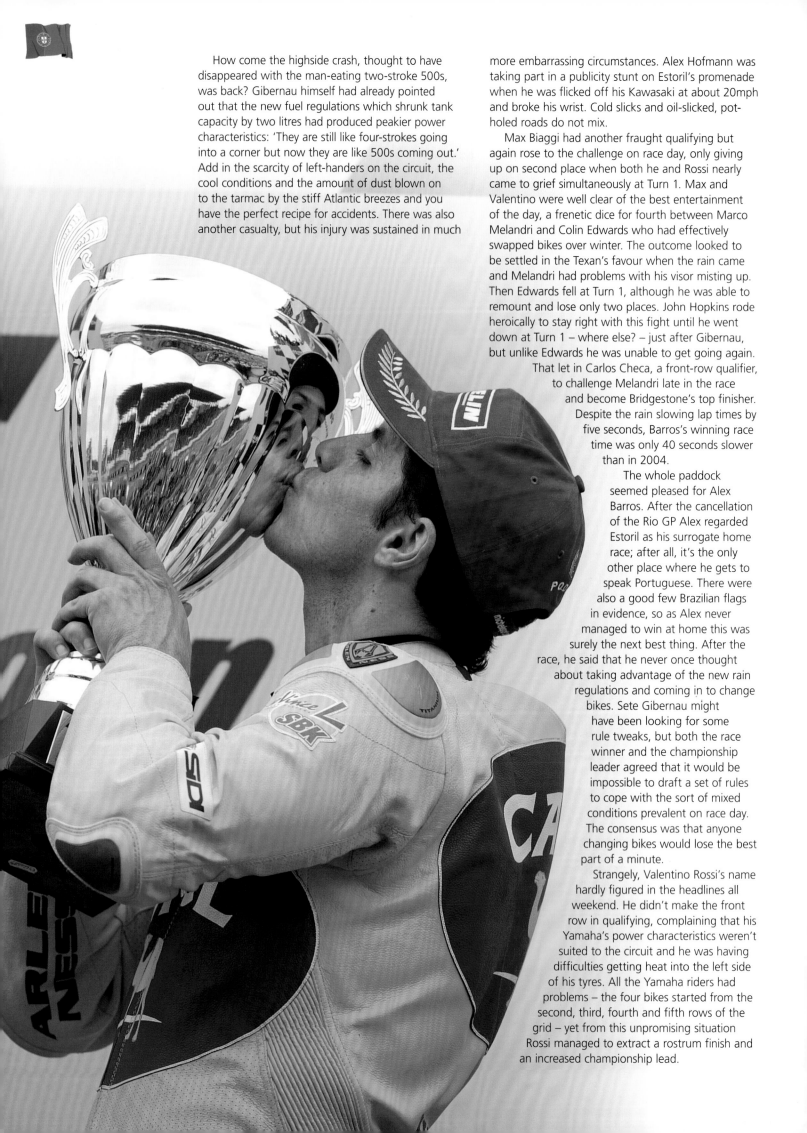

How come the highside crash, thought to have disappeared with the man-eating two-stroke 500s, was back? Gibernau himself had already pointed out that the new fuel regulations which shrunk tank capacity by two litres had produced peakier power characteristics: 'They are still like four-strokes going into a corner but now they are like 500s coming out.' Add in the scarcity of left-handers on the circuit, the cool conditions and the amount of dust blown on to the tarmac by the stiff Atlantic breezes and you have the perfect recipe for accidents. There was also another casualty, but his injury was sustained in much

more embarrassing circumstances. Alex Hofmann was taking part in a publicity stunt on Estoril's promenade when he was flicked off his Kawasaki at about 20mph and broke his wrist. Cold slicks and oil-slicked, pot-holed roads do not mix.

Max Biaggi had another fraught qualifying but again rose to the challenge on race day, only giving up on second place when both he and Rossi nearly came to grief simultaneously at Turn 1. Max and Valentino were well clear of the best entertainment of the day, a frenetic dice for fourth between Marco Melandri and Colin Edwards who had effectively swapped bikes over winter. The outcome looked to be settled in the Texan's favour when the rain came and Melandri had problems with his visor misting up. Then Edwards fell at Turn 1, although he was able to remount and lose only two places. John Hopkins rode heroically to stay right with this fight until he went down at Turn 1 – where else? – just after Gibernau, but unlike Edwards he was unable to get going again. That let in Carlos Checa, a front-row qualifier, to challenge Melandri late in the race and become Bridgestone's top finisher. Despite the rain slowing lap times by five seconds, Barros's winning race time was only 40 seconds slower than in 2004.

The whole paddock seemed pleased for Alex Barros. After the cancellation of the Rio GP Alex regarded Estoril as his surrogate home race; after all, it's the only other place where he gets to speak Portuguese. There were also a good few Brazilian flags in evidence, so as Alex never managed to win at home this was surely the next best thing. After the race, he said that he never once thought about taking advantage of the new rain regulations and coming in to change bikes. Sete Gibernau might have been looking for some rule tweaks, but both the race winner and the championship leader agreed that it would be impossible to draft a set of rules to cope with the sort of mixed conditions prevalent on race day. The consensus was that anyone changing bikes would lose the best part of a minute.

Strangely, Valentino Rossi's name hardly figured in the headlines all weekend. He didn't make the front row in qualifying, complaining that his Yamaha's power characteristics weren't suited to the circuit and he was having difficulties getting heat into the left side of his tyres. All the Yamaha riders had problems – the four bikes started from the second, third, fourth and fifth rows of the grid – yet from this unpromising situation Rossi managed to extract a rostrum finish and an increased championship lead.

RED LIGHT TO WHITE FLAG

Opposite Alex Barros
– damp but happy

Above Hopkins and Tamada
bite the dust

Below The dice between
Edwards and Melandri was
spiced up by the fact they
had effectively swapped bikes
over winter

If the rain had come 20 minutes earlier, the Portuguese GP could have been the first World Championship race in which riders changed bikes. The winter's major rule change stipulated that from 2005 on, MotoGP races will not be interrupted because of rain but will run 'flag to flag', as it is known, despite the fact that a flag is only used to finish a race nowadays and not to start it.

If Race Direction declares a race 'wet' before the start then riders have the option to come in and change bikes at any time after the start. They must leave the pits on a machine equipped with a different type of tyre from that which they came in on. In other words, if you begin the race on slicks and it starts raining you can come in and change to a bike equipped with either rain or intermediate tyres. If a race is declared 'dry' (look for officials holding up boards on the grid) but, as happened at Estoril, it starts to rain during the race, then

white flags are used to signal to the riders that they now have the option to come in and change bikes. It is still permissible to come into the pits and change wheels under any circumstances.

A pit-lane speed limit of 36mph is enforced via hardwired sensors, and any rider breaking the limit will be called in for a ride-through penalty.

The rule was brought in to avoid aggregate races, where spectators and TV viewers have to try and refer to the gaps between riders during the first part of the race in order to work out real race positions in the second part. Apart from the obvious problem of fans being short-changed, TV companies do not take kindly to schedules being ignored with the consequent extra satellite uplink costs. The balance that had to be found was between rider safety and commercial expediency, which is why the original plan for wheel-changing only was abandoned under pressure from the riders.

ESTORIL
PORTUGUESE GRAND PRIX

ROUND 2

RACE RESULTS

RACE DATE April 17th
CIRCUIT LENGTH 2.599 miles
NO. OF LAPS 28
RACE DISTANCE 72.772 miles
WEATHER Dry, 17°C
TRACK TEMPERATURE 19°C
WINNER Alex Barros
FASTEST LAP 1m 38.480s, 94.782mph, Alex Barros
PREVIOUS LAP RECORD 1m 38.423s, 95.052mph, Valentino Rossi, 2004

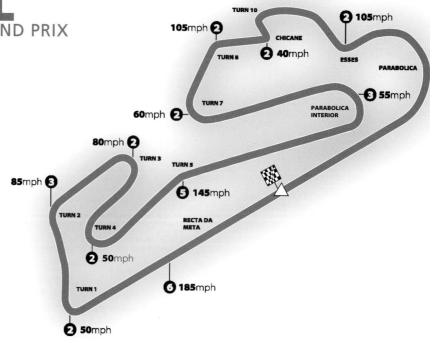

QUALIFYING

	Rider	Nationality	Team	Qualifying	Pole +	Gap
1	Barros	BRA	Camel Honda	1m 37.202s		
2	Gibernau	SPA	Movistar Honda MotoGP	1m 37.329s	0.127s	0.127s
3	Checa C.	SPA	Ducati Marlboro Team	1m 37.456s	0.254s	0.127s
4	Rossi	ITA	Gauloises Yamaha Team	1m 37.643s	0.441s	0.187s
5	Melandri	ITA	Movistar Honda MotoGP	1m 37.835s	0.633s	0.192s
6	Capirossi	ITA	Ducati Marlboro Team	1m 38.000s	0.798s	0.165s
7	Edwards	USA	Gauloises Yamaha Team	1m 38.003s	0.801s	0.003s
8	Biaggi	ITA	Repsol Honda Team	1m 38.009s	0.807s	0.006s
9	Hayden	USA	Repsol Honda Team	1m 38.123s	0.921s	0.114s
10	Nakano	JPN	Kawasaki Racing Team	1m 38.283s	1.081s	0.160s
11	Hopkins	USA	Team Suzuki MotoGP	1m 38.412s	1.210s	0.129s
12	Xaus	SPA	Fortuna Yamaha Team	1m 38.949s	1.747s	0.537s
13	Bayliss	AUS	Camel Honda	1m 39.033s	1.831s	0.084s
14	Roberts	USA	Team Suzuki MotoGP	1m 39.628s	2.426s	0.595s
15	Elias	SPA	Fortuna Yamaha Team	1m 39.836s	2.634s	0.208s
16	Rolfo	ITA	Team D'Antin – Pramac	1m 41.327s	4.125s	1.491s
17	Ellison	GBR	Blata WCM	1m 41.699s	4.497s	0.372s
18	Byrne	GBR	Team Roberts	1m 41.705s	4.503s	0.006s
19	Battaini	ITA	Blata WCM	1m 41.728s	4.526s	0.023s
20	Tamada	JPN	Konica Minolta Honda	1m 41.930s	4.728s	0.202s

FINISHERS

1 ALEX BARROS Fastest in every practice session, fastest in qualifying, fastest in warm-up and a runaway winner: a faultless weekend which only needed the lap record to be perfect. Despite the perilous conditions Alex was within 0.06 seconds of Rossi's 2004 record.

2 VALENTINO ROSSI Not a weekend he enjoyed, yet he still came out of it with an increased points lead. Never totally happy with the bike, so quite happy to pick up the points for second; and noticeably happy for Barros and quick to congratulate him on the slow-down lap.

3 MAX BIAGGI Relieved to get the team's first rostrum of the year after the horror show of the first race. Never threatened the leaders, but was able to back off when conditions turned nasty and make sure of third place.

4 MARCO MELANDRI Had to fight hard with Edwards for most of the race, and then with Checa in the closing stages. Rode the last eight laps with his visor partially open because of misting problems.

5 CARLOS CHECA The shoulder injury from pre-season testing and tyres that weren't working well until the closing stages of the race prevented him from backing up his front-row start.

Had a real go at Melandri on the last lap, though.

6 COLIN EDWARDS Looked to have fourth place sewn up when Melandri dropped back, but became another victim of the rain at Turn 1. Got back on and only lost two places.

7 NICKY HAYDEN Never happy with his bike's set-up, a situation that was exacerbated by the weather conditions on race day.

8 SHINYA NAKANO The new big-bang motor went less well than at Jerez, with acceleration out of the slow corners being the biggest problem. Just as in previous years, getting the power down was difficult and there wasn't enough of it.

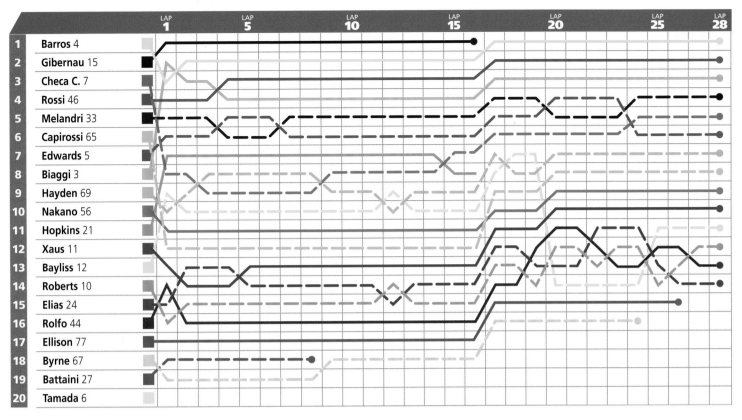

		LAP 1	LAP 5	LAP 10	LAP 15	LAP 20	LAP 25	LAP 28
1	Barros 4							
2	Gibernau 15							
3	Checa C. 7							
4	Rossi 46							
5	Melandri 33							
6	Capirossi 65							
7	Edwards 5							
8	Biaggi 3							
9	Hayden 69							
10	Nakano 56							
11	Hopkins 21							
12	Xaus 11							
13	Bayliss 12							
14	Roberts 10							
15	Elias 24							
16	Rolfo 44							
17	Ellison 77							
18	Byrne 67							
19	Battaini 27							
20	Tamada 6							

RACE

	Rider	Motorcycle	Race Time	Time +	Fastest Lap	Average Speed
1	Barros	Honda	47m 14.053s		1m 38.480s	197.543mph
2	Rossi	Yamaha	47m 16.824s	2.771s	1m 39.142s	197.543mph
3	Biaggi	Honda	47m 20.124s	6.071s	1m 38.848s	201.333mph
4	Melandri	Honda	47m 43.599s	29.546s	1m 39.102s	201.333mph
5	Checa C.	Ducati	47m 43.827s	29.774s	1m 39.556s	198.475mph
6	Edwards	Yamaha	47m 58.269s	44.216s	1m 39.584s	196.486mph
7	Hayden	Honda	48m 11.174s	57.121s	1m 39.492s	200.774mph
8	Nakano	Kawasaki	48m 13.900s	59.847s	1m 39.545s	194.249mph
9	Capirossi	Ducati	48m 21.771s	1m 07.718s	1m 40.013s	200.090mph
10	Xaus	Yamaha	48m 36.484s	1m 22.431s	1m 41.397s	190.707mph
11	Bayliss	Honda	48m 47.582s	1m 33.529s	1m 39.535s	198.350mph
12	Roberts	Suzuki	48m 48.104s	1m 34.051s	1m 41.328s	187.600mph
13	Rolfo	Ducati	48m 50.009s	1m 35.956s	1m 42.058s	196.424mph
14	Elias	Yamaha	48m 50.545s	1m 36.492s	1m 41.228s	196.797mph
15	Ellison	Blata	47m 19.474s	2 Laps	1m 43.229s	182.753mph
16	Byrne	Proton KR	47m 53.289s	4 Laps	1m 44.061s	190.956mph
	Gibernau	Honda	26m 30.320s	12 Laps	1m 38.513s	199.655mph
	Hopkins	Suzuki	26m 51.387s	12 Laps	1m 39.413s	196.610mph
	Battaini	Blata	14m 24.799s	20 Laps	1m 44.315s	182.505mph

CHAMPIONSHIP

	Rider	Team	Points
1	Rossi	Gauloises Yamaha Team	45
2	Barros	Camel Honda	38
3	Melandri	Movistar Honda MotoGP	29
4	Biaggi	Repsol Honda Team	25
5	Gibernau	Movistar Honda MotoGP	20
6	Nakano	Kawasaki Racing Team	19
7	Checa C.	Ducati Marlboro Team	17
8	Edwards	Gauloises Yamaha Team	17
9	Bayliss	Camel Honda	15
10	Capirossi	Ducati Marlboro Team	10
11	Hayden	Repsol Honda Team	9
12	Tamada	JIR Konica Minolta Honda	8
13	Xaus	Fortuna Yamaha Team	6
14	Elias	Fortuna Yamaha Team	6
15	Hofmann	Kawasaki Racing Team	5
16	Roberts	Team Suzuki MotoGP	4
17	Rolfo	Team D'Antin – Pramac	4
18	Hopkins	Team Suzuki MotoGP	2
19	Ellison	Blata WCM	1

9 LORIS CAPIROSSI Anxious not to fall and aggravate the ankle injury he'd suffered in Jerez, so a top-ten finish was acceptable under the circumstances.

10 RUBEN XAUS Coped with the tricky conditions brilliantly despite the small matter of three crashes in practice, including one in warm-up.

11 TROY BAYLISS Frankly, it was surprising he was fit to race after the bang on the head he sustained on Friday. Was up to seventh when he slid off coming into the chicane on lap 20. He got back on for five points.

12 KENNY ROBERTS Another rider never happy with his set-up, although he had a good dice with Rolfo and Elias before pulling out a gap and taking his first points of the season.

13 ROBERTO ROLFO Two races and two point-scoring rides, this time after a dice with ex-World Champion Roberts. Encouraged by his increased understanding of the bike and Dunlop's development work.

14 TONI ELIAS Added to team-mate Xaus's crashes with a big one of his own in practice, which left him with a very sore knee. Never regained his confidence in the bike.

15 JAMES ELLISON Followed Rolfo off the start but lost a bit of confidence when the rain started. Nevertheless, delivered WCM's first point of the season.

16 SHANE BYRNE Started from pit lane after his engine decided to tick over at about 10,000rpm. The problem was solved, but Shakey didn't really have a race – he had some extra testing time.

NON-FINISHERS

SETE GIBERNAU Crashed out of the lead while pushing hard when the proper rain hit Turn 1. Despite leading every lap bar two of the championship so far (while he was on two wheels), he was already 25 points adrift of Rossi. Still professing himself happy with the work he and the team have done.

JOHN HOPKINS Right there behind the Edwards/Melandri dice until the rain started and he became another victim of Turn 1. Unlike his fellow American he couldn't get going again, but did set the sixth-best lap time of the race.

FRANCO BATTAINI Forced to retire at mid-distance by a rear subframe breakage.

NON-STARTERS

ALEX HOFMANN Broke his scaphoid and ulna when he crashed on the Wednesday before the race during a publicity event on Estoril's seafront. Out for at least two races.

MAKOTO TAMADA One of several highside victims during practice and qualifying. Damaged his right wrist but needed further investigation to discover if the scaphoid was broken. Out for at least one race.

SHANGHAI
CHINESE GRAND PRIX

ROUND 3

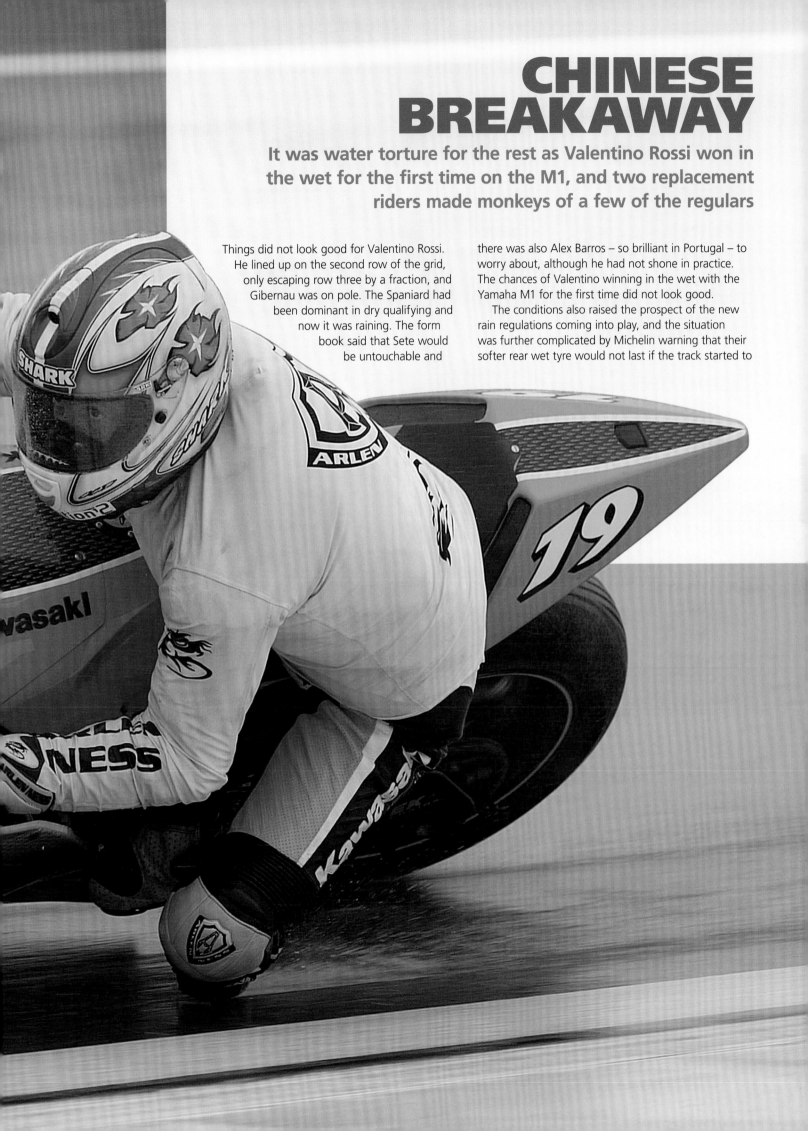

CHINESE BREAKAWAY

It was water torture for the rest as Valentino Rossi won in the wet for the first time on the M1, and two replacement riders made monkeys of a few of the regulars

Things did not look good for Valentino Rossi. He lined up on the second row of the grid, only escaping row three by a fraction, and Gibernau was on pole. The Spaniard had been dominant in dry qualifying and now it was raining. The form book said that Sete would be untouchable and there was also Alex Barros – so brilliant in Portugal – to worry about, although he had not shone in practice. The chances of Valentino winning in the wet with the Yamaha M1 for the first time did not look good.

The conditions also raised the prospect of the new rain regulations coming into play, and the situation was further complicated by Michelin warning that their softer rear wet tyre would not last if the track started to

dry to any significant degree. This led the company to advise its riders, in the strongest terms, to go with the harder rubber, a recommendation that would have a major effect on Sete Gibernau's race. He hadn't used it before race day, felt a vibration on the warm-up lap and so asked for a new tyre on the grid. There wasn't one. He had to race with what he'd got, and when he ran wide at the first corner it was obvious he had problems. Barros, the other perceived threat to Rossi, did himself no favours by jumping the start and being called in for a ride-through penalty.

Rain is always a leveller, and when it falls on a circuit that is brand new to everyone the effect is more pronounced than normal. That was evident on the first lap as Kenny Roberts effortlessly went to the front, proving both that he hadn't lost the drive that made him a World Champion and that Bridgestone had taken a major leap forward with their rain tyres. The only man that could go with him was Rossi, who was uncharacteristically forceful on the opening lap to get himself out of the cloud of spray that engulfed the pack. When Roberts's Suzuki suffered engine failure at the end of the fifth lap Rossi was thus left alone with a comfortable cushion over Gibernau.

At this point Olivier Jacque, deputising on the Kawasaki for Alex Hofmann, was down in seventh place. A lap later John Hopkins, who'd been right at the front in the first corner, ran off the track promoting the Frenchman to fourth. He took two laps to close on Max Biaggi and forced past on the brakes for the final corner at the end of lap nine. Jacque was now visibly the fastest man on the track and, with the rain persisting, there was no likelihood of his Bridgestones fading: quite the reverse. Gibernau, clearly uncomfortable but riding with a stoic brilliance (if that isn't a non sequitur), was despatched six laps later.

Valentino Rossi was then surprised to see the letter 'O' appear on his pit board instead of the 'Sete' that had been indicating the man behind him for the previous ten laps. His crew had not prepared a sign for the Frenchman and were hurriedly improvising with the absent Hofmann's board and duct tape. 'I saw "O" and didn't know who it was,' Rossi said later; 'I thought maybe a Chinese rider.' Next time round he was shown 'OJ' and a shrinking lead. He got the message.

Opposite many people thought Kenny Roberts would have won the race if his engine hadn't given up

Above Rossi and Jacque do a little mutual admiration after the flag

Right Jacque nearly T-boned Capirossi on his charge to the rostrum

Olivier was taking risks and closing the gap. Valentino upped his pace a little and, once he'd had a couple of warnings, Jacque decided that second place wasn't such a bad idea; but Rossi's lead had come down to under two seconds by the flag. It was Jacque's first rostrum in the top class and also Kawasaki's best-ever result in the MotoGP era. Spare a thought, then, for Kenny Roberts, on the same tyres, and Shinya Nakano, on the same bike and tyres as OJ – both went out early with mechanical failure.

All the luck was with the World Champion. On Saturday evening Valentino had been pessimistic about his chances, citing no grip on the right side of the front tyre, poor front-end set-up and lack of top speed on the long straights as his three major problems. Jerry Burgess was more optimistic: he pointed out that the Yamaha was always significantly slower than the Hondas and Ducatis; he also reckoned the team could sort the front end in Sunday warm-up, so they only had one problem not three. Nevertheless, when asked after the event what would have happened if the weather had been dry Rossi still maintained that he could only have shot for a rostrum finish, not the win.

As usual, though, events conspired to make Rossi's weekend even better than it looked. After his ride-through penalty Barros could only finish eleventh, despite setting the fastest lap of the race, while Gibernau was shoved aside on the last lap by his team-mate Marco Melandri, so didn't even make it to the rostrum. The Spaniard didn't finish the slow-down lap either, pulling to a halt at the end of the pit wall and then somewhat theatrically stalking back to his pit after taking a long look at his rear tyre. Michelin couldn't find anything amiss despite the fact that, even from the side of the track, it was obvious that all was not well with the Movistar Honda. Even an autopsy back in France failed to reveal any faults.

The other replacement rider who rattled a few cages was Jurgen van den Goorbergh. He finished sixth without having sat on the bike before he got to China, bringing the Konica Minolta Honda home with three other RCVs in front of him and two behind, not a comfortable situation for Nicky Hayden in ninth or the other Repsol rider, Max Biaggi, who was only two

seconds in front of the Dutchman. In case any deluded conspiracy theorists thought Max was somehow taking it easy, the Roman was starting his 187th consecutive GP and did an astonishing 201mph in the midst of the sodden pack.

Rossi's joy at the flag was unconfined. He congratulated Jacque warmly and confessed that it was the most unexpected victory of his career. Unless he's as good an actor as he is a rider, he wasn't lying. OJ had a few choice words to say as well. On Thursday he had confessed to feeling 'like a hair on the soup' after a year away from GPs; on Sunday afternoon he 'felt like a fish in water' – an apt metaphor, given the conditions.

So ended MotoGP's first race in the People's Republic, in a city that seemed much more capitalist than communist, especially if you ventured to the frighteningly fashionable riverside area called The Bund. Shanghai is the spearhead of China's economic expansion, and the possessor of the craziest, most dangerous traffic anyone in the paddock had ever seen. It was, as John Lennon once said, Far East, man...

Right James Ellison had the rare pleasure of leading Alex Barros for a few laps after the Brazilian had been called in for a ride-through penalty

NEW ORDER

The 25,000 people who braved the elements looked a little lost in the giant stands. A man from central government thought so too and told the deputy mayor of Shanghai, there to present a trophy, that this was not suitable for an event with the title of Grand Prix of China. He then ordered that in 2006 there should be 100,000 spectators.

Interestingly, the circuit attracted a good crowd for its inaugural F1 race in 2004, but MotoGP is still breaking through. The fans that were there made a disproportionately large amount of noise and wore enough yellow to show they certainly knew who the World Champion was. The circuit itself is superbly appointed with magnificent buildings including teams' offices built on stilts over the lake at the back of the paddock. However, the pre-eminence of F1 was clearly demonstrated by the track, which turned out to be not as exciting as it looked on paper. A Suzuki rider would find himself in bottom gear four times each lap, and the slow corners went on for ever. No-one found it very interesting, despite boasting the longest straight in the calendar which, incidentally, proved that the Ducati is still the fastest thing out there: Carlos Checa clocked over 211mph in practice.

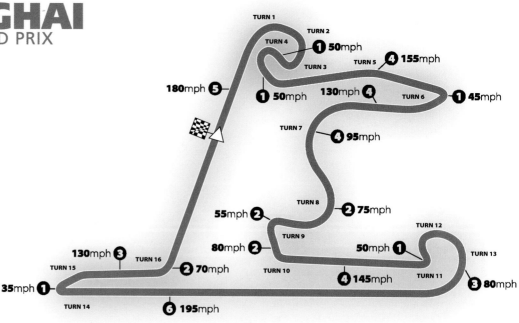

SHANGHAI
CHINESE GRAND PRIX

ROUND 3

RACE RESULTS

RACE DATE May 1st
CIRCUIT LENGTH 3.281 miles
NO. OF LAPS 22
RACE DISTANCE 72.182 miles
WEATHER Wet, 19°C
TRACK TEMPERTURE 21°C
WINNER Valentino Rossi
FASTEST LAP 2m 13.716s, 88.150mph, Alex Barros

QUALIFYING

	Rider	Nationality	Team	Qualifying	Pole +	Gap
1	Gibernau	SPA	Movistar Honda MotoGP	1m 59.710s		
2	Melandri	ITA	Movistar Honda MotoGP	1m 59.873s	0.163s	0.163s
3	Capirossi	ITA	Ducati Marlboro Team	2m 00.480s	0.770s	0.607s
4	Hopkins	USA	Team Suzuki MotoGP	2m 00.666s	0.956s	0.186s
5	Hayden	USA	Repsol Honda Team	2m 00.747s	1.037s	0.081s
6	Rossi	ITA	Gauloises Yamaha Team	2m 00.821s	1.111s	0.074s
7	Checa C.	SPA	Ducati Marlboro Team	2m 00.902s	1.192s	0.081s
8	Elias	SPA	Fortuna Yamaha Team	2m 01.081s	1.371s	0.179s
9	Roberts	USA	Team Suzuki MotoGP	2m 01.085s	1.375s	0.004s
10	Nakano	JPN	Kawasaki Racing Team	2m 01.098s	1.388s	0.013s
11	Barros	BRA	Camel Honda	2m 01.117s	1.407s	0.019s
12	Bayliss	AUS	Camel Honda	2m 01.328s	1.618s	0.211s
13	Edwards	USA	Gailoises Yamaha Team	2m 01.401s	1.691s	0.073s
14	Biaggi	ITA	Repsol Honda Team	2m 01.502s	1.792s	0.101s
15	Jacque	FRA	Kawasaki Racing Team	2m 02.072s	2.362s	0.570s
16	Xaus	SPA	Fortuna Yamaha Team	2m 02.869s	3.159s	0.797s
17	Rolfo	ITA	Team D'Antin – Pramac	2m 03.886s	4.176s	1.017s
18	Ukawa	JPN	Moriwaki Racing	2m 04.223s	4.513s	0.337s
19	Goorbergh	NED	Konica Minolta Honda	2m 04.594s	4.884s	0.371s
20	Battaini	ITA	Blata WCM	2m 05.468s	5.758s	0.874s
21	Ellison	GBR	Blata WCM	2m 06.496s	6.786s	1.028s

FINISHERS

1 VALENTINO ROSSI The first wet-weather win on the Yamaha M1, and after two days of practice which saw him on the back of the second row of the grid. It was his lowest qualifying position since Qatar 2004, and the first time he'd been over a second slower than pole since Donington 2001, yet he still won and the two men he feared most had bad days.

2 OLIVIER JACQUE Kawasaki's best result in MotoGP, and a compelling demonstration of the improvements in Bridgestone's rain tyres. A massively impressive achievement for a replacement rider, and even more impressive when it's taken into account that he started from 15th on the grid in foul conditions.

3 MARCO MELANDRI Another impressive race, this time from his best-ever qualifying position, put him second in the championship. Could be forgiven for again feeling he didn't get the attention he deserved, though, as most people only wanted to talk about the fact he wore Dovizioso's helmet to avoid misting problems with his own brand.

4 SETE GIBERNAU Right up to the sighting lap it all looked so good, as even the weather gods seemed to be on his side. Then vibration struck, and he performed minor miracles to stay in second place for as long as he did. A deficit of 37 points to Rossi is a daunting prospect for the rest of the season, however.

5 MAX BIAGGI Another frankly worrying qualifying performance followed by a storming

first lap and a gutsy ride in his 200th GP. Still insisting that the bike has major problems in corners. Fastest through the speed traps topping 201mph on race day.

6 JURGEN VAN DEN GOORBERGH Sat on the bike for the first time on Thursday morning, qualified 19th out of 21, then worked his way up from 12th at the end of the first lap. Decided not to take risks to make up more places, but made sure he didn't lose any either.

7 JOHN HOPKINS Led a GP for the first time and was looking good in fourth when he ran off the track and dropped back, but kept working to claw three places back.

8 COLIN EDWARDS Couldn't make use of his qualifying tyre so started from the fifth row of the grid, then got tangled up on the first lap.

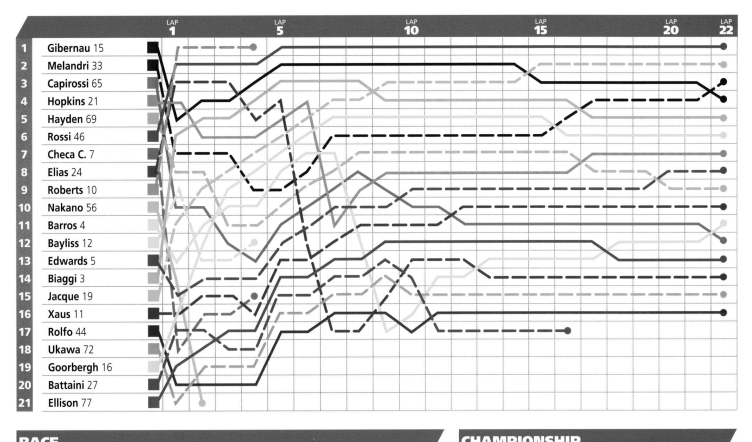

		LAP 1	LAP 5	LAP 10	LAP 15	LAP 20	LAP 22
1	Gibernau 15						
2	Melandri 33						
3	Capirossi 65						
4	Hopkins 21						
5	Hayden 69						
6	Rossi 46						
7	Checa C. 7						
8	Elias 24						
9	Roberts 10						
10	Nakano 56						
11	Barros 4						
12	Bayliss 12						
13	Edwards 5						
14	Biaggi 3						
15	Jacque 19						
16	Xaus 11						
17	Rolfo 44						
18	Ukawa 72						
19	Goorbergh 16						
20	Battaini 27						
21	Ellison 77						

RACE

	Rider	Motorcycle	Race Time	Time +	Fastest Lap	Average Speed
1	Rossi	Yamaha	50m 02.463s		2m 14.225s	198.102mph
2	Jacque	Kawasaki	50m 04.163s	1.700s	2m 14.133s	197.108mph
3	Melandri	Honda	50m 19.037s	16.574s	2m 14.717s	201.644mph
4	Gibernau	Honda	50m 21.369s	18.906s	2m 15.120s	198.413mph
5	Biaggi	Honda	50m 22.014s	19.551s	2m 15.626s	203.570mph
6	Goorbergh	Honda	50m 24.085s	21.622s	2m 15.524s	199.717mph
7	Hopkins	Suzuki	50m 28.346s	25.883s	2m 14.607s	199.842mph
8	Edwards	Yamaha	50m 33.496s	31.033s	2m 15.175s	195.927mph
9	Hayden	Honda	50m 41.762s	39.299s	2m 15.282s	198.164mph
10	Xaus	Yamaha	50m 43.454s	40.991s	2m 16.249s	182.008mph
11	Barros	Honda	50m 46.477s	44.014s	2m 13.716s	201.085mph
12	Capirossi	Ducati	50m 46.864s	44.401s	2m 15.755s	200.650mph
13	Ellison	Blata	50m 55.912s	53.449s	2m 15.400s	185.736mph
14	Elias	Yamaha	51m 08.316s	1m 05.853s	2m 16.520s	200.898mph
15	Ukawa	Moriwaki	51m 11.943s	1m 09.480s	2m 16.560s	187.289mph
16	Rolfo	Ducati	51m 17.756s	1m 15.293s	2m 16.853s	200.277mph
	Battaini	Blata	37m 35.911s	6 Laps	2m 17.391s	184.120mph
	Roberts	Suzuki	12m 36.308s	17 Laps	2m 16.591s	166.286mph
	Bayliss	Honda	9m 29.777s	18 Laps	2m 18.905s	171.382mph
	Checa C.	Ducati	9m 31.760s	18 Laps	2m 17.949s	180.268mph
	Nakano	Kawasaki	5m 38.031s	20 Laps	2m 30.849s	143.170mph

CHAMPIONSHIP

	Rider	Team	Points
1	Rossi	Gauloises Yamaha Team	70
2	Melandri	Movistar Honda MotoGP	45
3	Barros	Camel Honda	43
4	Biaggi	Repsol Honda Team	36
5	Gibernau	Movistar Honda MotoGP	33
6	Edwards	Gauloises Yamaha Team	25
7	Jacque	Kawasaki Racing Team	20
8	Nakano	Kawasaki Racing Team	19
9	Checa C.	Ducati Marlboro Team	17
10	Hayden	Repsol Honda Team	16
11	Bayliss	Camel Honda	15
12	Capirossi	Ducati Marlboro Team	14
13	Xaus	Fortuna Yamaha Team	12
14	Hopkins	Team Suzuki MotoGP	11
15	Goorbergh	JIR Konica Minolta Honda	10
16	Tamada	JIR Konica Minolta Honda	8
17	Elias	Fortuna Yamaha Team	8
18	Hofmann	Kawasaki Racing Team	5
19	Roberts	Team Suzuki MotoGP	4
20	Ellison	Blata WCM	4
21	Rolfo	Team D'Antin – Pramac	4
22	Ukawa	Moriwaki Racing	1

Good pace when he had a clear track but then hit gear-selection and tyre-wear problems.

9 NICKY HAYDEN Never happy with his set-up despite being fastest in one of the dry sessions. Got up to seventh then dropped back with vibration. The team later diagnosed a waterlogged sensor that had defaulted the engine management to safety mode.

10 RUBEN XAUS An atypically conservative approach to the race after being impressively fast in morning warm-up. Kept out of the way in the first corner and conserved his tyres, which allowed him to be as fast as the leading group at the end of the race. Still feeling he owes his team after his pre-season crashfest.

11 ALEX BARROS A lost opportunity thanks to disappointing qualifying and a ride-through penalty for a jumped start. Set the fastest lap of the race the penultimate time round and could surely have followed Melandri to the front of the race. Another victim of visor misting.

12 LORIS CAPIROSSI Went for a soft-compound rear tyre because the team thought the race would be drier than warm-up; this turned out to be a mistake. Doubly disappointing given his impressive qualifying.

13 JAMES ELLISON Delighted to score points for the second race in a row. Had problems with visor misting but was grateful to ride alone so he didn't have to deal with spray from bikes in front of him. Actually lapped faster than Rossi towards the end of the race.

14 TONI ELIAS A brilliant weekend right up to the start of the race. Good in both wet and dry practice, season's best qualifying by five places, a stunning start and then held third place for the first three laps, only to get a ride-through penalty. Amazingly, it wasn't for jumping the start but for lining up on the wrong grid slot.

15 TOHRU UKAWA Despite his only experience of the bike being in wet-weather testing, Ukawa couldn't get near his personal target of a top-ten finish. It was the bike's first outing on Michelins so the team were happy just to gather data.

16 ROBERTO ROLFO Never got near a set-up he thought was useable, never happy at any point in the weekend and very unhappy about finishing behind another Dunlop runner.

NON-FINISHERS

FRANCO BATTAINI Running right with his team-mate up to lap 11 when he started having serious visor-fogging trouble. Ran off the track, dropped the bike and couldn't restart.

KENNY ROBERTS In front and looking as comfortable as anybody could in the conditions when the motor broke a major component. And he had the right tyres.

TROY BAYLISS Another crash for the Aussie, who'd looked very good in warm-up. His team-manager's post-race statement seemed to criticise him for trying too hard too soon.

CARLOS CHECA 'I guess I found the limit,' he said, after losing the front braking for the last turn and aquaplaning on his back right up the pit access road.

SHINYA NAKANO An electrical problem on lap one turned into what felt like a misfire on lap two, so Shinya had to stand and watch his temporary team-mate take Kawasaki's best-ever result in MotoGP. Ouch.

NON-STARTERS

SHANE BYRNE Team Roberts did not attend because of material shortages.

MAKOTO TAMADA Had the wrist he injured in Portugal operated on a couple of days before the race.

ALEX HOFMANN Out with the wrist injury suffered before the Portuguese GP.

LE MANS
FRENCH GRAND PRIX

ROUND 4

DE L'OUEST

DUNLOP

NORMAL SERVICE IS RESUMED

Rossi versus Gibernau at lap-record pace all the way to the flag – it felt like a return to the status quo

For a track that riders aren't supposed to like very much and on which it is allegedly difficult to overtake, Le Mans often provides enthralling racing. After they both got bad starts, Valentino Rossi and Sete Gibernau came through the field to provide another thrilling climax to a French GP. Once they'd broken clear of long-time leader Colin Edwards they ran the last half-dozen laps of the

race at an astonishing pace, and although Gibernau couldn't put a move on Rossi he did push him to a new record time on the final lap.

All through the 2004 season and in the first three races of '05 Rossi and his team had used every available minute of track time to get the M1 working as they wanted it to – and they have usually needed it. In France

it was wet in practice as often as not, yet Valentino had none of the complaints about his bike and tyres that he'd regaled us with on Saturday in Shanghai. Last year at this venue the Yamaha had snapped sideways with worrying frequency and even Rossi couldn't get it on the rostrum; this year its behaviour was impeccable, despite the lack of set-up time. Granted, Le Mans is not the most challenging track for teams as regards set-up, but the contrast was striking. Rossi and Burgess later said the work had been done in the test after the Portuguese GP but the settings weren't used in China because that race was wet. When Rossi and Gibernau got to the front here it was all but impossible to pick a difference between the Honda and the Yamaha.

Before the finale a record crowd, boosted no doubt by Olivier Jacque's appearance on the Kawasaki, had seen two Americans set the pace. Nicky Hayden got the holeshot but Colin Edwards came round the outside at the high-speed first corner to put himself on the inside for the slow left-hand entry to the Dunlop chicane. He then led immaculately for 20 laps until Rossi, who had been back in sixth at the end of the first lap, came up the inside on the brakes for Garage Vert. Edwards left a little more space for his team-mate than he would for anyone else, only to find Sete Gibernau coming through nailed to Rossi's rear wheel. Colin exited the corner shaking his head ruefully. Later, the ever-quotable Edwards would say that he could have done 1m 34s laps all day but if you'd told him to do 1m 33s to save his life 'I'd have said put the gun to my head right now.' Rossi's last lap was 1m 33.678s, with Gibernau right behind him at 1m 33.906s; the only other man to get into the

33s was Marco Melandri who did 1min 33.965s five laps from the end of the race.

Gibernau's start was even less eye-catching than Rossi's. He'd had to wait for his hard rear tyre to start working before he could come up through the field from eighth place on lap five. His team had also made some major set-up adjustments after the morning warm-up and he took a couple of laps to feel comfortable with the bike. Nevertheless, he was the first man into the 33s as he chased down the leaders, and his arrival in third place pushed Rossi into a mistake. An attempt to overtake Edwards going into the chicane in the back straight saw Rossi get into the corner too fast and run over the kerbs on the way out: his loss of momentum not only let Colin retake the lead but allowed Sete to drive past into second place. The American tried to counter-attack but found he was asking too much of his tyres. Rossi took two laps to assess the situation before passing Gibernau and Edwards on consecutive laps to retake the lead and set up the final showdown. The Spanish rider was planning a last-lap pass but a small mistake on the penultimate round meant he was never quite close enough to try.

Two men who might have hoped to have a say in the result had their races ruined before the end of the first lap. Carlos Checa had looked dangerous in warm-up only to fall after being sideswiped by Max Biaggi, who was taking evasive action, in the first chicane. John Hopkins's chances of a good finish didn't even last that long. His Suzuki developed a mechanical fault on the warm-up lap so he had to swap to his spare bike, managing to get away before the field came round to

Opposite Both WCM riders crashed – Ellison in the race and Battaini (inset) spectacularly at Turn 1 during practice

Below The story of the first half of the race: Edwards leads, Gibernau stalks, Rossi waits

complete their first lap, so he could stick with his slick tyres (see the panel on page 77 for an explanation of the new rules).

Apart from the weather, the major contrast between Le Mans and the previous round in Shanghai was the relative fortune of the replacement riders. After his heroic race in China Kawasaki took every opportunity to showcase Olivier Jacque, keeping the man himself busy with personal appearances and autograph sessions. Jurgen van den Goorbergh got back on the Konica Minolta Honda once Tamada had decided he couldn't ride. However, there is a world of difference between a wet new track where no-one has tested and one where every team has gigabytes of data and each rider vast experience. Both their replacement stints came to an end after the French GP, but Jacque had already pocketed a testing contract and the promise of at least a couple more rides, this time as a wild card.

Team Roberts were back after missing the Chinese GP due to lack of hardware, but they had a miserable time. The new V4 KTM motor kept cutting out after only a few corners and they had to revert to their remaining old-spec motor for the race. It looked like an electronic fault but it turned out to be mechanical, the Austrian factory later diagnosing a problem with tolerances.

As the upcoming vital run of three GPs at Barcelona, Mugello and Assen was very much on the paddock's collective mind, it felt as if Le Mans had shown us the blueprint for what was to shape the pattern of the championship. As usual, Colin Edwards summed it up best when, referring to Gibernau and Rossi, he said: 'I really wanted to win that one but those two bastards were just too fast.'

Above The KTM powered KR Proton appeared for the first time but gave Shakey Byrne a torrid weekend

Below Rossi leads his team-mate

Opposite Yamaha team boss Davide Brivio on the rostrum with his riders

Above Makoto Tamada tried to ride the Konica Minolta Honda but the wrist he injured in Portuagl wouldn't let him and Jurgen van den Goorbergh got to carry on where he left off in China

REALITY CHECK

After the joy of the Chinese race where they finished second and sixth, replacement riders Olivier Jacque and Jurgen van den Goorbergh were brought down to earth in France when they finished eleventh and fourteenth.

Same bikes, same riders, but a vast difference in competitivity. Why? The race situations could not have been more different: Shanghai was a totally new track where no-one had tested but at Le Mans normal service was resumed and it showed. All the regular riders' experience and the teams' data came into play. Olivier and Jurgen's lack of testing time and especially of dry-weather testing showed through. Their performance also underlined how competitive the MotoGP class now is.

At Le Mans, a fraction over three-quarters of a second covered first to twelfth on the grid. Not that long ago you would get gaps of that order between adjacent riders. Go back to the heyday of Agostini and the MV Agusta and you can find results which tell you that Ago lapped the field twice!

In a field as competitive as MotoGP now is, you only have to be a few per cent off the pace to be relegated to the status of also ran. Take the relative Le Mans qualifying times of pole sitter Valentino Rossi and Olivier Jacque in thirteenth place. The Kawasaki man's time was slower than The Doctor's by just 1.26%. In the race their fastest laps differed by 2.18% and their total race times by exactly 2%. Rossi won the race and set the fastest lap, Olivier was twelfth and his fastest lap was the twelfth best of the nineteen competitors.

Given those sorts of margins, it is very difficult to say that Kawasaki or Bridgestone are doing a bad job. They also demonstrate how difficult it is to close that seemingly tiny gap.

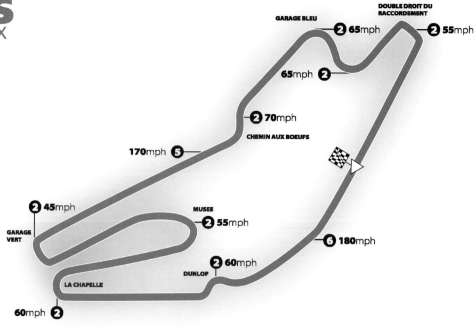

LE MANS
FRENCH GRAND PRIX

ROUND 4

RACE RESULTS

RACE DATE May 15th
CIRCUIT LENGTH 2.597 miles
NO. OF LAPS 28
RACE DISTANCE 72.716 miles
WEATHER Wet, 15°C
TRACK TEMPERATURE 21°C
WINNER Valentino Rossi
FASTEST LAP 1m 33.678s, 99.594mph, Valentino Rossi (record)
PREVIOUS LAP RECORD 1m 34.088s, 99.383mph, Max Biaggi, 2004

QUALIFYING

	Rider	Nationality	Team	Qualifying	Pole +	Gap
1	Rossi	ITA	Gauloises Yamaha Team	1m 33.226s		
2	Edwards	USA	Gauloises Yamaha Team	1m 33.449s	0.223s	0.223s
3	Melandri	ITA	Movistar Honda MotoGP	1m 33.465s	0.239s	0.016s
4	Gibernau	SPA	Movistar Honda MotoGP	1m 33.467s	0.241s	0.002s
5	Hayden	USA	Repsol Honda Team	1m 33.514s	0.288s	0.047s
6	Nakano	JPN	Kawasaki Racing Team	1m 33.536s	0.310s	0.022s
7	Hopkins	USA	Team Suzuki MotoGP	1m 33.594s	0.368s	0.058s
8	Biaggi	ITA	Repsol Honda Team	1m 33.699s	0.473s	0.105s
9	Checa C.	SPA	Ducati Marlboro Team	1m 33.727s	0.501s	0.028s
10	Capirossi	ITA	Ducati Marlboro Team	1m 33.773s	0.547s	0.046s
11	Barros	BRA	Camel Honda	1m 33.876s	0.650s	0.103s
12	Elias	SPA	Fortuna Yamaha Team	1m 33.991s	0.765s	0.115s
13	Jacque	FRA	Kawasaki Racing Team	1m 34.403s	1.177s	0.412s
14	Roberts	USA	Team Suzuki MotoGP	1m 35.068s	1.842s	0.665s
15	Bayliss	AUS	Camel Honda	1m 35.231s	2.005s	0.163s
16	Xaus	SPA	Fortuna Yamaha Team	1m 35.772s	2.546s	0.541s
17	Byrne	GBR	Team Roberts	1m 36.249s	3.023s	0.477s
18	Rolfo	ITA	Team D'Antin – Pramac	1m 36.319s	3.093s	0.070s
19	Goorbergh	NED	Konica Minolta Honda	1m 36.595s	3.369s	0.276s
20	Ellison	GBR	Blata WCM	1m 37.265s	4.039s	0.670s
21	Battaini	ITA	Blata WCM	1m 37.341s	4.115s	0.076s

FINISHERS

1 VALENTINO ROSSI No problems for the Doctor, who appears to have cured any ills with the Yamaha M1's handling and power delivery: pole, first place, fastest lap and a significantly extended points lead. Had to break the lap record last time round to keep Gibernau behind him, though.

2 SETE GIBERNAU Back to his best form after the traumas of the first three races. Worked his way through the field after a slow start to push Rossi to a new record time, and also set his own best time, on the last lap. Hard to see how he could have done more.

3 COLIN EDWARDS His first front-row start in MotoGP followed by a brilliant round-the-outside move at the first corner to take the lead. Held it for two-thirds of the race before the front two went past in one go. Honest and entertaining as ever, he said there was no way he could match their pace.

4 MARCO MELANDRI Not a bad result for a man who was in the Clinica Mobile until late on Saturday thanks to a nasty stomach bug. Elected to race with a hard rear tyre so didn't show at the front early on. Sneaked up on Biaggi to take fourth and consolidate second in the championship.

5 MAX BIAGGI The now customary lacklustre qualifying compounded by a vicious crash in warm-up that left him with massive bruising to his lower back was followed by the equally customary heroics in the race: at least half-a-dozen overtaking moves.

6 NICKY HAYDEN Brilliant in the first part of the race and looking good in fourth when a mechanical problem hit ten laps from the flag. The rear wheel started pattering violently on the way into corners, indicating some sort of problem with his slipper clutch.

7 LORIS CAPIROSSI Third early on after a great start but faded towards half-distance when his medium-compound rear started to lose grip. The whole team wasn't helped by lack of dry practice so early in their relationship with suppliers Bridgestone and the consequent lack of data.

8 SHINYA NAKANO A great start from the second row, but then trouble judging his

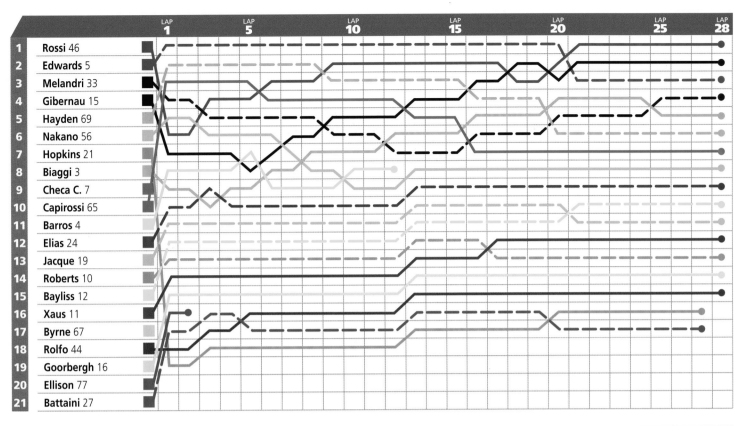

1	Rossi 46
2	Edwards 5
3	Melandri 33
4	Gibernau 15
5	Hayden 69
6	Nakano 56
7	Hopkins 21
8	Biaggi 3
9	Checa C. 7
10	Capirossi 65
11	Barros 4
12	Elias 24
13	Jacque 19
14	Roberts 10
15	Bayliss 12
16	Xaus 11
17	Byrne 67
18	Rolfo 44
19	Goorbergh 16
20	Ellison 77
21	Battaini 27

RACE

	Rider	Motorcycle	Race Time	Time +	Fastest Lap	Average Speed
1	Rossi	Yamaha	44m 12.223s		1m 33.678s	184.742mph
2	Gibernau	Honda	44m 12.605s	0.382s	1m 33.906s	185.985mph
3	Edwards	Yamaha	44m 17.934s	5.711s	1m 34.366s	182.132mph
4	Melandri	Honda	44m 19.499s	7.276s	1m 33.965s	182.443mph
5	Biaggi	Honda	44m 19.926s	7.703s	1m 34.206s	199.282mph
6	Hayden	Honda	44m 33.993s	21.770s	1m 34.355s	185.550mph
7	Capirossi	Ducati	44m 36.887s	24.664s	1m 34.658s	182.256mph
8	Nakano	Kawasaki	44m 48.163s	35.940s	1m 34.856s	182.940mph
9	Elias	Yamaha	44m 50.285s	38.062s	1m 35.191s	182.008mph
10	Bayliss	Honda	45m 04.830s	52.607s	1m 35.786s	178.838mph
11	Jacque	Kawasaki	45m 05.525s	53.302s	1m 35.720s	180.454mph
12	Xaus	Yamaha	45m 12.565s	1m 00.342s	1m 35.991s	179.149mph
13	Roberts	Suzuki	45m 12.737s	1m 00.514s	1m 35.763s	178.279mph
14	Goorbergh	Honda	45m 30.216s	1m 17.993s	1m 36.706s	183.872mph
15	Rolfo	Ducati	45m 44.456s	1m 32.233s	1m 36.258s	180.765mph
16	Hopkins	Suzuki	44m 50.726s	1 Lap	1m 35.406s	180.951mph
17	Battaini	Blata	45m 22.642s	1 Lap	1m 39.642s	167.280mph
	Barros	Honda	19m 10.033s	16 Laps	1m 34.740s	184.369mph
	Ellison	Blata	3m 26.375s	26 Laps	1m 38.996s	164.795mph
	Byrne	Proton KR				
	Checa C.	Ducati				

CHAMPIONSHIP

	Rider	Team	Points
1	Rossi	Gauloises Yamaha Team	95
2	Melandri	Movistar Honda MotoGP	58
3	Gibernau	Movistar Honda MotoGP	53
4	Biaggi	Repsol Honda Team	47
5	Baros	Camel Honda	43
6	Edwards	Gauloises Yamaha Team	41
7	Nakano	Kawasaki Racing Team	27
8	Hayden	Repsol Honda Team	26
9	Jacque	Kawasaki Racing Team	25
10	Capirossi	Ducati Marlboro Team	23
11	Bayliss	Camel Honda	21
12	Checa C.	Ducati Marlboro Team	17
13	Xaus	Fortuna Yamaha Team	16
14	Elias	Fortuna Yamaha Team	15
15	Goorbergh	JIR Konica Minolta Honda	12
16	Hopkins	Team Suzuki MotoGP	11
17	Tamada	JIR Konica Minolta Honda	8
18	Roberts	Team Suzuki MotoGP	7
19	Hofmann	Kawasaki Racing Team	5
20	Rolfo	Team D'Antin – Pramac	5
21	Ellison	Blata WCM	4
22	Ukawa	Moriwaki Racing	1

braking for the first turn. When he got that sorted his engine developed a minor misfire, so couldn't challenge Capirossi for the honour of being top Bridgestone finisher.

9 TONI ELIAS His first top-ten finish in MotoGP despite being held up by the first-lap crash at the chicane. Unfortunately crashed heavily in testing the Monday after the race, suffering fractures to the ulna and radius in his left arm plus a cracked fibula.

10 TROY BAYLISS Happy to come out on top of a good dice with Jacque but not happy with his finishing position or feeling with the bike. Hoped to make a breakthrough in testing the Monday after the race.

11 OLIVIER JACQUE Some braking problems and a trip up the escape road

at the Chemin aux Boeufs chicane meant OJ was never going to repeat the miracle of Shanghai, but he enjoyed his dice with Bayliss, as did the crowd.

12 RUBEN XAUS A cautious race for a few points after another fraught practice and a crash when it started to rain. Still frustrated by his inability to come to terms with the Yamaha after his years on Ducati V-twins.

13 KENNY ROBERTS Good pace towards the end which at least showed the Bridgestone tyres lasted the race well, but really another depressing weekend for the Suzuki team.

14 GOORBERGH Found riding the RGV in the dry a very different proposition from the wet Chinese race. A good start meant he avoided the crash at the chicane, but then

made a mistake trying to pass Bayliss and lost a couple of places. Treated the rest of the race as a test session.

15 ROBERTO ROLFO Looked good in warm-up but tangled in Checa's crash, which put him 20 seconds adrift of the pack. Better rhythm in the second half of the race when he'd calmed down a bit.

16 JOHN HOPKINS An electrical problem on the warm-up lap with a servo motor that operated the throttle butterflies of one cylinder bank meant he was coming into the pits to change his bike while the rest were disappearing towards Turn 1.

17 FRANCO BATTAINI Did all that could be expected of him, and brought the bike home a lap down on the field.

NON-FINISHERS

ALEX BARROS Lost the rear going into the last left-hander while trying to catch Melandri and Biaggi. Took a big hit to his back from the bike; lucky to get away without any serious damage.

JAMES ELLISON Got a little over-ambitious when he saw van den Goorbergh in front of him on lap three and crashed without injury.

SHANE BYRNE For once this weekend a crash that wasn't down to a mechanical problem but to the rider grabbing too big a handful of throttle and highsiding himself on the first lap.

CARLOS CHECA Taken out by Biaggi at the chicane on the first lap and unable to restart. Another cruel blow for Ducati, as Carlos was fastest in warm-up by 0.6sec on a track where he always goes well. Team-manager Livio Suppo toured the press room after the event reminding journos of Ducati's catalogue of bad luck so far this season.

NON-STARTERS

ALEX HOFMANN Still recovering from the injuries he received before the Portuguese GP.

MAKOTO TAMADA Tried to ride in the first session but gave up after seven laps and handed the bike to van den Goorbergh, who'd also replaced him in China.

MUGELLO
ITALIAN GRAND PRIX

ROUND 5

ITALY 4, REST OF THE WORLD 0

Sometimes there is a race so sublime that you know you'll be talking about it in decades to come. This was one of those races

Can it get any better? One of the world's finest race tracks, set in a glorious Tuscan valley and bathed in sunshine, echoing to the screams of 90,000 fans as four Italians led the world's best home. Marco Melandri reported that he could actually hear the crowd during the race! If you ever find yourself growing weary of the commercialism or politics of the sport, re-watch the video of this race and be reminded why you love motorcycle racing.

Mugello 2005 had everything from the renaissance of Max Biaggi to the collapse of Sete Gibernau's

remaining title hopes, plus Ducati's first rostrum of the year. Four Italians on three different makes of motorcycle all took turns at leading before the Doctor had the final say. Rossi may have won again but, for once, he had the decency to look like he'd had to work for his victory; when the helmet came off Valentino was as red in the face and as sweaty as the guys behind him.

The man who pushed him hardest was his old rival, Max Biaggi, who had by far his best qualifying of the season so far and also set a new lap record in the race. Despite a get-off in warm-up for the second race

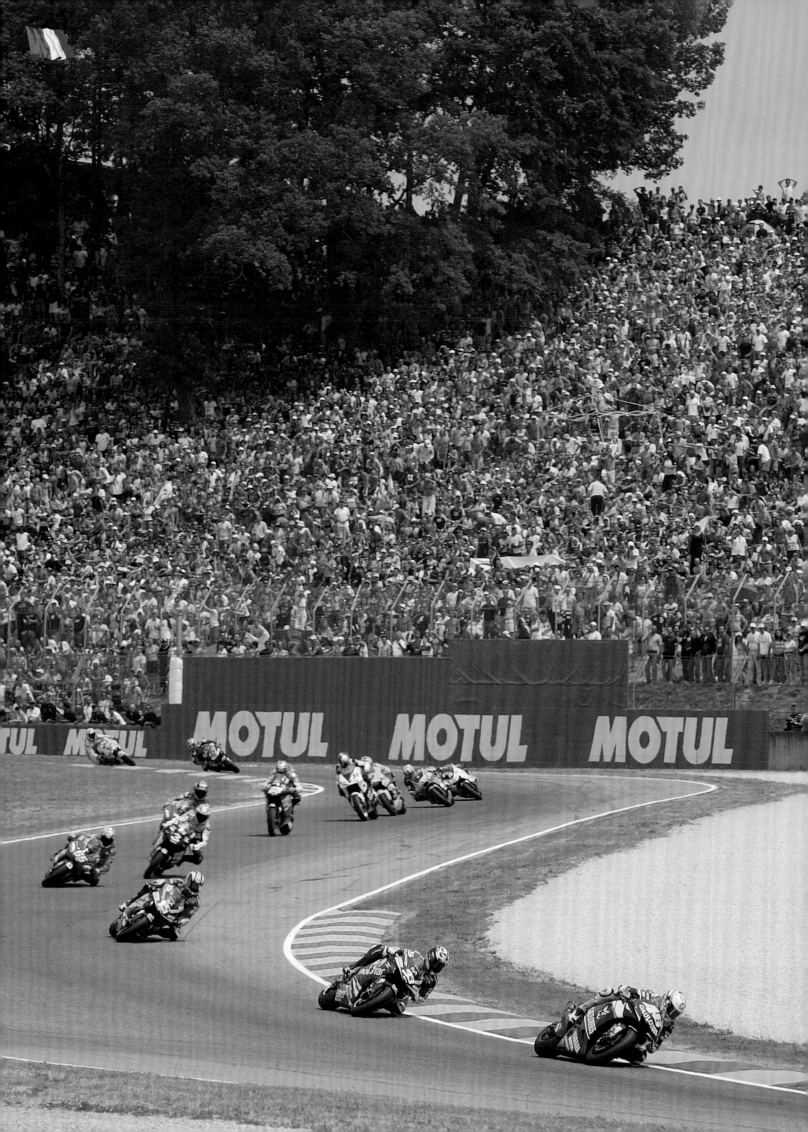

Opposite Early on in the race and Sete Gibernau is the only foreigner spoiling the Italian party

Above Max Biaggi was back to form: third on the grid and second in the race with the fastest lap to go third in the championship

Below right At last, a rostrum for the Bridgestone-shod Ducati and Loris Capirossi

running Max was back to his best, although still not completely happy with the bike, especially the front end. Even on a TV screen it was possible to make out his front wheel pattering violently into the downhill right-hander at Correntaio. Nevertheless, Rossi only broke his challenge three laps from the flag. By that time the four Italians had split into two pairs, with Capirossi and Melandri attacking each other at every opportunity. Loris had at least four goes at outbraking Marco at the first corner, only to run wide and be re-passed immediately before he made a move stick. The action was so hectic that Capirossi resorted to looking at the giant TV screens around the circuit to see what was going on.

The fact that Melandri could run with his illustrious fellow countrymen showed just what a force he has become this year, as did the fact that no-one was surprised to see him in such august company. Despite finishing fourth for the third time in five races he declared it far and away his best performance so far. As he passed Rossi and Biaggi in one go as they braked for Turn 1, to take the lead just before half-distance, then indulged in a gloves-off dice with Capirossi for third, that could be regarded as a massive understatement.

The Ducati rider, and the factory, were uncharacteristically happy with their third place, the team's first rostrum of the year and their first on Bridgestone tyres. Team-manager Livio Suppo was able to shave off his beard in celebration before it grew to Old Testament proportions. The tall, elegant Ingrid Capirossi, usually the epitome of Italian cool, lost it completely and ran squawking down pit lane, her

designer high heels in her hands, shoving security men aside to embrace her husband in parc fermé. In Italy racing really does matter, as the record-breaking TV audience showed. Mediaset's Italia Uno channel had a market share of 47 per cent and an average of 7.6 million viewers.

A great day for Italy, then, but a bad one for Spain. Sete Gibernau clung on to Rossi for one lap before being passed by Melandri and then, on lap four, by Biaggi, who'd made a bad start and been sixth at the

Above Believe it or not, this is Mugello on race day

Below Competitiveness at last for Ducati

the title had gone. The Doctor agreed, and nominated Biaggi and Melandri as the threats for the rest of the season. Yes, Rossi was being nice about Biaggi. He took great trouble to shake hands with him on the slow-down lap and was fulsome in his praise of the Repsol Honda rider. Max even went as far as to put his arm round Valentino's shoulders in the post-race press conference. Rossi was genuinely glad to see Capirossi on the rostrum – he used to be a fan after all – but his relationship with Melandri has definitely cooled. Vale is always happy to see people do well, provided he does not consider them a threat to his title or status.

The returning Makoto Tamada couldn't raise his game to the heights of his Mugello fourth place in 2003, and the young gun most likely to make an impact, Toni Elias, was absent due to a nasty collection of fractures suffered during testing at Le Mans the day after the French GP. He was replaced by David Checa, younger brother of Carlos, who qualified within two-and-a-half seconds of pole-man Rossi.

Checa the elder's fifth place completed Ducati's joy, making them the only team to get both riders in the top five. The new-generation Bridgestones helped, as did the fact that Ducati's test team had spent a lot of time at Mugello. Interestingly, Loris Capirossi made a significant change to his style by abandoning his usual treatment of the throttle as an on/off switch and going for a more progressive attitude to the twistgrip. Ducati were the only Bridgestone team to challenge the Michelin men; Suzuki didn't manage to get a bike into the top ten (which makes John Hopkins's fifth place in qualifying all the more praiseworthy), while Nakano's Kawasaki came in a distant tenth.

end of the first lap. Gibernau never looked comfortable and on lap six the seemingly inevitable happened when he slid out. He had no excuses but was a little puzzled as to how it could all go so right through practice and qualifying and then completely wrong on race day. Whatever the reason for Sete's crash, it left him 67 points adrift of Rossi and conceding that his chances of

However, all Italy's praise was being heaped upon the head of Valentino Rossi. As usual, he donned a new crash helmet design for the occasion of his home race with 'Il Laureato' (the Graduate) on the back, a reference to the honorary degree in communications recently awarded him by the University of Urbino, the town of his birth. In Italy, anyone with a university degree can call themselves dottore (doctor), so Valentino was now a real doctor. He even wore the academic mortarboard he'd sported at the degree ceremony on the rostrum, complete with Michelin sticker. Later he reported that his mother was at least as emotional about her son getting a university degree as she was about his winning the race.

Right Sete Gibernau contemplates the wreckage of his championship chances as he is ferried back to the paddock by a marshal

Below Academic mortar board firmly in place and specially painted helmet in hand, Valentino Rossi revels in what he called his most emotional victory of the year

RULE CHANGES

As expected, the MSMA (Motor Sports Manufacturers Association) announced that from the 2007 season maximum capacity of MotoGP machines would be reduced from 990cc to 800cc, with tank capacity lowered by another litre, on top of the reduction at the start of the '05 season, to 21 litres. This capacity limit will stay in force for five years. The move was considered necessary to slow down the rate at which lap times are decreasing – in round figures, about one second per year. In addition, MotoGP bikes are such different beasts from what went before that they crash in different ways and at different places. Overall, the danger is that traditional circuits are in danger of being outgrown. Riders seem to be in favour of the move, with Valentino Rossi saying that the 900cc bikes would now pass into legend as monsters.

Honda, who had the presidency of the MSMA when the decision

was taken, were widely perceived as driving the change, but the vote was unanimous. It should be noted, though, that KTM did not have a vote on this issue as they were in their first year of competition in MotoGP and they would later cite the new regulation as one of the reasons for their withdrawal from the class.

Minimum weight limits will also all be increased, with the exception of the lowest limit, for twin-cylinder machines, which was lowered by 2kg. The MSMA also formally outlawed two-strokes from MotoGP but confirmed the continuation of the 250cc class without change until 2009.

The main question being asked in the paddock was: just how much slower would an 800cc bike be once the engineers had spent a couple of years developing revvier, peakier motors? The answer seemed to be not a lot. In fact no-one seemed to expect much of a slow down at all.

MUGELLO
ITALIAN GRAND PRIX

ROUND 5

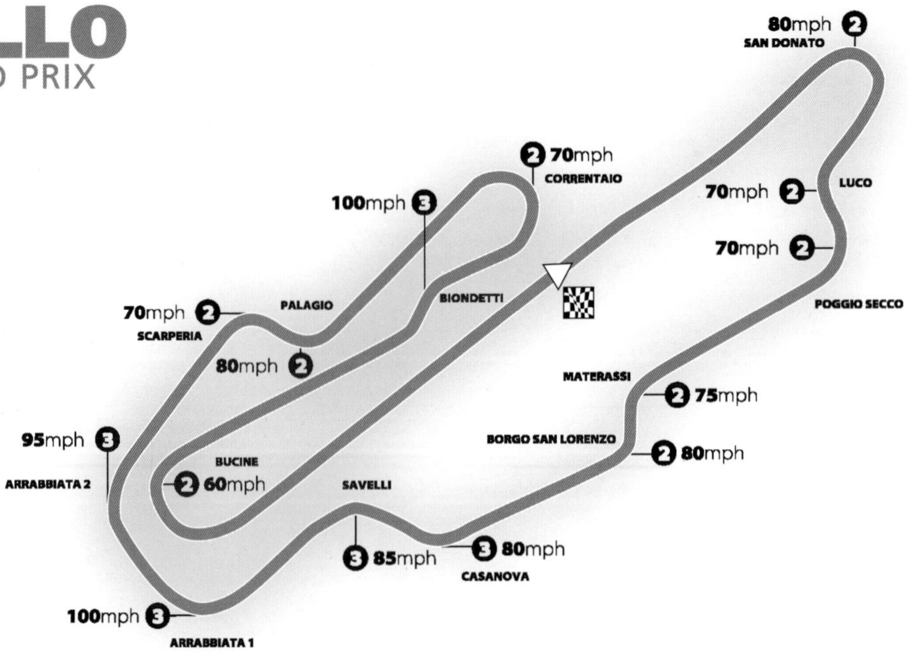

RACE RESULTS

RACE DATE June 5th
CIRCUIT LENGTH 3.259 miles
NO. OF LAPS 23
RACE DISTANCE 74.794 miles
WEATHER Dry, 27°C
TRACK TEMPERATURE 42°C
WINNER Valentino Rossi
FASTEST LAP 1m 50.117s, 106.312mph, Max Biaggi (record)
PREVIOUS LAP RECORD 1m 51.133s, 105.578mph, Sete Gibernau, 2004

Circuit map labels:
- 80mph SAN DONATO 2
- 70mph 2 CORRENTAIO
- 100mph 3
- 70mph 2 LUCO
- 70mph 2
- PALAGIO
- BIONDETTI
- POGGIO SECCO
- 70mph 2 SCARPERIA
- 80mph 2
- MATERASSI
- 75mph 2
- 95mph 3 ARRABBIATA 2
- BUCINE
- 60mph 2
- BORGO SAN LORENZO
- 80mph 2
- SAVELLI
- 85mph 3
- 80mph 3 CASANOVA
- 100mph 3 ARRABBIATA 1

QUALIFYING

	Rider	Nationality	Team	Qualifying	Pole +	Gap
1	Rossi	ITA	Gauloises Yamaha Team	1m 49.223s		
2	Gibernau	SPA	Movistar Honda Team	1m 49.361s	0.138s	0.138s
3	Biaggi	ITA	Repsol Honda Team	1m 49.458s	0.235s	0.097s
4	Hayden	USA	Repsol Honda Team	1m 49.546s	0.323s	0.088s
5	Hopkins	USA	Team Suzuki MotoGP	1m 49.556s	0.333s	0.010s
6	Capirossi	ITA	Ducati Marlboro Team	1m 49.633s	0.410s	0.077s
7	Melandri	ITA	Movistar Honda Team	1m 49.805s	0.582s	0.172s
8	Checa C.	SPA	Ducati Marlboro Team	1m 49.811s	0.588s	0.006s
9	Nakano	JPN	Kawasaki Racing Team	1m 49.856s	0.633s	0.045s
10	Tamada	JPN	Konica Minolta Honda	1m 49.951s	0.728s	0.095s
11	Roberts	USA	Team Suzuki MotoGP	1m 50.052s	0.829s	0.101s
12	Edwards	USA	Gauloises Yamaha Team	1m 50.176s	0.953s	0.124s
13	Barros	BRA	Camel Honda	1m 50.281s	1.058s	0.105s
14	Hofmann	GER	Kawasaki Racing Team	1m 51.056s	1.833s	0.775s
15	Xaus	SPA	Fortuna Yamaha Team	1m 51.585s	2.362s	0.529s
16	Checa D.	SPA	Fortuna Yamaha Team	1m 51.610s	2.387s	0.025s
17	Bayliss	AUS	Camel Honda	1m 51.764s	2.541s	0.154s
18	Byrne	GBR	Team Roberts	1m 52.117s	2.894s	0.353s
19	Rolfo	ITA	Team D'Antin – Pramac	1m 53.010s	3.787s	0.893s
20	Ellison	GBR	Blata WCM	1m 54.177s	4.954s	1.167s
21	Battaini	ITA	Blata WCA	1m 54.820s	5.597s	0.643s

FINISHERS

1 VALENTINO ROSSI An almost perfect weekend, only the lap record escaping the Doctor. After just five rounds of the championship he looked to have yet another title in his grasp – and it was his fourth win in a row at Mugello.

2 MAX BIAGGI His second rostrum of the year, but this time in with a chance of victory. Indeed, he was fast right from the first practice session. Valentino versus Max at lap-record pace for the win was just like old times, so was this the Mugello effect or a genuine renaissance?

3 LORIS CAPIROSSI Another beneficiary of the home-race effect? Given his team-mate's success, this looked like a genuine return to form for both Loris and the Bologna factory. His typically brilliant start to lead into the first corner and the battle with Melandri were thrilling to watch.

4 MARCO MELANDRI Looked like he had machinery problems but reported he was simply riding close to and over the edge. Lost out to Capirossi's Ducati in the fast sections but made it up in the slower Esses. Nearly crashed five laps from the flag but only lost third place by a tenth of a second. And all from his lowest grid position so far this year.

5 CARLOS CHECA The fastest man on track mid-race when he was hunting down Nicky Hayden. Not so happy early on with a full fuel load, but delighted to end his run of crashes and contribute to the Ducati team's best weekend yet in '05.

6 NICKY HAYDEN The closest he's been to the leaders all year and some good lap times early on when he went past Checa, but not happy with sixth place. Never found the feeling with the bike he'd had in qualifying and not helped by a bad start.

7 ALEX BARROS Judging by his race pace unaffected by injuries picked up in his French crash, but 13th in qualifying meant he had too much work to do early on. Reckoned he'd have been fighting for a podium if he'd started nearer the front.

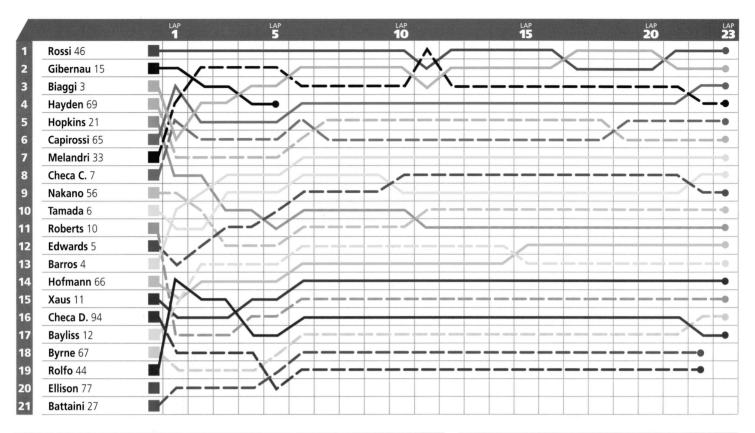

		LAP 1	LAP 5	LAP 10	LAP 15	LAP 20	LAP 23
1	Rossi 46						
2	Gibernau 15						
3	Biaggi 3						
4	Hayden 69						
5	Hopkins 21						
6	Capirossi 65						
7	Melandri 33						
8	Checa C. 7						
9	Nakano 56						
10	Tamada 6						
11	Roberts 10						
12	Edwards 5						
13	Barros 4						
14	Hofmann 66						
15	Xaus 11						
16	Checa D. 94						
17	Bayliss 12						
18	Byrne 67						
19	Rolfo 44						
20	Ellison 77						
21	Battaini 27						

RACE

	Rider	Motorcycle	Race Time	Time +	Fastest Lap	Average Speed
1	Rossi	Yamaha	42m 42.994s		1m 50.291s	203.322mph
2	Biaggi	Honda	42m 43.353s	0.359s	1m 50.117s	205.931mph
3	Capirossi	Ducati	42m 46.868s	3.874s	1m 50.728s	206.988mph
4	Melandri	Honda	42m 46.973s	3.979s	1m 50.338s	204.999mph
5	Checa C.	Ducati	42m 50.892s	7.898s	1m 50.856s	208.666mph
6	Hayden	Honda	42m 51.198s	8.204s	1m 50.974s	204.129mph
7	Barros	Honda	42m 54.566s	11.572s	1m 50.963s	203.508mph
8	Tamada	Honda	43m 08.388s	25.394s	1m 51.388s	203.570mph
9	Edwards	Yamaha	43m 08.479s	25.485s	1m 51.504s	202.576mph
10	Nakano	Kawasaki	43m 19.543s	36.549s	1m 52.136s	197.232mph
11	Hopkins	Suzuki	43m 24.631s	41.637s	1m 52.208s	200.525mph
12	Hofmann	Kawasaki	43m 26.653s	43.659s	1m 52.145s	199.655mph
13	Bayliss	Team	43m 26.910s	43.916s	1m 52.120s	202.576mph
14	Xaus	Yamaha	43m 34.569s	51.575s	1m 52.712s	197.915mph
15	Roberts	Suzuki	43m 53.269s	1m 10.275s	1m 52.531s	198.972mph
16	Byrne	Proton KR	43m 55.576s	1m 12.582s	1m 53.907s	201.395mph
17	Rolfo	Ducati	43m 56.041s	1m 13.047s	1m 53.273s	205.559mph
18	Battaini	Blata	43m 01.858s	1 Lap	1m 55.335s	185.612mph
19	Checa D.	Yamaha	44m 23.120s	1 Lap	1m 53.725s	196.548mph
	Gibernau	Honda	9m 22.690s	18 Laps	1m 50.938s	202.700mph
	Ellison	Blata				

CHAMPIONSHIP

	Rider	Team	Points
1	Rossi	Gauloises Yamaha Team	120
2	Melandri	Movistar Honda MotoGP	71
3	Biaggi	Repsol Honda Team	67
4	Gibernau	Movistar Honda MotoGP	53
5	Barros	Camel Honda	52
6	Edwards	Gauloises Yamaha Team	48
7	Capirossi	Ducati Marlboro Team	39
8	Hayden	Repsol Honda Team	36
9	Nakano	Kawasaki Racing Team	33
10	Checa C.	Ducati Marlboro Team	28
11	Jacque	Kawasaki Racing Team	25
12	Bayliss	Camel Honda	24
13	Xaus	Fortuna Yamaha Team	18
14	Hopkins	Team Suzuki MotoGP	16
15	Tamada	JIR Konica Minolta Honda	16
16	Elias	Fortuna Yamaha Team	15
17	Goorbergh	JIR Konica Minolta Honda	12
18	Hofmann	Kawasaki Racing Team	9
19	Roberts	Team Suzuki MotoGP	8
20	Rolfo	Team D'Antin – Pramac	5
21	Ellison	Blata WCM	4
22	Ukawa	Moriwaki Racing	1

8 MAKOTO TAMADA Still suffering from his Estoril wrist injury and missing vital track time. Quickly lost contact with the leaders and then found his suspension set-up was too soft exiting corners. Put a great move on Edwards on the last lap to keep hold of eighth, the same position as at Jerez.

9 COLIN EDWARDS On Friday looked as if he'd pick up where he left off at Le Mans, but no matter what the team did they couldn't improve the bike. 'I'm as mystified as anyone,' said Colin. Didn't get off the line well but passed a lot of people on the first lap and through the race before being mugged by Tamada.

10 SHINYA NAKANO Handicapped by instability on the brakes and a lack of acceleration out of the faster corners. Won a great battle with Hopkins, then said he couldn't have done more with the machinery available to him. The team agreed.

11 JOHN HOPKINS Three laps from the end decided that a finish was better than a crash and had to concede to Nakano (who John said was riding really well). Earned high praise from his team-manager for his effort and discipline. Definitely got the best out of an 'awesome' qualifying tyre.

12 ALEX HOFMANN Happy to be back after a three-race layoff and set a good pace right from the first session. Hit trouble mid-race when he thought he felt a misfire, after which engine braking became inconsistent. His wrist troubled him but not enough to need painkillers.

13 TROY BAYLISS Another very difficult weekend. Never got any feeling for the bike on the highly technical track.

14 RUBEN XAUS Went through the million-Euro barrier in crash damage costs in practice, then rode what his team-manager called his best race so far. Let Edwards go, then had a tough job with the straight-line speed of Rolfo's Ducati. Finally refused to concede to Roberts and was catching the group ahead of him.

15 KENNY ROBERTS Both Suzukis got in the points for the first time this year, but team-manager Paul Denning described Kenny as 'quite lost in terms of the direction to go' to try and get what he wants from the bike.

16 SHANE BYRNE No reliability problems from the KTM motor and less than two-and-a-half seconds outside the points. Ultimate top speed was impressive but lack of torque meant the bike didn't get there quickly enough. A definite cause for optimism.

17 ROBERTO ROLFO Suffered badly from rear tyre degradation which saw him 'unable to control the bike' at the end of the race. Lost touch with Xaus and Roberts after fighting with them in the early stages, and couldn't hold off Byrne at the end.

18 FRANCO BATTAINI A machine 25mph down on top speed is going to have a hard time at Mugello, so getting to the flag was the best Franco could hope for.

19 DAVID CHECA Had to come in early because he chose a rear tyre that was too soft, then circulated on his own but was closing on the group in front. Generally a satisfactory debut.

NON-FINISHERS

SETE GIBERNAU Desperately wanted to win the race but crashed on the fourth lap trying to run with the pace of the leaders. Blamed himself for the calamitous outcome of a weekend that had looked so good right up to race day.

JAMES ELLISON Didn't get round the first lap thanks to a broken valve, one of a spate of such failures that has troubled the WCM team.

TO HAVE AND HAVE NOT

You needed a factory Yamaha or a Honda on Michelins to look good in Barcelona. No-one else got a sniff of a rostrum position

The season so far was summed up by a Marco Melandri malapropism, delivered in the post-race press conference: 'The championship will be between Valentino and Rossi.' He quickly realised his error and hastened to explain that he'd meant Valentino and Sete, but no-one was listening – they were too busy laughing. Sitting alongside his team-mate Sete had quickly stifled a laugh then adopted a suitably unamused demeanour, but that little slip of the tongue would serve very well as a metaphor for his entire weekend.

After Jerez all Sete would say was that he was very happy with everything he'd done, and he would have been well justified in saying the same again after Barcelona. Gibernau started from pole position, led 18 of the 25 laps, set the second-fastest lap of the race and beat his team-mate Melandri, yet he was defeated again by an imperious Valentino Rossi. It's a measure of the Italian's dominance that no-one was surprised, including

Sete Gibernau's home crowd. Barcelona is the epicentre of MotoGP and the Catalan fans are probably more knowledgeable than any other crowd in the world. Usually, when a Catalan racer is half a second in front at his home GP the stands are a riot of fireworks, flags and noise you can hear above the bikes. When Pedrosa was leading the 250 race 106,000 people screamed him on to victory and then took raucous delight in Dani's first 250 win at home in Barcelona. So shouldn't they have been going completely mental for Sete Gibernau, another son of Barcelona? Shouldn't they have been recalling the last corner at Jerez and baying for Rossi's blood, as did the crowd down south? What happened was highly illuminating. As Sete struggled to pull away from Rossi – who never allowed the gap to rise much above half a second – the fans sat there nervously and waited for the inevitable. It happened three laps from the end when Valentino made his pass, broke the lap record and won by a second.

After the Mugello race the previous week Rossi had said, 'I make my attack three laps from the end...' The Barcelona crowd knew it was coming again, everyone watching at home on TV knew it was coming again, and Sete Gibernau was in no doubt either. Equally, they were certain there was nothing anyone could do about it. We are no longer surprised by miracles. Rossi then completed his victory lap without being pelted with bottles; in fact he wasn't even booed and a large chunk of the grandstand opposite the podium appeared to be wearing yellow, here in Sete's home town. There was no Jerez backlash.

The real issue at Catalunya was tyres, not surprising

as race time was an astonishing 47 seconds quicker than the previous year. Despite the pre-season test in March, all three tyre companies seemed surprised by the nature of the new surface. The Bridgestone users suffered most; and after Sunday morning warm-up all of them were advised, in the strongest possible terms, to switch to a hard, 'safe' tyre. This frustrated any thoughts Loris Capirossi and Ducati might have had of repeating their 2003 win at this track. Michelin brought many more front tyres than usual and even went so far as to ship in new designs overnight on Friday. The track was always tricky for the tyre engineers, mainly because of significant variations in the temperature of the tarmac during race day, but now it seemed to be abrasive as well and several riders reported that tyre

Above Waiting for the inevitable: Gibernau leads Rossi

Below Marco Melandri enjoyed himself showing off to the photographers

Above Gibernau's home crowd didn't seem that upset that Rossi won

Below John Hopkins' race was curtailed by tyre troubles

choice (Edwards) or degradation (Gibernau) had blunted their challenge. Michelin's competition chief, Nicholas Goubert, reported that the new surface meant it was just like going to a totally new racetrack and that the temperature differences between the March tests and a June race meant data from the test weren't really much use. All three manufacturers used double- and even triple-compound tyres to try and cope with the demands.

Not that you would have guessed anyone had any problems at the start of the race, for it looked like a six-lap production-bike sprint at a Brands Hatch club meeting. The circuit record lasted just two laps before Alex Barros went faster amid a brawl between Rossi and the Hondas of Gibernau, Melandri, Hayden, Biaggi, Tamada and Barros himself. The two Movistar team-mates, in particular, seemed anxious to beat each other up, and Sete had to take avoiding action at the tight left-hander as he came within millimetres of tailgating Marco. It took four laps for Gibernau and Rossi to make a break on the pack and another lap for the Spaniard to slip past into the lead going into the first turn. Nicky Hayden, setting a new lap record, led the pursuit as Barros and Melandri continued to try and pass each other at least twice a lap. For a short while it looked as if the returning Makoto Tamada would add to the fun, but he slid out when his front tyre cried enough. Bridgestone's worries were realised, forcing first Hofmann and then Hopkins to pit for new rubber.

That left two fights on track, the duel for first and then Nicky Hayden trying to fight off Barros and Melandri for the final rostrum position. Both battles were decided with three laps to go. Rossi set lap record

on the circuit that included the pass and followed that up with another two only marginally slower. Sete later said that he'd lost grip on the left side of his tyre eight laps from the flag so couldn't respond – and lest anyone think that is an excuse, Rossi also said he noted that his rival had a tyre problem. Hayden hit trouble with his front tyre and lost two places, leaving Melandri to take third after a few more exchanges of paint between the blue Honda and the yellow one.

It was very noticeable that, after the race, Rossi went to great pains to say how well Gibernau had ridden, even going so far as to mention that at mid-distance he'd thought the Spaniard would be able to pull away. For once Valentino even looked a little hot and bothered after the race, just to emphasise how hard he'd had to try. No doubt with Jerez in mind, and aware of some of the criticism his behaviour after that race had attracted, he also thanked the Spanish fans for the way they'd treated him, revealing that he had been a little worried before the event. 'It shows', he said, 'that our sport has true fans.'

POWER GAMES

Above Kawasaki's Yoda-san contemplates the unequal struggle

Below Rossi and his minders plan their escape route

The Circuit of Catalunya is reckoned to be a good track to test on as its mix of fast and slow corners with a good bit of elevation change and a long, fast straight examines every aspect of a bike's performance. If a bike works here, it should work anywhere. Conversely, if a bike has a weak spot it will be shown up here and there will be no disguising the problem.

At the end of the 2004 season it was obvious that Bridgestone were making rapid progress in their tyre war with Michelin. This pushed the French company into even greater efforts over winter, and the way in which lap records have been regularly demolished this season is as much down to their tyres as the motorcycle manufacturers.

Bridgestone were not idle over winter. The Chinese GP showed how much their rain tyres have improved, while they have always made excellent qualifying tyres. As for race tyres, the Bridgestone fronts have always been good but the performance of their rears seemd to plateau at this point in the season. The problems the Japanese company experienced this weekend severely handicapped their teams, Ducati, Suzuki and Kawasaki. However, the two Japanese bike makers could not put all their problems down to their rubber. Now that the pattern of the season was established, it was obvious that Suzuki and Kawasaki were not giving their riders the engines they needed. Even Shinya Nakano was starting to come out with some very un-Japanese remarks about his bike and senior staff like Yoda-san were making lightly coded statements to the effect that they needed more power delivered in a more useable fashion. They read like messages to head office back in Japan, not press releases. Over at Suzuki much the same attitude prevailed, while most of us wondered how two factories with such luminous four-stroke racing histories could remain so uncompetitive.

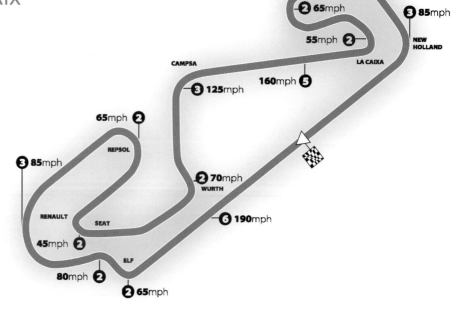

CATALUNYA
CATALAN GRAND PRIX

ROUND 6

RACE RESULTS

RACE DATE June 12th
CIRCUIT LENGTH 2.937 miles
NO. OF LAPS 25
RACE DISTANCE 73.425 miles
WEATHER Dry, 36°C
TRACK TEMPERATURE 36°C
WINNER Valentino Rossi
FASTEST LAP 1m 43.195s,
102.240mph, Valentino Rossi (record)
PREVIOUS LAP RECORD 1m 44.641s,
101.055mph, Sete Gibernau, 2004

QUALIFYING

	Rider	Nationality	Team	Qualifying	Pole +	Gap
1	Gibernau	SPA	Movistar Honda MotoGP	1m 42.337s		
2	Melandri	ITA	Movistar Honda MotoGP	1m 42.390s	0.053s	0.053s
3	Rossi	ITA	Gauloises Yamaha Team	1m 42.723s	0.386s	0.333s
4	Biaggi	ITA	Repsol Honda Team	1m 42.756s	0.419s	0.033s
5	Hayden	USA	Repsol Honda Team	1m 42.847s	0.510s	0.091s
6	Caporossi	ITA	Ducati Marlboro Team	1m 42.992s	0.655s	0.145s
7	Edwards	USA	Gauloises Yamaha Team	1m 43.109s	0.772s	0.117s
8	Checa C.	SPA	Ducati Marlboro Team	1m 43.129s	0.792s	0.020s
9	Barros	BRA	Camel Honda	1m 43.159s	0.822s	0.030s
10	Tamada	JPN	Konica Minolta Honda	1m 43.207s	0.870s	0.048s
11	Hopkins	USA	Team Suzuki MotoGP	1m 43.291s	0.954s	0.084s
12	Nakano	JPN	Kawasaki Racing Team	1m 43.607s	1.270s	0.316s
13	Roberts	USA	Team Suzuki MotoGP	1m 43.787s	1.450s	0.180s
14	Hofmann	GER	Kawasaki Racing Team	1m 43.864s	1.527s	0.077s
15	Bayliss	AUS	Camel Honda	1m 44.122s	1.785s	0.258s
16	Xaus	SPA	Fortuna Yamaha Team	1m 44.193s	1.856s	0.071s
17	Rolfo	ITA	Team D'Antin – Pramac	1m 44.934s	2.597s	0.741s
18	Checa D.	SPA	Fortuna Yamaha Team	1m 45.310s	2.973s	0.376s
19	Byrne	GBR	Team Roberts	1m 45.636s	3.299s	0.326s
20	Ellison	GBR	Blata WCM	1m 46.750s	4.413s	1.114s
21	Battaini	ITA	Blata WCM	1m 47.599s	5.262s	0.849s

FINISHERS

1 VALENTINO ROSSI Career win number 73 off his 100th front-row start (47 and 59th in the top class), and there can't have been many better. Didn't set pole and had some complaints about the right side of his front tyre, but when it mattered he was untouchable.

2 SETE GIBERNAU Did everything that could be expected of him, but said the left side of his rear tyre was shot eight laps from the flag. Not afraid of the close combat early on and ran a scorching pace when he led, yet still beaten on his home track.

3 MARCO MELANDRI Even happier than at Mugello, as he reckoned his race pace here

was far superior. Led early on, then lost ground to the leaders when embroiled in the fight for third. Fausto Gresini was delighted to have two bikes on the rostrum in his 150th GP as a team-manager.

4 ALEX BARROS Fought for the final rostrum place until the flag – tried to get past Melandri twice on the last lap – and not too disappointed with fourth as it proved he could run at the leaders' pace. Wasn't able to use his favoured weapon, the demon outbraking manoeuvre, as he had brake problems from the sixth lap on.

5 NICKY HAYDEN Deeply frustrated to have a good weekend yet only finish fifth when he thought third was within his grasp. Bullied out of the last rostrum position in the final

couple of laps when he lost ground after a pass and couldn't get back on terms with the two men in front of him.

6 MAX BIAGGI Never in the fight and disappointed not to have carried forward momentum gained at Mugello. The team gave him a set-up to improve stability on the brakes, but it came at the expense of handling. Finished four seconds behind his team-mate.

7 COLIN EDWARDS Caught out by the tarmac's extreme temperature changes. Saturday morning's rear tyre turned out to be too soft on Sunday afternoon so couldn't get any grip at full lean in the second half of the race. Had to stand the bike up and widen his lines.

8 TROY BAYLISS Followed up a distinctly average qualifying with what he reckoned was

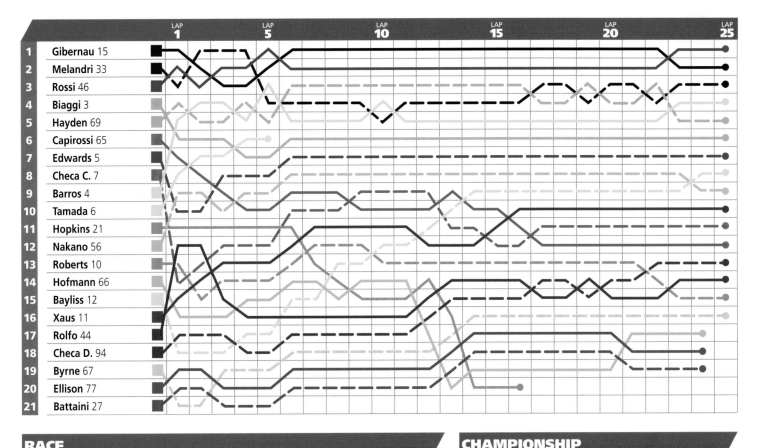

RACE

	Rider	Motorcycle	Race Time	Time +	Fastest Lap	Average Speed
1	Rossi	Yamaha	43m 16.487s		1m 43.195s	200.525mph
2	Gibernau	Honda	43m 17.581s	1.094s	1m 43.253s	199.717mph
3	Melandri	Honda	43m 24.297s	7.810s	1m 43.422s	202.700mph
4	Barros	Honda	43m 24.691s	8.204s	1m 43.498s	202.265mph
5	Hayden	Honda	43m 24.760s	8.273s	1m 43.389s	199.966mph
6	Biaggi	Honda	43m 28.538s	12.051s	1m 43.508s	202.514mph
7	Edwards	Yamaha	43m 35.249s	18.762s	1m 43.840s	199.158mph
8	Bayliss	Honda	43m 59.118s	42.631s	1m 44.365s	197.480mph
9	Nakano	Kawasaki	44m 03.125s	46.638s	1m 44.097s	195.987mph
10	Xaus	Yamaha	44m 03.179s	46.692s	1m 44.962s	195.865mph
11	Checa C.	Ducati	44m 16.844s	1m 00.357s	1m 44.646s	200.650mph
12	Capirossi	Ducati	44m 20.351s	1m 03.864s	1m 44.889s	221.777mph
13	Checa D.	Yamaha	44m 20.472s	1m 03.985s	1m 45.820s	197.729mph
14	Rolfo	Ducati	44m 26.745s	1m 10.258s	1m 45.420s	201.333mph
15	Roberts	Suzuki	44m 40.218s	1m 23.731s	1m 44.793s	194.498mph
16	Byrne	Proton KR	44m 51.111s	1m 34.624s	1m 46.726s	195.118mph
17	Hofmann	Kawasaki	43m 43.269s	1 Lap	1m 44.439s	195.243mph
18	Ellison	Blata	43m 52.521s	1 Lap	1m 48.208s	182.008mph
19	Battaini	Blata	43m 56.686s	1 Lap	1m 48.391s	185.301mph
	Hopkins	Suzuki	31m 26.247s	9 Laps	1m 44.475s	198.102mph
	Tamada	Honda	8m 47.428s	20 Laps	1m 43.757s	199.655mph

CHAMPIONSHIP

	Rider	Team	Points
1	Rossi	Gauloises Yamaha Team	145
2	Melandri	Movistar Honda MotoGP	87
3	Biaggi	Repsol Honda Team	77
4	Gibernau	Movistar Honda MotoGP	73
5	Barros	Camel Honda	65
6	Edwards	Gauloises Yamaha Team	57
7	Hayden	Repsol Honda Team	47
8	Capirossi	Ducati Marlboro Team	43
9	Nakano	Kawasaki Racing Team	40
10	Checa C	Ducati Marlboro Team	33
11	Bayliss	Camel Honda	32
12	Jacque	Kawasaki Racing Team	25
13	Xaus	Fortuna Yamaha Team	24
14	Hopkins	Team Suzuki MotoGP	16
15	Tamada	JIR Konica Minolta Honda	16
16	Elias	Fortuna Yamaha Team	15
17	Goorbergh	JIR Konica Minolta Honda	12
18	Hofmann	Kawasaki Racing Team	9
19	Roberts	Team Suzuki MotoGP	9
20	Rolfo	Team D'Antin – Pramac	7
21	Ellison	Blata WCM	4
22	Checa D	Fortuna Yamaha Team	3
23	Ukawa	Moriwaki Racing	1

the worst start of his career. Took three laps to catch the pack, then made ten overtakes to get his best finish since the first race of the year.

9 SHINYA NAKANO First Bridgestone finisher again, on a tough day for the Japanese tyre company. Got a good start but spent the last ten laps with virtually no rear grip and couldn't fight off Bayliss.

10 RUBEN XAUS Although his finishing position didn't compare with his sixth place in '04, Ruben and his team were again content with a job well done and his third top-ten finish of the year.

11 CARLOS CHECA Like all other Bridgestone runners raced with the safe option, a hard-compound rear tyre, and suffered accordingly. Dropped back after handlebar

shake shook his brake pads away from the discs and he took two grabs of the lever and locked the tyre.

12 LORIS CAPIROSSI Qualified sixth and was as high as seventh before lack of rear grip sent him back downfield. It was, he said, like riding in the wet. Set the fastest speed of the weekend through the trap: 205.3mph (330.3km/h).

13 DAVID CHECA Scored his first MotoGP points despite only getting on the bike on Saturday after Toni Elias realised he couldn't continue. Delighted with his race.

14 ROBERTO ROLFO Well inside the top ten going into the first corner and convinced he could run the same pace as the Bayliss group, but his rear tyre wouldn't go. Much

like the Bridgestones, his Dunlop was sliding dramatically from the seventh lap on.

15 KENNY ROBERTS Kept going despite the same tyre troubles as the other Bridgestone riders. After the previous race his team had seemed critical of him, this time they couldn't praise him enough: they reckoned his tyre couldn't have done another lap.

16 SHANE BYRNE Just like the previous race was one place off his first point of the year, but this time he was over ten seconds adrift of Roberts. The bike that had worked so well at Mugello just wouldn't respond in Barcelona. Shakey did not enjoy the race one little bit.

17 ALEX HOFMANN The first of two Bridgestone runners to pit because of tyre-induced vibration. Changed rubber and ran at the

same pace as Edwards and Biaggi for the next five laps, which only added to his frustration.

18 JAMES ELLISON Thought he had a cunning plan to prolong the useful life of his Dunlops by using a wider tyre. Actually slowed him down and the tyre went off after the same number of laps as his original choice. Doh!

19 FRANCO BATTAINI Followed his team-mate home, but the WCMs were never going to stand a chance of being competitive in dry weather.

ASSEN
DUTCH TT

ROUND **7**

HISTORY MAN

Valentino Rossi became the first Yamaha rider ever to win five races in a row. It was a fitting send-off for the most challenging stretch of tarmac in the calendar

Again it took a record on the final lap, under the severest of pressure, but Valentino Rossi made yet another little piece of history. The difference this time was that the man turning the screw wasn't Sete Gibernau or Max Biaggi but Marco Melandri. As Rossi himself noted, his nearest challenger this season isn't just fast, he's young. 'So young!' said Valentino after the race. 'He's two-and-a-half years younger than me.' Being challenged by a man younger than himself is a new experience for Rossi. The thirty-somethings he'd previously had to worry about, on the other hand, had

a terrible time. Gibernau never kick-started his weekend after his crew chief was hospitalised for the first day of practice, and Biaggi had the weekend from hell, at least up until race day.

The one thing everyone agreed was that the upcoming amputation of the entire northern loop of the fastest track in the calendar was a tragedy. Rossi spoke for them all: 'In the Safety Commission, all the riders were crying because this is the last time they will ride the real Assen. It will become just another track.' Then, more in sorrow than anger, he added, 'for a car park...',

a reference to the redevelopment scheduled to take place that will include a hotel and museum complex to be known as TT World, plus 7000 much-needed parking spaces. Valentino has always been acutely aware of the history of the sport and his place in it – and it was very easy to read into his words an intention to see the wonderful old track out with something special. And that's what happened, although not quite in the way the Doctor would have imagined.

For once, the effort needed to set pole seemed to take a lot out of him, with Rossi actually looking exhausted at the end of the session. That lap on its own would have been a fitting memorial to the old circuit, and after an overnight storm of massive intensity washed the track and radically altered its grip characteristics no-one really expected the race to be of such high quality. Valentino threw away any advantage he'd gained in qualifying with a bad start, while Melandri hit the front and stayed there for the first half of the race. Marco had finished no lower than fourth in the first six rounds of 2005 and he'd made it onto the rostrum three times, mightily impressive for his first year on a Honda and good enough to put him second in the championship after the third race of the year. Melandri has won both 125 and 250 races at Assen – indeed, his maiden win in GPs was a victory in the 125 class here in 1998, which made him the youngest rider ever to win at this historic venue. Anyone who breaks their duck at Assen tends to be a bit special, and his first ride at the TT on an RCV211V was most certainly that.

After Rossi had worked his way through the field, tracked Melandri for a couple of laps and then taken the lead, the younger man still had the pace to go with the World Champion, a man who reckoned his bike was 'perfect' and his Michelin tyres were 'really good' on a track he loves. The current wisdom is that to beat Valentino you must carve out perfect laps for the whole race. Marco could only point to one mistake, just after Rossi took the lead, which he reckoned cost him eight-tenths of a second, while an excess of wheelspin half way round the last lap blunted his final challenge. The man who nearly profited from Melandri's big mistake was Colin Edwards, who had a very good view of Marco nearly ramming Rossi at the De Strubben horseshoe left. The American had already fought his way up from a bad start and now the red mist came down as he pushed hard to try and catch the front two. Discretion returned with big front-wheel slides at the same corner on consecutive laps, Colin settling for his second rostrum of the year while making sure that Nicky Hayden didn't catch him in the closing stages.

If you were looking for a man who'd suffered a bad weekend, it had to be Max Biaggi. He ended Friday $6000 the poorer thanks to fines imposed for riding in an irresponsible manner and for doing a practice start before the session had ended. The victim of both incidents was none other than Marco Melandri, who claimed his fast laps were spoiled when he came across Max dawdling on the racing line and then doing that practice start. Ironically, Biaggi was also involved in an incident at the revised right/left at the end of the Veenslang which culminated in Franco Battaini clinging to the back of the Honda after Max had gone straight on entering the fast chicane, run across the gravel and

Opposite Shinya Nakano contemplates another struggle against the odds

Below The field charges into Haarbocht for the last time; in 2006 they'll be turning right just after the pit lane exit

Above Blue was the colour to be seen in on the rostrum

Opposite This is not a doctored picture: Melandri has run on at the new chicane and narrowly missed collecting Biaggi as he rejoined the track

Below Melandri harried Rossi right to the flag

collected the WCM rider when he came back on track. In truth, the blame for that one probably lay with the new track layout, but Max does have a reputation for such behaviour which may explain why he was hit with a $5000 fine for his miscreant riding and only $1000 for the seemingly much more dangerous illegal practice start.

Marco Melandri wasn't waiting for Race Direction to consider the case: he pulled alongside Max on the slow-down lap, offered his opinion of proceedings and then sideswiped the Repsol Honda in the chicane. Biaggi just about stayed on. Back in pit lane Max's Uncle Valerio abused Marco, then shook him warmly by the

throat and promptly had his pass withdrawn. Biaggi was summoned on race morning by Tanaka-san, his Repsol Honda team-manager, to be told he considered that: (1) Max should have looked before he re-entered the track and collected Battaini, and (2) such a famous MotoGP racer and factory Honda rider should not do something as dangerous as a practice start before qualifying was over. He also made it clear there was absolutely no question of appealing against Race Direction's decision. Interestingly, although Race Direction did not sanction Melandri for his part in the pushing match, Mr Tanaka and HRC general manager Mr Ishii went to see Marco's team-manager, Fausto Gresini, to make it clear they considered the incident to be closed.

Max's personal press release on the subject (not the one put out through the Repsol team's PR machinery) placed all the blame on Melandri. This will not have done Biaggi's already strained relationship with HRC any good. The relationship the paddock was now watching with interest, though, was that between Rossi and Melandri. In previous years they've always seemed to get on well, but no-one who has threatened the Doctor's dominance has come out of the encounter unscathed, as first Max Biaggi and then Sete Gibernau could attest. Then there is the emergence of Melandri as Honda's only consistent challenger to consider, a matter complicated by the fact he was not one of the three men favoured with a full factory bike at the start of the year. Who will the rumoured updated RCV go to? At the beginning of the year HRC made it clear they would wait for a pattern to emerge before putting their effort behind one rider. Did Assen provide the focus HRC needed?

HAPPY BIRTHDAY

MotoGP 2005 wasn't just the last time a GP will be held on the 6km circuit, it was also the 75th Dutch TT. Assen is unique in that there has been a Grand Prix at the track every year since 1949, when the modern World Championship was inaugurated. The track itself has undergone many changes since its first incarnation, in 1925, as a 17-mile loop of closed public roads, but it has always maintained the character of a road circuit with a crown in the centre of much of the track, banked corners and nothing that could honestly be called a straight. Despite the fact that the bikes aren't upright for any length of time the track is (or was) the fastest in the calendar. There couldn't be a greater contrast with modern tracks such as Shanghai, which Valentino Rossi characterises as set numbers of fast and slow corners, one long straight and a couple of short straights joined up using a computer.

In defence of Assen's management it should be said that they have spent a lot of money on significant improvements over the last few years, both for paddock users and the paying public. The 'floating' Timmer Bocht grandstand overlooking the final chicane, opened just before the 2005 race, is a prime example. However, there is no doubt that something unique is being lost. Road-derived circuits that place a premium on a rider's ability to carry speed through interlinked corners display the subtlety of motorcycle racing to its best advantage: think the first part of Donington or the difference between Motegi and the sadly missed Suzuka. While the necessarily safe new tracks are built to host Formula 1, Phillip Island will be left to carry the torch and will also become the fastest track at which MotoGP races.

ASSEN
DUTCH TT

ROUND 7

RACE RESULTS

RACE DATE June 25th
CIRCUIT LENGTH 3.726 miles
NO. OF LAPS 19
RACE DISTANCE 70.794 miles
WEATHER Dry, 23°C
TRACK TEMPERATURE 30°C
WINNER Valentino Rossi
FASTEST LAP 2m 00.991s,
110.630mph, Valentino Rossi
PREVIOUS LAP RECORD 1m 59.472s,
112.852mph, Valentino Rossi, 2004

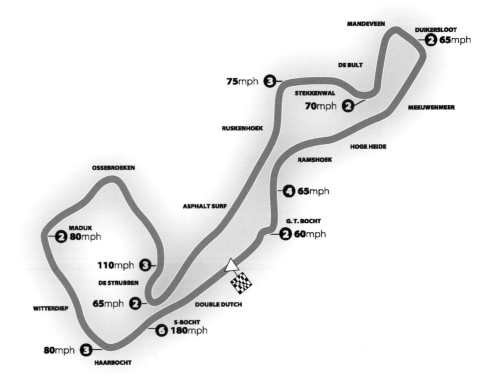

QUALIFYING

	Rider	Nationality	Team	Qualifying	Pole +	Gap
1	Rossi	ITA	Gauloises Yamaha Team	1m 58.936s		
2	Gibernau	SPA	Movistar Honda MotoGP	1m 59.247s	0.311s	0.311s
3	Melandri	ITA	Movistar Honda MotoGP	1m 59.632s	0.696s	0.385s
4	Nakano	JPN	Kawasaki Racing Team	1m 59.760s	0.824s	0.128s
5	Hayden	USA	Repsol Honda Team	1m 59.784s	0.848s	0.024s
6	Edwards	USA	Gauloises Yamaha Team	2m 00.006s	1.070s	0.222s
7	Capirossi	ITA	Ducati Marlboro Team	2m 00.136s	1.200s	0.130s
8	Barros	BRA	Camel Honda	2m 00.232s	1.296s	0.096s
9	Biaggi	ITA	Repsol Honda Team	2m 00.281s	1.345s	0.049s
10	Hofmann	GER	Kawasaki Racing Team	2m 00.298s	1.362s	0.017s
11	Tamada	JPN	Konica Minolta Honda	2m 00.656s	1.720s	0.358s
12	Hopkins	USA	Team Suzuki MotoGP	2m 00.810s	1.874s	0.154s
13	Checa C.	SPA	Ducati Marlboro Team	2m 00.883s	1.947s	0.073s
14	Bayliss	AUS	Camel Honda	2m 01.216s	2.280s	0.333s
15	Roberts	USA	Team Suzuki MotoGP	2m 01.836s	2.900s	0.620s
16	Xaus	SPA	Fortuna Yamaha Team	2m 01.854s	2.918s	0.018s
17	Checa D.	SPA	Fortuna Yamaha Team	2m 02.639s	3.703s	0.785s
18	Rolfo	ITA	Team D'Antin – Pramac	2m 02.704s	3.768s	0.065s
19	Byrne	GBR	Team Roberts	2m 03.442s	4.506s	0.738s
20	Ellison	GBR	Blata WCM	2m 03.488s	4.552s	0.046s
21	Battaini	ITA	Blata WCM	2m 06.527s	7.591s	3.039s

FINISHERS

1 VALENTINO ROSSI Another hard-fought victory made him the first Yamaha rider ever to win twice in the top class at Assen, and the first to win five races in a row. Had to break the lap record again on the last lap to do it, however.

2 MARCO MELANDRI Pushed Rossi all the way. His best-ever result in MotoGP and his best-ever race in the class, as befits the rider who became the youngest Assen winner, taking 125 victory in 1998 at 15 years of age.

3 COLIN EDWARDS His progress from average qualifying and start almost exactly paralleled that of team-mate Rossi: they ended the first lap fifth and seventh and came first and third in the race. Two big front-wheel slides at Turn 2 dissuaded him from pushing at the end of the race.

4 NICKY HAYDEN Ended up a lonely fourth after having to gamble with settings because of the big change in track conditions. Another season's best performance but still not really happy because he wasn't in contention for the rostrum, let alone the win.

5 SETE GIBERNAU Described the race as one of his worst in recent times. Never found a set-up he was happy with, a situation not helped by his race engineer Juan Martinez spending Friday in the medical centre suffering severe migraine.

6 MAX BIAGGI Fined $6000 for a variety of offences in practice and qualifying, then finished an eventful three days with a lacklustre race thanks, he said, to a lack of grip. Still managed five overtakes, though.

7 ALEX BARROS Had a 'frankly terrible' race at the track that is statistically his best. Chose a softer tyre than most – which didn't suit the colder conditions – because he hadn't got on with the harder one in qualifying.

8 SHINYA NAKANO Great qualifying but lack of top-end power handicapped him in the race, causing Kawasaki's technical director, Ichiro Yoda, to say the factory needed to speed up engine development. Still managed to be the top Bridgestone finisher.

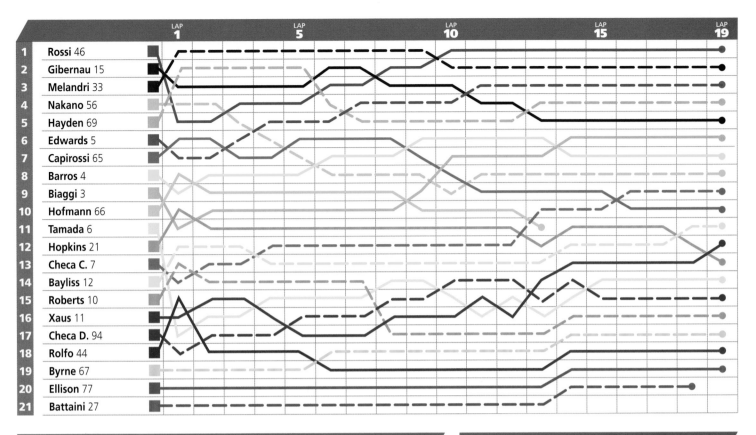

		LAP 1			LAP 5					LAP 10					LAP 15				LAP 19
1	Rossi 46																		
2	Gibernau 15																		
3	Melandri 33																		
4	Nakano 56																		
5	Hayden 69																		
6	Edwards 5																		
7	Capirossi 65																		
8	Barros 4																		
9	Biaggi 3																		
10	Hofmann 66																		
11	Tamada 6																		
12	Hopkins 21																		
13	Checa C. 7																		
14	Bayliss 12																		
15	Roberts 10																		
16	Xaus 11																		
17	Checa D. 94																		
18	Rolfo 44																		
19	Byrne 67																		
20	Ellison 77																		
21	Battaini 27																		

RACE

	Rider	Motorcycle	Race Time	Time +	Fastest Lap	Average Speed
1	Rossi	Yamaha	38m 41.808s		2m 00.991s	185.985mph
2	Melandri	Honda	38m 43.391s	1.583s	2m 01.177s	189.899mph
3	Edwards	Yamaha	38m 49.451s	7.643s	2m 01.488s	185.239mph
4	Hayden	Honda	38m 51.936s	10.128s	2m 01.702s	186.606mph
5	Gibernau	Honda	38m 56.603s	14.795s	2m 01.864s	186.730mph
6	Biaggi	Honda	39m 03.383s	21.575s	2m 02.152s	186.792mph
7	Barros	Honda	39m 04.533s	22.725s	2m 02.222s	187.227mph
8	Nakano	Kawasaki	39m 08.285s	26.477s	2m 02.526s	178.155mph
9	Checa C.	Ducati	39m 12.029s	30.221s	2m 02.678s	185.239mph
10	Capirossi	Ducati	39m 12.273s	30.465s	2m 02.052s	186.482mph
11	Bayliss	Honda	39m 25.610s	43.802s	2m 03.255s	181.324mph
12	Xaus	Yamaha	39m 31.672s	49.864s	2m 03.642s	180.392mph
13	Hopkins	Suzuki	39m 32.638s	50.830s	2m 02.430s	186.047mph
14	Tamada	Honda	39m 35.178s	53.370s	2m 04.005s	183.810mph
15	Checa D.	Yamaha	39m 36.773s	54.965s	2m 03.997s	182.380mph
16	Roberts	Suzuki	39m 48.747s	1m 06.939s	2m 03.502s	174.737mph
17	Byrne	Proton KR	39m 48.807s	1m 06.999s	2m 03.896s	183.375mph
18	Rolfo	Ducati	40m 10.856s	1m 29.048s	2m 05.897s	178.901mph
19	Ellison	Blata	40m 25.576s	1m 43.768s	2m 06.514s	170.512mph
	Battaini	Blata	39m 22.537s	1 Lap	2m 09.650s	169.517mph
	Hofmann	Kawasaki	26m 52.136s	6 Laps	2m 02.457s	182.380mph

CHAMPIONSHIP

	Rider	Team	Points
1	Rossi	Gauloises Yamaha Team	170
2	Melandri	Movistar Honda MotoGP	107
3	Biaggi	Repsol Honda Team	87
4	Gibernau	Movistar Honda MotoGP	84
5	Barros	Camel Honda	74
6	Edwards	Gauloises Yamaha Team	73
7	Hayden	Repsol Honda Team	60
8	Capirossi	Ducati Marlboro Team	49
9	Nakano	Kawasaki Racing Team	48
10	Checa C.	Ducati Marlboro Team	40
11	Bayliss	Camel Honda	37
12	Xaus	Fortuna Yamaha Team	28
13	Jacque	Kawasaki Racing Team	25
14	Hopkins	Team Suzuki MotoGP	19
15	Tamada	JIR Konica Minolta Honda	18
16	Elias	Fortuna Yamaha Team	15
17	Goorbergh	JIR Konica Minolta Honda	12
18	Hofmann	Kawasaki Racing Team	9
19	Roberts	Team Suzuki MotoGP	9
20	Rolfo	Team D'Antin – Pramac	7
21	Checa D.	Fortuna Yamaha Team	4
22	Ellison	Blata WCM	4
23	Ukawa	Moriwaki Racing	1

9 CARLOS CHECA Boxed in at the start, after dismal qualifying. Got going at two-thirds' distance once the fuel load lightened and he felt more comfortable in the corners.

10 LORIS CAPIROSSI In contrast to his team-mate had a good start to the race but slipped down the order once his tyres went off. His public pronouncements were politically correct ('I don't want to blame anybody') but the strain is starting to show: 'Some riders are used to finishing well back, I'm neither used to this nor happy about it.'

11 TROY BAYLISS Had another frustrating weekend at a track he knows well, and likes. Still struggling to come to terms with the Honda, still desperately unhappy with his performance.

12 RUBEN XAUS Didn't have any feeling for the bike at the start, then got shot-blasted by stones from Tamada's rear wheel at the chicane. Set his best lap three from home and beat Hopkins in the closing yards.

13 JOHN HOPKINS Yet again, scant reward for three days of wholehearted effort. Ran with Biaggi early on, was the fastest Bridgestone man mid-race, but a quickshifter problem three laps from the flag combined with tyre wear slowed him drastically.

14 MAKOTO TAMADA Described it as the worst race of his MotoGP career and was mortified that his fastest lap was three seconds slower than Rossi's. Never found any feel and ran into problems with arm pump, probably due to a ferocious fitness campaign after his wrist operation.

15 DAVID CHECA Third and final replacement ride for Fortuna Yamaha, and his best. In front of Tamada and team-mate Xaus early on, but hit on the forearm by a small rock thrown up when the Japanese retook him five laps in. Suffered severe bruising that hampered him significantly. Nevertheless, did his prospects of future employment no harm at all.

16 KENNY ROBERTS Said that the character of the circuit combined with the nature of the Suzuki meant he was always going to have problems. He was right.

17 SHANE BYRNE Once again was only hundredths of a second behind Roberts's Suzuki and set his best time of the race trying – 'really trying' – to get him on the last lap. Also felt the bike improved as the race went on.

18 ROBERTO ROLFO Much like his Barcelona race, Roby got a good start and thought he could run with Bayliss, but felt his rear tyre go off after just a couple of laps. From then on it was a pretty lonely ride.

19 JAMES ELLISON Another race, another finish on a fast track where the WCM was totally outgunned. Had to be content with beating his team-mate.

20 FRANCO BATTAINI Will remember the meeting chiefly for his collision with Max Biaggi during practice, an incident that left Franco clinging to the Repsol Honda.

NON-FINISHERS

ALEX HOFMANN Pulled in when the chain started to jump its sprockets. The real question is why it started jumping; the engine was taken away for investigation.

NON-STARTER

TONI ELIAS Didn't try to ride as still not fully fit following his Le Mans crash, giving David Checa a third race on the Fortuna Yamaha.

LAGUNA SECA
US GRAND PRIX

ROUND 8

AMERICAN BEAUTY

Nicky Hayden delighted his home crowd with a masterful win, and at the same time put a damper on Yamaha's 50th birthday party

The long-awaited return of MotoGP to the United States was a strange experience. Any doubts about the country's appetite for the sport evaporated in the face of the sell-out crowd, the array of high-profile event sponsors and the parade of A-list stars in the paddock. Yamaha's one-off reversion to their 1970s American black-and-yellow livery was a master stroke, and the collection of their ex-champions from Giacomo Agostini and Kel Carruthers to Eddie Lawson and Wayne Rainey gave the event extra gravitas. But – and it's a big but – there were some serious problems both on and off track. Marco Melandri was the loudest complainant, calling the track 'a scandal', which drew an uncharacteristic volley of expletives from team-mate Sete Gibernau who suggested he should make his views known to the Safety Commission rather than mouthing off to the press. That must have made for an interesting atmosphere in the Movistar Honda garage.

Prime among the on-track issues were lack of run-off and the bumpy surface. While it is true that the organisers had done

Laguna experience – and two days later Rossi lined up second on the grid. The next-best Laguna debut was Makoto Tamada's, in ninth. 'Personally it would be good if I can be on the podium; I don't want to speak of victory,' said Rossi, again referring to the experience of Hayden, Bayliss and Edwards.

Meanwhile, off track, there were problems with traffic, not helped by particularly bone-headed local police although, as British fans know, such jams are not unique to Laguna. More surprising were the paucity of paddock facilities for both teams and media, and the unreliability of the services. There was no power to pit-lane monitors during the first practice session so we were treated to the sight of Yamaha manager, Davide Brivio, sitting in the media centre phoning times over to his teams. It was difficult to reconcile all this with the fact that Silicon Valley is a mere 50 miles up the road to San Francisco.

Yamaha weren't the only ones with a new party frock; Suzuki turned out in Red Bull colours for Laguna, with Kenny Roberts sporting a special helmet which, rather pleasingly, paid homage to his dad's original 1970s American eagle design. Nicky Hayden also had a new paint job on his Arai plus a great deal of pressure on his shoulders. Half way through his third year with the Honda factory team, and still without a win, indeed without a rostrum finish so far in 2005, Hayden was suffering the longest fallow period of his career. If he didn't get that elusive win at home in the US where would it happen? If he was feeling the burden, though, Nicky didn't show it. On the contrary, having his brothers around, both racing in the AMA championship

Opposite Edwards and Rossi sweep out of the Corkscrew in vain pursuit of Hayden

Above John Hopkins shows off Suzuki's one-off Red Bull livery

Below This is the section of track that really got the riders' attention: Turn 1. That's a concrete wall in the bottom left of the picture

all that was asked of them, with considerable financial help from Yamaha and Red Bull, the closeness of concrete fences on the outside of the high-speed kink that is Turn 1 and on the run-up to the Corkscrew drew comment from everyone except the Americans. There are very few racetracks that repay local knowledge in the way that Laguna Seca does, so the field was given an especially extended practice session on Friday. The Doctor followed Bayliss for a few laps and reported that it helped him realise he needed to change his style, to be 'more physical'. Of the top ten, after that one-hour session, only Gibernau and Rossi had had no previous

support events, made him look more relaxed than normal and in the numerous press conferences he certainly didn't allow Rossi to play his usual mind games.

Right from the first laps Hayden had looked the favourite for the event. Despite its vertiginous nature, the Corkscrew is not a particularly demanding corner; however, the downhill run to the final corner that follows is the key to Laguna. Nicky was visibly faster and more comfortable in this critical section than anyone, even the other Americans, his front tyre seemingly glued to the tarmac. His speed through this final corner, backed up by his holeshot off pole, gave him a lead of over a second after the first lap of the race. After that, he never made a mistake. The Yamahas of Rossi and Edwards pressed, but if they gained Nicky responded immediately. The big sort-out for the chasers came at the top of the Corkscrew on lap 4 when Edwards pushed inside Bayliss and Biaggi to take third. Gibernau took advantage to get Biaggi and then outbrake Bayliss at Turn 11. Biaagi, who had taken third off Bayliss in the left before the run-up to the Corkscrew, ended the lap in sixth. Gibernau's race was remarkable given the complete disaster of practice and qualifying on his 'unridable' Honda, and even though he only ended up fifth he described it as one of the best, if not the best, race of his season.

Edwards set the fastest lap of the race on lap 5 as he closed on his team-mate before passing him in the same place he'd earlier taken the two Hondas simultaneously. It was a move born of profound track knowledge and not a little courage. Instead of moving to the right of the track through the uphill Turn 6 Edwards hung to the left, giving himself a straight-line outbraking opportunity after the apex which then put him exactly where his victim didn't want him, on the entrance to the Corkscrew. Colin made passing Valentino Rossi look easy at Laguna. In the closing stages Edwards thought he had second place sewn up but, going into the last lap, Rossi suddenly teleported himself across a two-second gap to Edwards's back wheel. The American dug deep, and Valentino later reported having a vision of two yellow Yamahas in the dirt, after which he decided to settle for third.

To the unbridled joy of the crowd, Colin followed Nicky across the line for an American one–two. It was Honda's first-ever win at Laguna Seca and ended a streak of 72 GPs without an American winner (the last was Kenny Roberts at Motegi in 2000, the race after he clinched his world title). Hayden then broke new ground by taking his dad Earl for a victory lap on the back of the Repsol Honda. He'd been dreaming about bringing this dirt-tracker's tradition to MotoGP and he broke through a line of officials at high speed to make it come true. To date, Nicky hasn't been fined for this contravention of regulations.

There followed a joyous rostrum celebration bracketed by a daft dance beforehand and tears during the anthem. It was a genuinely moving moment, as were Nicky's words of thanks to his parents for their sacrifices to send him and his brothers racing. Older brother Roger Lee did feel forced to point out, though, that not all the Haydens dance as badly as Nicky.

In the end everybody, including Brad Pitt and Michael Jordan, but with the possible exception of Marco Melandri, enjoyed the Laguna Seca experience more than they'd expected. It is doubtful, however, if they will be as forgiving of the place's faults when they go back again.

OLD SCHOOL

As part of the company's 50th birthday celebrations Yamaha put their factory team in yellow and black for Laguna Seca, the colours in which Kenny Roberts won the 1978, '79 and '80 world 500cc titles. They weren't factory colours but the livery of Yamaha America for whom Kenny rode before venturing onto the world stage. They are the colours in which he won his first title after epic duels with Barry Sheene, the colours in which the motorcycling world outside of the USA first saw King Kenny. Yamaha's factory colours are red and white, as seen on many generations of TZs and YZRs over the years. Today's Yamaha bosses saw the idea as a tribute to the American riders who have won for them and as a suitable celebration of the return of MotoGP to the USA. Two other American riders won three world titles for Yamaha; Eddie Lawson in the 1980s and Wayne Rainey in the 1990s. Both were at Laguna.

To many American fans, the history of Yamaha is the history of Kenny Roberts, and despite some recent friction between the two parties, King Kenny was happy to attend the celebrations.

Kenny's best memory of Yamaha? Lying in a Japanese hospital bed after breaking his back testing in the winter of 1979, wondering if he will walk again never mind race, and wondering what he'll do for money, seeing as how he never signed a contract for the upcoming season. Then in comes the race team manager with a bunch of papers: 'Ken-san, must sign contract.'

Yamaha USA also had their great dirt riders present plus Giacomo Agostini, on the grounds he won Daytona for them in 1973, his first race on a Yamaha, his first race on a two stroke and his first race in the USA! In a splendid act of nonconformism, Ago, resplendent in black and yellow, could always be found lunching at HRC's portacabin facility on the grounds it was run by his fellow Bergamesco and the food at Yamaha was inedible.

Opposite Nicky Hayden celebrates his first MotoGP victory in front of his home fans

Above What the black-and-yellow celebration was all about: Kenny Roberts glory days of the late 1970s and early '80s

Below At last, a point for Shakey Byrne and Team Roberts

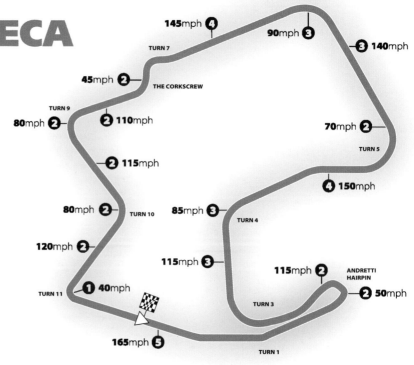

LAGUNA SECA
US GRAND PRIX

ROUND 8

RACE RESULTS

RACE DATE July 10th
CIRCUIT LENGTH 2.243 miles
NO. OF LAPS 32
RACE DISTANCE 71.776 miles
WEATHER Dry, 23°C
TRACK TEMPERATURE 52°C
WINNER Nicky Hayden
FASTEST LAP 1m 23.915s,
96.020mph, Colin Edwards (record)

QUALIFYING

	Rider	Nationality	Team	Qualifying	Pole +	Gap
1	Hayden	USA	Repsol Honda Team	1m 22.670s		
2	Rossi	ITA	Yamaha Factory Racing	1m 23.024s	0.354s	0.354s
3	Barros	BRA	Honda Pons	1m 23.312s	0.642s	0.288s
4	Bayliss	AUS	Honda Pons	1m 23.358s	0.688s	0.046s
5	Edwards	USA	Yamaha Factory Racing	1m 23.469s	0.799s	0.111s
6	Hopkins	USA	Red Bull Suzuki	1m 23.493s	0.823s	0.024s
7	Biaggi	ITA	Repsol Honda Team	1m 23.596s	0.926s	0.103s
8	Checa C.	SPA	Ducati Team	1m 23.597s	0.927s	0.001s
9	Tamada	JPN	Konica Minolta Honda	1m 23.750s	1.080s	0.153s
10	Nakano	JPN	Kawasaki Racing Team	1m 23.799s	1.129s	0.049s
11	Melandri	ITA	Movistar Honda MotoGP	1m 23.905s	1.235s	0.106s
12	Roberts	USA	Red Bull Suzuki	1m 24.011s	1.341s	0.106s
13	Gibernau	SPA	Movistar Honda MotoGP	1m 24.145s	1.475s	0.134s
14	Capirossi	ITA	Ducati Team	1m 24.257s	1.587s	0.112s
15	Hofmann	GER	Kawasaki Racing Team	1m 24.480s	1.810s	0.223s
16	Xaus	SPA	Fortuna Yamaha Team	1m 24.741s	2.071s	0.261s
17	Elias	SPA	Fortuna Yamaha Team	1m 25.462s	2.792s	0.721s
18	Rolfo	ITA	Team D'Antin – Pramac	1m 25.881s	3.211s	0.419s
19	Byrne	GBR	Team Roberts	1m 25.937s	3.267s	0.056s
20	Ellison	GR	Blata WCM	1m 26.800s	4.130s	0.863s
21	Battaini	ITA	Blata WCM	1m 28.435s	5.765s	1.635s

FINISHERS

1 NICKY HAYDEN Not just his first win but a weekend of total domination: fastest in every session (except first free practice), pole position, an astonishing opening lap and a dominant win. Taking dad Earl pillion for an extra victory lap was the perfect way to celebrate the return of MotoGP to the USA.

2 COLIN EDWARDS Beat his team-mate for the first time to complete an American one–two, and worked hard for it after getting boxed in on the first corner. The pass on Rossi at the top of the Corkscrew was a thing of beauty. It was also the first time he scored consecutive rostrum finishes in MotoGP.

3 VALENTINO ROSSI Said all weekend he'd be happy to get on the rostrum and didn't appear too disappointed when his wish came true, maybe because his championship lead went from 63 to 79 points. Ominously said he'd learnt a lot from the Americans this year.

4 MAX BIAGGI Fourth from seventh on the grid, but another weekend of mixed messages. Was fourth in qualifying with a few minutes to go but couldn't take advantage of his qualifying tyres after making suspension adjustments. Enjoyed the scrap with Gibernau, which he described as 'tough but always fair'. Generous in praise of his team-mate.

5 SETE GIBERNAU A quite remarkable race after terrible qualifying that saw him start from 13th on the grid. Was as high as fourth after the mass mugging of Biaggi on lap 4. Came out of the weekend wondering why he goes so well after bad qualifying and so disappointingly after qualifying well.

6 TROY BAYLISS Equalled his best finish of the year, at Jerez, but wasn't too happy. Fastest in the first session and thought his previous experience at Laguna should have helped carry that form through to the race. At least he was seen to smile again during a race weekend.

7 MAKOTO TAMADA Happy to be competitive after fitness problems and

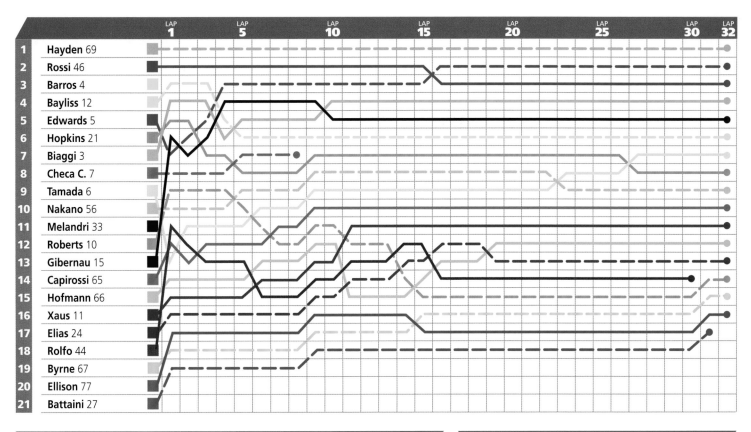

		LAP 1	LAP 5	LAP 10	LAP 15	LAP 20	LAP 25	LAP 30	LAP 32
1	Hayden 69								
2	Rossi 46								
3	Barros 4								
4	Bayliss 12								
5	Edwards 5								
6	Hopkins 21								
7	Biaggi 3								
8	Checa C. 7								
9	Tamada 6								
10	Nakano 56								
11	Melandri 33								
12	Roberts 10								
13	Gibernau 15								
14	Capirossi 65								
15	Hofmann 66								
16	Xaus 11								
17	Elias 24								
18	Rolfo 44								
19	Byrne 67								
20	Ellison 77								
21	Battaini 27								

RACE

	Rider	Motorcycle	Race Time	Time +	Fastest Lap	Average Speed
1	Hayden	Honda	45m 15.374s		1m 23.984s	157.711mph
2	Edwards	Yamaha	45m 17.315s	01.941s	1m 23.915s	155.101mph
3	Rossi	Yamaha	45m 17.686s	02.312s	1m 24.207s	155.536mph
4	Biaggi	Honda	45m 19.590s	04.216s	1m 24.280s	155.722mph
5	Gibernau	Honda	45m 19.852s	04.478s	1m 24.294s	153.237mph
6	Bayliss	Honda	45m 37.755s	22.381s	1m 24.787s	155.039mph
7	Tamada	Honda	45m 37.867s	22.493s	1m 24.654s	153.982mph
8	Hopkins	Suzuki	45m 38.522s	23.148s	1m 24.783s	156.033mph
9	Nakano	Kawasaki	45m 38.999s	23.625s	1m 24.706s	150.627mph
10	Capirossi	Ducati	45m 41.497s	26.123s	1m 24.702s	150.875mph
11	Xaus	Yamaha	45m 58.886s	43.512s	1m 25.254s	148.266mph
12	Hofmann	Kawasaki	46m 06.331s	50.957s	1m 25.437s	150.565mph
13	Elias	Yamaha	46m 06.717s	51.343s	1m 25.371s	148.887mph
14	Roberts	Suzuki	46m 29.123s	1m 13.749s	1m 25.187s	150.068mph
15	Byrne	Proton KR	46m 39.630s	1m 24.256s	1m 26.495s	149.322mph
16	Ellison	Blata	46m 39.898s	1m 24.524s	1m 26.773s	150.005mph
17	Battaini	Blata	46m 20.215s	1 Lap	1m 28.638s	144.040mph
	Rolfo	Ducati	43m 19.959	2 Laps	1m 25.951s	150.102mph
	Checa C.	Ducati	11m 28.318	24 Laps	1m 24.694s	156.468mph
	Melandri	Honda				
	Barros	Honda				

CHAMPIONSHIP

	Rider	Team	Points
1	Rossi	Gauloises Yamaha Team	186
2	Melandri	Movistar Honda MotoGP	107
3	Biaggi	Repsol Honda Team	100
4	Gibernau	Movistar Honda MotoGP	95
5	Edwards	Gauloises Yamaha Team	93
6	Hayden	Repsol Honda Team	85
7	Baros	Camel Honda	74
8	Capirossi	Ducati Marlboro Team	55
9	Nakano	Kawasaki Racing Team	55
10	Bayliss	Camel Honda	47
11	Checa C.	Ducati Marlboro Team	40
12	Xaus	Fortuna Yamaha Team	33
13	Tamada	JIR Konica Minolta Honda	27
14	Hopkins	Team Suzuki MotoGP	27
15	Jacque	Kawasaki Racing Team	25
16	Elias	Fortuna Yamaha Team	18
17	Hofmann	Kawasaki Racing Team	13
18	Goorbergh	JIR Konica Minolta Honda	12
19	Roberts	Team Suzuki MotoGP	11
20	Rolfo	Team D'Antin – Pramac	7
21	Checa D.	Fortuna Yamaha Team	4
22	Ellison	Blata WCM	4
23	Byrne	Team Roberts	1
24	Ukawa	Moriwaki Racing	1

regarded Laguna as a positive experience. On the wrong end of a shoving match on the first lap and clipped a track marker post later on; both incidents spoiled his rhythm. His Turn 1 pass on Hopkins was breathtaking.

8 JOHN HOPKINS Battled with Bayliss and Tamada all race but didn't have the grunt to pull away. Elevated race-day temperatures forced him to use a hard tyre he hadn't got on with in practice, making his achievement of being top Bridgestone finisher all the more praiseworthy.

9 SHINYA NAKANO A hard first race at Laguna, in which he learnt a lot from Hopkins and Bayliss. Only 1.3sec off sixth place at the flag but still bemoaning the Kawasaki's lack of top-end power.

10 LORIS CAPIROSSI Gastroenteritis meant he missed Friday afternoon practice and was far from fully fit for the rest of the weekend. Loris has won a 250 GP at Laguna, so he might have expected to do better. Under the circumstances he declared himself satisfied with his race.

11 RUBEN XAUS Another fraught weekend, made more so by the fact he'd won a World Superbike race at the track in 2003. Took five laps to get into his stride, then lapped at about a second slower than the leading group – that, and a few points, cheered his team up.

12 ALEX HOFMANN Was in 13th just before half way when he found a false neutral at the last corner which dropped him behind

Rolfo and Elias. Had to fight back past them and Roberts to his final finishing place.

13 TONI ELIAS Still in severe pain from his wrist and needing injections to race, but they wore off after just five laps of this very physical track. Typically, he gritted his teeth and followed Hofmann home.

14 KENNY ROBERTS The one American who didn't shine at his home GP, despite being in the top ten in the early stages of his first race at home since winning the world title in 2000.

15 SHANE BYRNE At last a World Championship point, but another difficult weekend for the whole team. Reliability was a plus point, being led by Ellison and Rolfo for large chunks of the race most certainly wasn't.

16 JAMES ELLISON A brilliant ride, the highlight of which was leading Shakey Byrne for half-a-dozen laps, then tailing him for the rest of the race and finishing a mere quarter-second adrift of the last point.

17 FRANCO BATTAINI His sit-back 250 style meant he never got the feel he needed from the front, which in turn meant he never got to grips with the circuit.

NON-FINISHERS

ROBERTO ROLFO The hard-luck story of the race. Well in the points, then ran out of petrol with a lap to go thanks to lack of grip which generated massive wheelspin.

CARLOS CHECA Up to sixth, right behind Bayliss and looking good, when he lost the front at Turn 2 on lap 9.

MARCO MELANDRI Vociferous in his dislike of the track from the moment he got there, which turned into a self-fulfilling prophecy. Two crashes in practice and a third on the last corner of the first lap turned Laguna into the first bad weekend of Marco's season. In the previous seven races had not finished lower than fourth.

ALEX BARROS Thought he could have taken pole, but for being baulked on his last fast lap, and felt he was in with a chance of the win. Then became an innocent victim of Melandri's crash, despite the fact he claimed to have left him room.

DONINGTON
BRITISH GRAND PRIX

ROUND 9

ROSSI'S SEVENTH SYMPHONY

He crossed the line playing air violin, although miming paddling a canoe might have been more appropriate. Valentino's seventh win of the year was one of his best

There have only ever been two wet GPs at Donington Park, but when it rains there it really rains. As Valentino Rossi said, he felt like he was at the controls of a powerboat, not a racing motorcycle. It looked like it too. TV pictures clearly showed bikes leaving a visible

wake all the way from McLeans up to Coppice. That would seem to indicate there was a good deal of standing water on the track, which in turn may explain the extraordinary number of crashes. At Shanghai, where the weather was just as bad, there were only

four crashes in the race and some of them were down to visor misting rather than the surface. At Donington there were twelve crashes and dozens more near-misses. The Chinese track is brand new and its surface proved incredibly grippy in the wet, as Assen's has always been, but the Donington surface is only a year old so the discrepancy is hard to explain. Riders complained not just of the minimal grip available but of the variable nature of what there was. Marco Melandri was particularly vehement in his criticism, just as he was at Laguna Seca. This time it was Rossi who suggested he should take his complaints to the Safety Commission.

The Chinese GP was the first wet race that Rossi won on the M1 so it was no surprise that he was competitive in the Midlands. Neither was it unexpected that the men who pulled away with him were Kenny Roberts, who led in Shanghai until stopped by mechanical failure, and Alex Barros, who won in patchy conditions in Portugal. What was surprising was the crushing way in which Valentino took the victory.

The story unfurled in three wet phases. First there was the crashfest of the first four laps which saw Biaggi, Xaus, Hayden, Melandri and Bayliss slide out before Gibernau, who had opened up a significant lead, came to grief with Rossi in pursuit. It was horribly reminiscent of Portugal where Sete had also crashed while leading, letting Barros in for the win. Hopkins then hit the front but only because his visor was fogging up and he hoped being out of the spray would help it clear. His plan didn't work: he ran off the track and crashed. The two British riders had crashed in sympathy by the time Hopper got his bike back to the pits, and both Barros and Roberts

had entered corners with a foot down.

The second phase of the race was about the breakaway group of Rossi, Roberts, Barros and Edwards pulling out a significant lead over the opposition. Tamada was then fifth, around 12 seconds behind whoever was fourth, which was usually Edwards. Barros did most of the leading and although the group frequently fanned out in line abreast going into corners it was simply to keep out of the spray, which Rossi described as being so bad as to be painful. Valentino

Opposite Rossi's biggest moment of the race: out of the saddle at Redgate

Above Barros pushes to the front at the Melbourne Loop

Below Rossi has a grandstand view as Gibernau slides out of the lead at Redgate Corner

didn't make a good start but performed one minor miracle at the Fogarty Esses on the first lap when he outbraked five people. Now he outbraked himself at the same place and dropped back to fourth, a couple of seconds behind the leaders. One lap later he was back on the rear wheel of third-place man Edwards. Quite unbelievably, his lap time was over two seconds quicker than that of the leader, Barros. It was the fastest lap of the race so far, at 1m 47.875s, nearly a second quicker than anyone else had gone. This was when the World Champion took risks to get back in contention – it helped him understand what he could do in the conditions – but he waited.

Roberts's impressive performance underlined the competitiveness of Bridgestone's wet-weather tyres, as did Checa and Capirossi's surge towards the leaders in the final stages of the race. The Ducati riders were the fastest men on track until Rossi embarked on the third and final phase of his plan. On lap 22 he pushed past Barros going into the penultimate corner, the Melbourne Loop, to set a new fastest lap and take the lead. Next time round he went exactly a second and a half faster. Unlike in the early laps, where even the Doctor had been pinged out of the saddle a few times, this charge looked totally controlled. TV showed his progress graphically: Rossi going into Coppice as Barros and Roberts came out of McLeans, then Rossi at the bottom of Craner Curves as his pursuers came out of Redgate – he'd built up a lead of 3.3 seconds in less than a lap and a half. And he hadn't finished. On lap 24 he set the fastest lap of the race, at 1m 45.377s; no-one else even got into the 1m 46s bracket. Just to rub it in he did another 1m 45s lap next time round as well. His fastest lap was only

Above Ducati's good showing was another indication of the progress of Bridgestone's rain tyres

Below Rossi makes the break

fifteen-thousandths of a second off being a whole two seconds faster than anyone else managed. You would be hard put to find a better demonstration of absolute superiority under the most arduous of conditions. Any terminal cynic who'd harboured the last remnants of doubt about Rossi's talent had them utterly quashed.

Kenny Roberts saw Rossi make his move and tried to go with him: 'Three corners later I thought "Okay, I'm racing Alex." ' Kenny saved his own move for Coppice on the last lap, where he'd observed Barros having problems on the brakes, normally the Brazilian's strength. Roberts went through on the inside going in, Alex re-passed him, then Kenny squared the corner off, nailed the second apex and pushed Barros out towards the edge of the track on the exit: job done. It was a brilliantly thought-out and executed move, but once again it raised the question of whether one should applaud his two (so far) great races this season or criticise him for not riding as hard as his team-mate when conditions aren't so favourable for the Suzuki. Alex conceded that Kenny 'had played his card well' and had to be content with the lowest step on the rostrum to celebrate his 250th GP.

When Rossi's first 1m 45s lap time flashed up on the monitors Randy Mamola, not usually a man lost for words, was reduced to a heartfelt one-word response: 'Jesus,' he said quietly, then said it again slightly louder. This was a race that achieved the impossible. As well as reducing Mamola to near-silence it made the sodden, frozen spectators, all 75,000 of them, forget their discomfort, turn to each other and mouth 'How did he do that?' A very good question. The violin playing? Roughly translated, it means: 'Now you are dancing to my tune.'

Top Valentino crosses the line playing air violin thus simultaneously paying tribute to his 'symphony' of a qualifying lap and showing that everyone else is dancing to his tune

Above James Ellison picks the WCM Blatta out of the Coppice Corner gravel trap, he was one of numerous crashers

IN THE COURTS

The week before the Donington race, Alex Barros found himself on the wrong end of a judgement from the Paris Court of Arbitration. He was ordered to pay US $2.9-million plus interest to Altadis (the Franco-Spanish tobacco firm that owns the Gauloises and Fortuna brands). He was also ordered to pay $150,000 in court costs and another $180,000 as a contribution to Altadis's costs. The court's decision is final, no appeal is possible.

This judgement arose from what Altadis claimed was a breach of contract by the Brazilian in that he signed a two-year contract to ride a Gauloises sponsored Yamaha for the 2003 and '04 seasons but decided to defect to Repsol Honda for the 2004 season. Altadis then invoked the penalty clause in their contract. The Paris Court of Arbitration is a respected independent body, and a little investigation in the paddock revealed that a good number of the high rollers in motorcycle

racing and other sports lodge agreements and contracts with the court. Not surprisingly, Altadis expressed its 'full satisfaction' with the judgement and made the point that it had taken action not just in its own interests but 'for the good of the sport itself', a comment that cannot have been lost on racers in the MotoGP paddock or Formula 1. Barros simply stated that his representatives were studying the situation and that 'he respects the decisions of the court'.

Despite the fact that technically there is no appeal to the Paris Court, knowledgeable people within the paddock said that negotiations between the parties' lawyers would drag on long enough to ensure that Barros would be able to race in 2006 and beyond without being stalked by the French equivalent of bailiffs. Nevertheless, in a sport where contracts have often been of less value than the paper they were written on, this was a timely reality check.

DONINGTON
BRITISH GRAND PRIX

ROUND 9

RACE RESULTS

RACE DATE July 24th
CIRCUIT LENGTH 2.500 miles
NO. OF LAPS 29
RACE DISTANCE 72.500 miles
WEATHER Wet, 15°C
TRACK TEMPERATURE 13°C
WINNER Valentino Rossi
FASTEST LAP 1m 45.377s,
85.211mph, Valentino Rossi
PREVIOUS LAP RECORD 1m 29.973s,
100.026mph, Colin Edwards, 2004

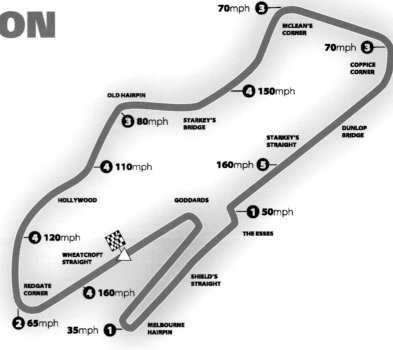

QUALIFYING

	Rider	Nationality	Team	Qualifying	Pole +	Gap
1	Rossi	ITA	Gauloises Yamaha Team	1m 27.897s		
2	Gibernau	SPA	Movistar Honda MotoGP	1m 28.182s	0.285s	0.285s
3	Melandri	ITA	Movistar Honda MotoGP	1m 28.295s	0.398s	0.113s
4	Barros	BRA	Camel Honda	1m 28.394s	0.497s	0.099s
5	Hayden	USA	Repsol Honda Team	1m 28.415s	0.518s	0.021s
6	Edwards	USA	Gauloises Yamaha Team	1m 28.656s	0.759s	0.241s
7	Bayliss	AUS	Camel Honda	1m 28.720s	0.823s	0.064s
8	Biaggi	ITA	Repsol Honda Team	1m 28.726s	0.829s	0.006s
9	Tamada	JPN	Konica Minolta Honda	1m 28.976s	1.079s	0.250s
10	Hopkins	USA	Team Suzuki MotoGP	1m 29.231s	1.334s	0.255s
11	Capirossi	ITA	Ducati Marlboro Team	1m 29.731s	1.834s	0.500s
12	Nakano	JPN	Kawasaki Racing Team	1m 29.742s	1.845s	0.011s
13	Checa C.	SPA	Ducati Marlboro Team	1m 29.816s	1.919s	0.074s
14	Xaus	SPA	Fortuna Yamaha Team	1m 29.890s	1.993s	0.074s
15	Hofmann	GER	Kawasaki Racing Team	1m 30.151s	2.254s	0.261s
16	Roberts	USA	Team Suzuki MotoGP	1m 30.260s	2.363s	0.109s
17	Elias	SPA	Fortuna Yamaha Team	1m 30.342s	2.445s	0.082s
18	Byrne	GBR	Team Roberts	1m 31.026s	3.129s	0.684s
19	Rolfo	ITA	Team D'Antin – Pramac	1m 31.180s	3.283s	0.154s
20	Ellison	GBR	Blata WCM	1m 31.791s	3.894s	0.611s
21	Battaini	ITA	Blata WCM	1m 32.684s	4.787s	0.893s

FINISHERS

1 VALENTINO ROSSI Anyone harbouring lingering doubts about his talent had them well and truly quashed. His fastest lap, set as he broke away from Roberts and Barros, was all but two seconds quicker than the next-best man – an incredible margin considering the appalling conditions.

2 KENNY ROBERTS His old masterful self; he may even have been a little emotional on the rostrum. The pass to take Barros was brilliantly planned and clinically executed. However, still difficult not to wonder why he hasn't been further up the order when conditions are less favourable to the Suzuki.

3 ALEX BARROS The last rostrum position was a fitting reward for a fine race on his 250th GP start. Encountered some front-end problems which prevented him braking as hard as he'd have liked, and also laid him open to Roberts's last-lap attack.

4 COLIN EDWARDS A weird weekend: never really happy with set-up until Sunday warm-up but ended the race third in the championship, only one point behind Melandri. Got into fourth early on, then kept getting up to the leaders only to drop off their pace again.

5 CARLOS CHECA Set the fourth-fastest lap of the race at mid-distance, another testimony to Bridgestone's new rain tyres. Carved through the pack after spinning off the line and finishing the first lap in 17th. Closed up on a watchful Edwards in the final stages.

6 LORIS CAPIROSSI For a rider who's never been happy in the rain this was a splendid ride. Got up behind team-mate Checa on lap 6 and tracked him all the way to the flag to give Ducati an encouraging result after another depressing qualifying performance.

7 MAKOTO TAMADA Second – and last! – Honda home in his first wet race on Michelins. Was fifth for a few laps before being passed by both Ducatis and circulating at the same pace as the leaders from laps 15 to 25.

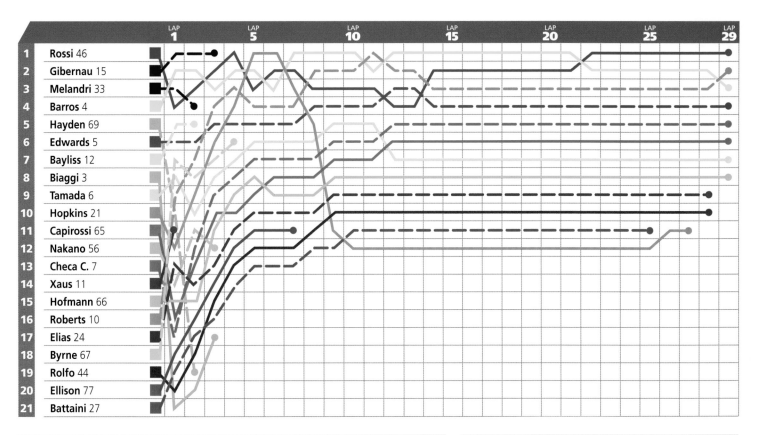

	LAP 1	LAP 5	LAP 10	LAP 15	LAP 20	LAP 25	LAP 29
1	Rossi 46						
2	Gibernau 15						
3	Melandri 33						
4	Barros 4						
5	Hayden 69						
6	Edwards 5						
7	Bayliss 12						
8	Biaggi 3						
9	Tamada 6						
10	Hopkins 21						
11	Capirossi 65						
12	Nakano 56						
13	Checa C. 7						
14	Xaus 11						
15	Hofmann 66						
16	Roberts 10						
17	Elias 24						
18	Byrne 67						
19	Rolfo 44						
20	Ellison 77						
21	Battaini 27						

RACE

	Rider	Motorcycle	Race Time	Time +	Fastest Lap	Average Speed
1	Rossi	Yamaha	52m 58.675s		1m 45.377s	147.768mph
2	Roberts	Suzuki	53m 01.844s	3.169s	1m 47.630s	146.774mph
3	Barros	Honda	53m 02.681s	4.006s	1m 47.362s	145.469mph
4	Edwards	Yamaha	53m 08.967s	10.292s	1m 47.702s	143.543mph
5	Checa C.	Ducati	53m 11.695s	13.020s	1m 47.539s	146.526mph
6	Capirossi	Ducati	53m 21.996s	23.321s	1m 47.693s	150.627mph
7	Tamada	Honda	53m 36.508s	37.833s	1m 48.570s	144.164mph
8	Hofmann	Kawasaki	53m 43.292s	44.617s	1m 48.730s	145.283mph
9	Elias	Yamaha	54m 02.294s	1 Lap	1m 53.114s	131.923mph
10	Rolfo	Ducati	54m 35.570s	1 Lap	1m 54.030s	142.735mph
11	Hopkins	Suzuki	53m 32.212s	2 Laps	1m 47.697s	150.005mph
	Battaini	Blata	49m 13.898s	4 Laps	1m 55.141s	138.572mph
	Ellison	Blata	13m 51.696s	22 Laps	1m 55.561s	138.261mph
	Byrne	Proton KR	7m 34.397s	25 Laps	1m 50.673s	141.492mph
	Gibernau	Honda	5m 37.179s	26 Laps	1m 50.698s	144.661mph
	Nakano	Kawasaki	5m 54.335s	26 Laps	1m 55.475s	136.708mph
	Biaggi	Honda	6m 30.818s	26 Laps	1m 52.942s	135.775mph
	Melandri	Honda	3m 49.265s	27 Laps	1m 51.663s	142.797mph
	Bayliss	Honda	3m 49.512s	27 Laps	1m 51.307s	137.018mph
	Hayden	Honda	4m 26.220s	27 Laps	2m 00.400s	138.510mph
	Xaus	Yamaha	2m 00.489s	28 Laps	2m 00.489s	131.736mph

CHAMPIONSHIP

	Rider	Team	Points
1	Rossi	Gauloises Yamaha Team	211
2	Melandri	Movistar Honda MotoGP	107
3	Edwards	Gauloises Yamaha Team	106
4	Biaggi	Repsol Honda Team	100
5	Gibernau	Movistar Honda MotoGP	95
6	Barros	Camel Honda	90
7	Hayden	Repsol Honda Team	85
8	Capirossi	Ducati Marlboro Team	65
9	Nakano	Kawasaki Racing Team	55
10	Checa C.	Ducati Marlboro Team	51
11	Bayliss	Camel Honda	47
12	Tamada	JIR Konica Minolta Honda	36
13	Xaus	Fortuna Yamaha Team	33
14	Hopkins	Team Suzuki MotoGP	32
15	Roberts	Team Suzuki MotoGP	31
16	Jacque	Kawasaki Racing Team	25
17	Elias	Fortuna Yamaha Team	25
18	Hofmann	Kawasaki Racing Team	21
19	Rolfo	Team D'Antin – Pramac	13
20	Goorbergh	JIR Konica Minolta Honda	12
21	Checa D.	Fortuna Yamaha Team	4
22	Ellison	Blata WCM	4
23	Byrne	Team Roberts	1
24	Ukawa	Moriwaki Racing	1

8 ALEX HOFMANN His best result in MotoGP – and it could have been even better had he not taken avoiding action when Elias braked early at the Esses on lap 2 and lost five places. Another Bridgestone user who could run at the same pace as Checa.

9 TONI ELIAS Discovered the meaning of the word aquaplane; after losing the front a few times decided to settle for some points.

10 ROBERTO ROLFO With his exemplary wet-weather record hoped for a better result, or at least a better race but, just like in China, found the '04 Ducati–Dunlop pairing a tricky combination. Happy with the points if not the result.

11 JOHN HOPKINS Right up with the leaders (including his team-mate) until a misting visor caused him to run off track and crash at Schwantz's. Got the bike back to the pits for running repairs, then went out again to collect points.

NON-FINISHERS

FRANCO BATTAINI Was on for his first points of the season but crashed out a lap from the flag.

JAMES ELLISON Conditions should have suited the WCM but the bike lacks sophisticated electronic engine management, let alone traction control.

Spat off in a nasty-looking highside at Coppice.

SHANE BYRNE Looked good for some serious points until he crashed on the brakes for the Melbourne Loop at the end of lap 5. He was in sixth place at the time.

SETE GIBERNAU Lasted one more corner than his team-mate, crashing out of the lead at Redgate at the beginning of lap 4.

SHINYA NAKANO Had a clutch problem on the line, then had trouble changing down the gearbox in the race. Missed a gear going into Redgate at the start of the fourth lap and joined Gibernau in the gravel trap.

MAX BIAGGI A good start, but fell at the Old Hairpin on the first lap, then repeated the performance three laps later. Reported absolutely no traction, even on the straight, in the first four gears.

MARCO MELANDRI One lap after Hayden, he did the same trick at Goddards. Still second in the championship, but only just. Like in the USA, he took a Camel Honda with him.

TROY BAYLISS An innocent victim of Melandri's crash: did well to avoid the Italian but tipped off on the grass after taking evasive action.

NICKY HAYDEN The first victim of Goddards. He went down at the end of the second lap, got the bike back into the pits but the handlebar was broken. Mad at himself as he'd watched plenty of people crash there in earlier races.

RUBEN XAUS Yet another crash. He lasted until McLeans on the second lap before getting too enthusiastic with the throttle while in 11th place.

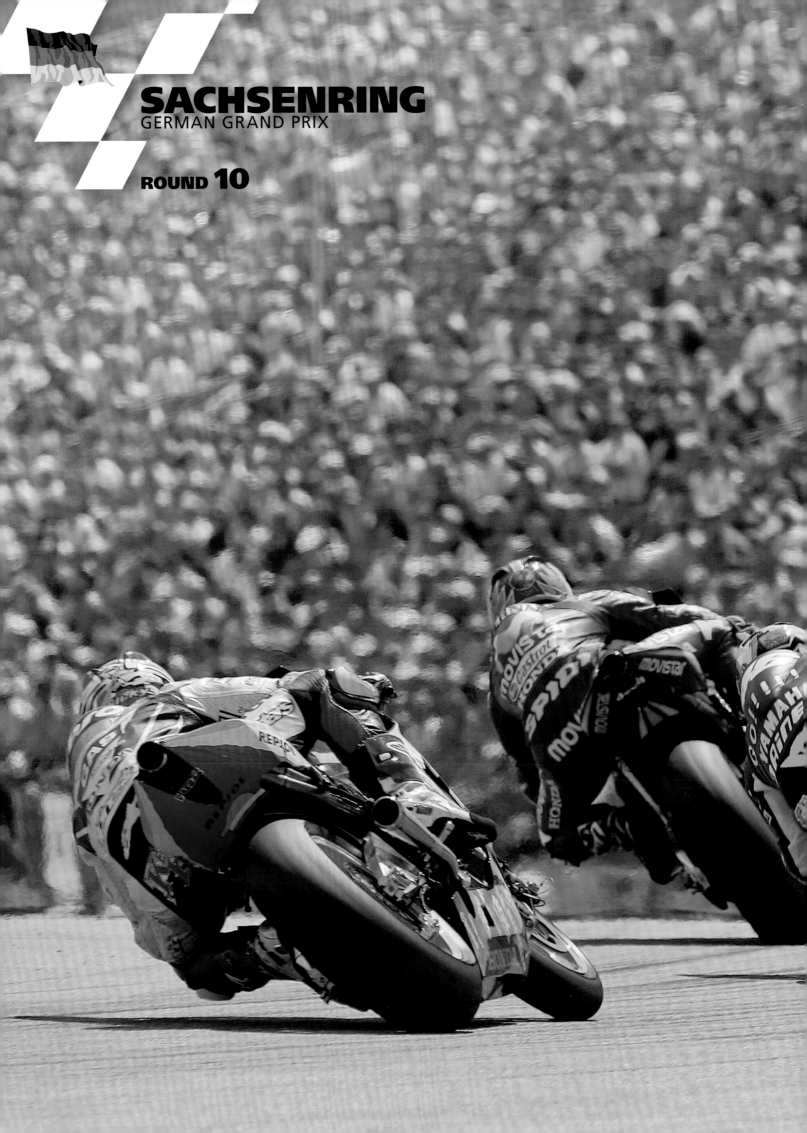

SACHSENRING
GERMAN GRAND PRIX

ROUND 10

MAGIC NUMBERS

Valentino Rossi's 50th premier-class win came in his 150th Grand Prix start and put him level with Mike Hailwood on 76 wins in all classes. Typically, he apologised to the memory of Mike the Bike

By his own admission Valentino Rossi does not like the Sachsenring, and through Friday and Saturday it looked like it. He fell off on Friday and could only finish the day 13th fastest, then he couldn't get on the front row in Saturday's qualifying. In the Doctor's view the first part of the track is too slow for a MotoGP bike and he doesn't get on with the predominantly left-handed nature of the place. That's not unusual for European racers brought up on mainly clockwise tracks. Americans, however, think otherwise, especially if they have a background in dirt-track. Nicky Hayden was pretty good on the ovals and admits he still feels happiest in fast lefts, which may have helped him set his second pole position. It was a nice 24th birthday present, but Hayden himself was acutely aware that he needs to back up his win at Laguna Seca to avoid accusations of being just a home-town hero. Suggestions

Opposite above A highly embarrassing heap of Kawasakis at the first turn of the team's home race

Opposite below After the restart Nicky Hayden leads the pack

Left More first-turn mayhem: Shakey Byrne tags Carlos Checa and mercifully rolls clear of trouble.

that a rostrum would be a satisfactory result were met with something as near to disdain as this unfailingly polite young man could muster. Interestingly, Rossi's view of Hayden is that he is indeed superb in fast lefts. 'He rides very well on the left and the control when he slides is very good. He has the possibility to arrive at the top.' Then comes the 'but': 'He needs to improve on other tracks, he needs more experience at tracks like Assen.'

One interesting subplot among the factory Honda riders concerned the much-rumoured new bike alleged to be in preparation. Word had it that Biaggi and Gibernau – but not Hayden – had a new chassis with revised swingarm pivot position. Certainly the sight of Biaggi's bike being wheeled to and fro from the scrutineering bay by Repsol mechanics to be weighed indicated that something was going on. Gibernau denied knowledge of any such new equipment; which caused Nicky Hayden to grin hugely and suggest Sete should attend church more often. Some HRC sources said the new bike, when it comes, would be visibly quite different from its predecessor. Another suggested that the mystery chassis was in fact something that was tried at the pre-season Phillip Island tests and was now being revisited in case it had been rejected too hastily. The really interesting aspect of this little drama was that HRC weren't allowing Nicky to get involved in it. Clearly, team bosses believed that he was doing pretty well with what he had and certainly didn't need the distraction of new parts to evaluate.

That other fast young American, John Hopkins, was looking forward to the chance to drive a Red Bull-sponsored F1 car in the summer break, with driver

Vitantonio Luzzi getting the chance to try Hopkins's Suzuki. The plan was abandoned after Hopper suffered a heavy crash on Friday. He highsided in fourth gear, breaking a bone in his foot, cracked at least one rib, damaged a thumb ligament in his right hand, bruised his back severely and suffered a chipped tooth. That painful collection meant John qualified behind his team-mate Kenny Roberts for the first time this year, as well as having serious ramifications in the race.

Kawasaki had high hopes at what is effectively the team's home race. Alex Hofmann was coming off a couple of good races, and Olivier Jacque was having his third ride of the season, this time as a wild card rather than a replacement. Bridgestone's multi-compound tyres

appeared to have taken a big step forward after a few races where their teams had been severely disadvantaged. But Harald Eckl and his team's hopes were dashed at the very first corner of the race when Byrne set off a chain reaction that saw the Team KR rider in the dirt after he clipped the back of Checa's Ducati. Hofmann and Jacque then collided while taking avoiding action. The other early retirement was James Ellison who had been nothing short of brilliant, spinning it up through the fast, blind right-hander behind the pits despite the WCM's two-stroke-like powerband, and going not just faster in qualifying than his team-mate Battaini but quicker than Shakey Byrne and Roby Rolfo as well.

Another crash brought out the red flags just as a four-man breakaway consisting of Hayden, Rossi, Barros and Gibernau was opening up a significant gap over the field. The cause of the stoppage was John Hopkins, who nearly matched the violence of his Friday crash when his strapped and numbed left foot accidentally nudged the gear lever and the quickshifter slammed the gearbox into first.

From the restart Barros and Hayden never felt as comfortable and couldn't quite stay with the pace set by Rossi and, especially, Gibernau. Nicky did for the first lap, and although he never led another lap he was able to head Rossi for half-a-dozen laps and take the third podium place. Barros was a fixture in fourth place until three laps from the flag when he finally lost out to a persistent Max Biaggi who had worked hard in the annulled part of the race to make up for an awful start. He took full advantage of the restart but never troubled the front three. Max's Sachsenring was a microcosm of his season so far.

The hero of the restarted race was Shinya Nakano

who occupied sixth place for the whole 25 laps, though the lap chart doesn't tell the full story. He closed a big gap to get to just over a second behind the Barros/Biaggi duel, but then opted for discretion after a couple of front-end slides. It was the first time all season that Kawasaki had looked competitive in the dry; at the flag Shinya was just 4.5 seconds behind the victor and his team rightly greeted him as if he'd won the race.

Just who the winner would be was unclear until the start of the last lap. Gibernau had led since the third lap, with Rossi stalking him. Valentino's move at the fast right on the penultimate lap looked like a rehearsal, but we never got to find out whether Sete would repeat his epic 2003 victory over Rossi because he outbraked himself at the end of the front straight and the Doctor accepted the invitation to dive through on the inside. There was nearly enough room for Hayden to get through as well. Neither party made too much of the incident afterwards, although Sete made the slightly bizarre suggestion that he had been momentarily distracted by his crew celebrating – prematurely – on the pit wall. He also said, as he'd done for much of the year, that he'd ridden well and was happy to be fighting for the victory. Rossi merely said he didn't know whether he could have won without Gibernau's 'small mistake'.

In honesty, it was an anti-climactic end to the race. After Rossi's elegant tribute to Mike Hailwood all that was left was to calculate that his lead had again grown and was now 120 points. The next day Yamaha announced they had retained Valentino Rossi's services for another year. It's a fair bet that he had a more relaxing holiday than anyone else on the MotoGP grid.

Opposite above Rossi takes control

Below Sete Gibernau on his way to another blow to his confidence

NUMBERS GAME

Valentino Rossi equalled Mike Hailwood's total of 76 wins in all classes when he won at the Sachsenring. The flag he took round on his slow-down lap read 'Rossi 76; Hailwood 76; I'm sorry Mike'. Valentino claims that numbers mean nothing to him but nevertheless 'to arrive at Mike the Bike is special.'

Note that he used the old nickname 'Mike the Bike'; he is a student of the sport. 'When someone younger arrives at your level, it is always disappointing,' he said, 'so I decided to apologise.' Only Angel Nieto (90) and Giacomo Agostini (123) have won more races.

So how does Rossi's record stack up against the heroes of the past? Because of the different number of races completed by everyone, it is necessary to deal in percentages. Including the German GP, Rossi had won 50 of his 90 races in 500cc and MotoGP for a win rate of 56 per cent. Ago won 68 out of 119 and Hailwood 37 out of 65, which gives both men a win rate of 57 per cent. The best in

this particular league is John Surtees with 65 per cent, but he only ran 34 500cc GPs and if anyone could be said to have had very little opposition in their career it is Surtees. Looking at the record books, the really striking thing about Ago's record is that he never finished third or fourth on the MV. He won or was beaten by Hailwood (early in his career) or Phil Read (late in his career). He finished between fifth and ninth only seven times and all of them were after he'd left MV.

Percentage podium finishes give another picture. Once again the striking thing is that those great rivals Hailwood and Agostini are again inseparable on 74 per cent. Rossi has a quite astonishing 83 per cent, while the second-best man in this league is Wayne Rainey on 77 per cent. The comparative lack of reliability of the machines Ago and Hailwood rode (with the same factor applying to Rainey, to a lesser extent), suggests these three

percentages should be slightly closer together – but no sensible correction would show anything other than Valentino Rossi with a substantially better record than anybody.

Is he the best ever? Who can say? The only certainty is that any discussion must involve comparison with the all-time greats.

SACHSENRING
GERMAN GRAND PRIX

ROUND 10

RACE RESULTS

RACE DATE July 31st
CIRCUIT LENGTH 2.281 miles
NO. OF LAPS 25
RACE DISTANCE 57.025 miles
WEATHER Dry, 21°C
TRACK TEMPERATURE 29°C
WINNER Valentino Rossi
FASTEST LAP 1m 23.705s,
97.887mph, Sete Gibernau (record)
PREVIOUS LAP RECORD 1m 24.056s,
97.698mph, Alex Barros, 2004

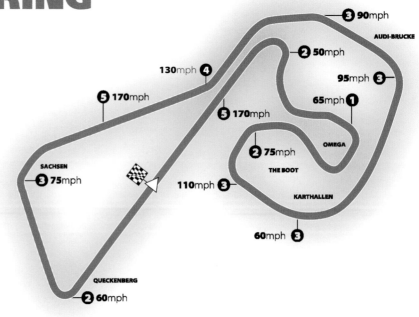

QUALIFYING

	Rider	Nationality	Team	Qualifying	Pole +	Gap
1	Hayden	USA	Repsol Honda Team	1m 22.785s		
2	Gibernau	SPA	Movistar Honda MotoGP	1m 22.889s	0.104s	0.104s
3	Barros	BRA	Camel Honda	1m 22.932s	0.147s	0.043s
4	Rossi	ITA	Gauloises Yahama Team	1m 22.973s	0.188s	0.041s
5	Melandri	ITA	Movistar Honda MotoGP	1m 23.051s	0.266s	0.078s
6	Biaggi	ITA	Repsol Honda Team	1m 23.054s	0.269s	0.003s
7	Edwards	USA	Gauloises Yamaha Team	1m 23.139s	0.354s	0.085s
8	Capirossi	ITA	Ducati Marlboro Team	1m 23.174s	0.389s	0.035s
9	Roberts	USA	Team Suzuki MotoGP	1m 23.212s	0.427s	0.038s
10	Hopkins	USA	Team Suzuki MotoGP	1m 23.296s	0.511s	0.084s
11	Checa C.	SPA	Ducati Marlboro Team	1m 23.341s	0.556s	0.045s
12	Nakano	JPN	Kawasaki Racing Team	1m 23.382s	0.597s	0.041s
13	Hofmann	GER	Kawasaki Racing Team	1m 23.405s	0.620s	0.023s
14	Jacque	FRA	Kawasaki Racing Team	1m 23.715s	0.930s	0.310s
15	Tamada	JPN	Konica Minolta Honda	1m 23.860s	1.075s	0.145s
16	Bayliss	AUS	Camel Honda	1m 23.916s	1.131s	0.056s
17	Elias	SPA	Fortuna Yamaha Team	1m 24.421s	1.636s	0.505s
18	Xaus	SPA	Fortuna Yamaha Team	1m 24.605s	1.820s	0.184s
19	Ellison	GBR	Blata WCM	1m 24.988s	2.203s	0.383s
20	Rolfo	ITA	Team D'Antin – Pramac	1m 25.011s	2.226s	0.023s
21	Byrne	GBR	Team Roberts	1m 25.713s	2.928s	0.702s
22	Battaini	ITA	Blata WCM	1m 26.154s	3.369s	0.441s

FINISHERS

1 VALENTINO ROSSI Would he have won without Gibernau's mistake? The man himself says he doesn't know, but it would have been worth watching. Came back from a highly uncharacteristic crash in the first session at a track he admits to not liking to take his 76th victory from 150 starts in all GP classes.

2 SETE GIBERNAU Maintained he was happy with his form and the fact he was again fighting for the win, but it's difficult to assess the damage to his confidence wrought by giving victory away. Could his first fastest lap of the season really make up for it?

3 NICKY HAYDEN Celebrated his birthday with pole position, then ran his best race of the year so far – outside the USA – despite being unsettled by the restart. Led the first lap, overtook Rossi at mid-distance and always looked a threat. Disappointed not to win but confident he'd learnt a great deal.

4 MAX BIAGGI Came out on top of a splendid battle with Barros but never looked like a contender for the podium; annoyed as he feels he can still win. Dropped down another place in the championship, to fifth. Lots of activity in practice suggested new or modified parts.

5 ALEX BARROS Three crashes in practice and qualifying, but fastest on Friday afternoon despite doing just seven laps and crashing twice

in the session! Disappointed with fifth but, like last year, ran into serious tyre problems eight laps from the end and couldn't hold off Biaggi.

6 SHINYA NAKANO Top Bridgestone rider and able to run with the top men again thanks to a quantum leap in performance from the Japanese tyre company. Only 4.5 seconds behind Rossi at the flag and just adrift of the Biaggi/Barros dice: by far the most encouraging result for Team Green since Jerez.

7 MARCO MELANDRI After crashing out of the last two races even seventh place was a relief. Never regained his feel for the bike after the restart despite being quickest in morning warm-up. Went for the summer break with confidence slightly restored and just holding onto second place in the championship.

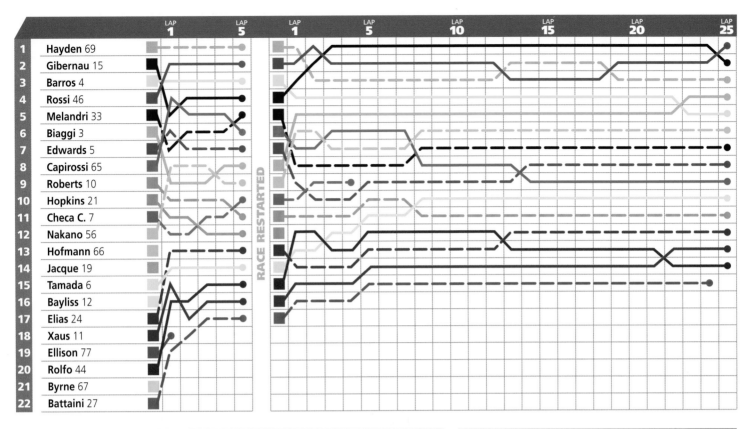

	LAP 1	LAP 5	LAP 1	LAP 5	LAP 10	LAP 15	LAP 20	LAP 25
1	Hayden 69							
2	Gibernau 15							
3	Barros 4							
4	Rossi 46							
5	Melandri 33							
6	Biaggi 3							
7	Edwards 5							
8	Capirossi 65							
9	Roberts 10							
10	Hopkins 21							
11	Checa C. 7							
12	Nakano 56							
13	Hofmann 66							
14	Jacque 19							
15	Tamada 6							
16	Bayliss 12							
17	Elias 24							
18	Xaus 11							
19	Ellison 77							
20	Rolfo 44							
21	Byrne 67							
22	Battaini 27							

RACE RESTARTED

RACE

	Rider	Motorcycle	Race Time	Time +	Fastest Lap	Average Speed
1	Rossi	Yamaha	35m 04.434s		1m 23.782s	174.924mph
2	Gibernau	Honda	35m 05.119s	0.685s	1m 23.745s	176.974mph
3	Hayden	Honda	35m 05.319s	0.885s	1m 23.847s	175.669mph
4	Biaggi	Honda	35m 06.799s	2.365s	1m 23.805s	175.794mph
5	Barros	Honda	35m 07.289s	2.855s	1m 23.799s	175.296mph
6	Nakano	Kawasaki	35m 08.991s	4.557s	1m 23.858s	173.494mph
7	Melandri	Honda	35m 16.703s	12.269s	1m 23.991s	175.234mph
8	Edwards	Yamaha	35m 19.283s	14.849s	1m 24.242s	173.122mph
9	Capirossi	Ducati	35m 27.923s	23.489s	1m 23.708s	177.099mph
10	Tamada	Honda	35m 32.263s	27.829s	1m 24.333s	176.788mph
11	Roberts	Suzuki	35m 46.533s	42.099s	1m 24.261s	169.020mph
12	Elias	Yamaha	35m 51.738s	47.304s	1m 25.049s	174.613mph
13	Xaus	Yamaha	36m 04.609s	1m 00.175s	1m 26.001s	171.195mph
14	Rolfo	Ducati	36m 12.148s	1m 07.714s	1m 24.869s	172.811mph
15	Battaini	Blata	35m 21.155s	1 lap	1m 27.079s	163.490mph
	Checa C.	Ducati	5m 40.304s	21 laps	1m 23.987s	153.982mph
	Hopkins	Suzuki				
	Bayliss	Honda				
	Ellison	Blata				
	Jacque	Kawasaki				
	Hofmann	Kawasaki				
	Byrne	Proton KR				

CHAMPIONSHIP

	Rider	Team	Points
1	Rossi	Gauloises Yamaha Team	236
2	Melandri	Movistar Honda MotoGP	116
3	Gibernau	Movistar Honda MotoGP	115
4	Edwards	Gauloises Yamaha Team	114
5	Biaggi	Repsol Honda Team	113
6	Barros	Camel Honda	101
7	Hayden	Repsol Honda Team	101
8	Capirossi	Ducati Marlboro Team	72
9	Nakano	Kawasaki Racing Team	65
10	Checa C.	Ducati Marlboro Team	51
11	Bayliss	Camel Honda	47
12	Tamada	JIR Konica Minolta Honda	42
13	Roberts	Team Suzuki MotoGP	36
14	Xaus	Fortuna Yamaha Team	36
15	Hopkins	Team Suzuki MotoGP	32
16	Elias	Fortuna Yamaha Team	29
17	Jacque	Kawasaki Racing Team	25
18	Hofmann	Kawasaki Racing Team	21
19	Rolfo	Team D'Antin – Pramac	15
20	Goorbergh	JIR Konica Minolta Honda	12
21	Checa D.	Fortuna Yamaha Team	4
22	Ellison	Blata WCM	4
23	Battaini	Blata WCM	1
24	Byrne	Team Roberts	1

8 COLIN EDWARDS A difficult weekend after a run of three splendid races that took him from sixth to third in the table. Like Rossi had problems in practice but never made the same big jump forward. Lost out massively in the third sector, from the left at the top of the hill through the blind downhill right-hander behind the pits.

9 LORIS CAPIROSSI Passed Nakano and Melandri early on for sixth, then had a couple of front-wheel slides in the fast downhill section. Dropped back when the rear also started moving towards the end of the race and was taken by Edwards. Good pace in warm-up when the Ducatis were second and third.

10 MAKOTO TAMADA Not happy at a track he doesn't really get on with. Like several others felt happier with his bike in the first,

annulled part of the race. Got a bad start, clawed a couple of places back, then had a lonely race.

11 KENNY ROBERTS Back to his usual finishing position after the triumph of Donington Park. 'Today was about where I expect to finish in the dry. Basically that's where we seem to be bike-wise right now.' However, the team was encouraged by Bridgestone's progress.

12 TONI ELIAS Still suffering from his wrist injury; pain-killing injections before the race wore off with ten laps to go. Sachsenring is not the place to be hauling a MotoGP bike around with a weakened arm.

13 RUBEN XAUS A little lucky to avoid the Bayliss crash and relieved to get home and score a few points. Said he is starting to understand how to ride the bike and set it up.

14 ROBERTO ROLFO A good start but the softer rear Dunlop the team decided on turned out to be a mistake; able to stay with Tamada until it went off. Looked like he was riding in the rain while the rest were in the dry. Disappointed because he likes the track – it's where he took his first 250 GP victory.

15 FRANCO BATTAINI At last, a point! Stuck to the job and, despite being lapped, finally got his WCM home in the top 15.

NON-FINISHERS

CARLOS CHECA Lost the front at the final corner of lap 5 while trying to make up ground on Melandri. But his massive fourth-gear highside in practice will be what's remembered, at the

fastest part of the track, with enough violence to rip both tyres off their rims. Carlos got up, walked to the barrier, leant on it, took one deep breath, walked back to the pits and went faster on his second bike.

NON-STARTERS*

TROY BAYLISS Slowed by the first-turn melée, then got his head down to catch Tamada. Crashed when he lost the front trying to make a pass.

OLIVIER JACQUE One of the shortest wild-card appearances on record: went down in a heap with team-mate Hofmann at the first corner. Unsurprisingly, their interpretation of events differed.

JOHN HOPKINS Crashed when his already injured foot nudged the quickshifter and selected bottom gear. The resulting highside left him lying winded on the track and brought out the red flags.

ALEX HOFMANN Tried to make room for the over-excited Byrne and got collected by his temporary team-mate Jacque. Not a good home GP, and he didn't blame Byrne for the crash.

SHANE BYRNE Got a great start but arrived at Turn 1 a little hot but, in his own words, not 'tragically' so. Made contact with Checa, then went down.

JAMES ELLISON Stopped when he felt his boot slipping off the footrest due to oil being blown out of an engine breather. Not a just reward for some superb riding in practice and qualifying.

BRNO
CZECH GRAND PRIX

ROUND **11**

PETROL CRISIS

Lady Luck found a new way to persecute Sete Gibernau, Team Roberts fell out terminally with KTM, but Loris Capirossi and the Ducati team were smiling for the first time this year. Rossi? He won another thriller

The very least Sete Gibernau deserved was second place. Everyone was agreed on that, including Valentino Rossi. This time the two of them swapped places several times in an epic battle with the outcome looking uncertain until the last lap. It wasn't the usual pattern – Gibernau leading, Rossi stalking him before carrying out a calculated mugging with three laps to go. And they weren't as

far ahead of the competition as usual: Capirossi, Barros and Biaggi were queuing up to take advantage of any mistakes. This time Gibernau stalked Rossi for much of the middle section of the race and it wasn't until the last corner of the penultimate lap that Valentino appeared to make the decisive move. The Doctor put himself on the outside of the Spaniard going into the left-handed first part of the ess bend at the top of the hill in order to be on the inside for the right-hander onto the straight. He then pulled out what looked to be a small but

unassailable lead. Could Gibernau fight back one more time on a track where he had beaten Rossi in a similar hand-to-hand battle a year previously?

The only good thing to be said about what happened next to Sete is that it didn't take place while he was in the lead. Coming up the hill for the final time his Honda spluttered to a halt. It's hard to imagine a more cruel blow to a rider's confidence and aspirations. The chances, admittedly tenuous, of a win and second place in the championship were both snatched away within sight of the flag. As if racing Valentino Rossi wasn't difficult enough anyway.

What happened? Simple, he ran out of fuel. Or not so simple, because team-mate Melandri still had a litre in his tank and, with no first-gear corners or stop-and-go sections, Brno is not a fuel-critical circuit. There had been no mistake with the fuel calculations and the correct volume had been put in the tank. Further investigation revealed a fault in the electronics that manage the fuel-injection system: it had decided to run the motor rich. Sete was not happy and demanded an explanation. He went so far as to spend a chunk of testing time on the Monday after race weekend trying to make sense of the fault. Just to add to the intra-team tension, he was also spotted hanging out rather ostentatiously in Ducati's hospitality unit.

Tension was just as high further down pit lane where Team Roberts and KTM were falling out both terminally and publicly. That left Shane Byrne unemployed – his wages and the Michelin tyre bill were both paid by the Austrian company. KTM maintained that it was no longer tenable for them to carry those costs as well as supplying engines. All the company ever wanted

to do, said KTM's Kurt Nicholl, was to be an engine supplier. He was also keen to point out that there had never been a formal contract between the parties. Some blame was also laid at the door of the upcoming 800cc regulations. KTM could see no point in continuing to develop a motor that could only be used for one season. The MSMA, of which KTM is a member, had voted unanimously for the 800cc rule but, as this was their first year in the class, the company was excluded from voting on matters affecting MotoGP.

Team Roberts's Chuck Aksland was equally keen to point to an email from Nicholl, with a February date, as a letter of intent to supply engines, tyres and rider. His position was that KTM had been living that agreement for over half a season. This public stand-off resulted in Team Roberts putting both the KTM-engined V4 and one of their old Proton V5s through scrutineering. Moments before first practice Byrne didn't know whether he should get into his leathers or not, as his old mate Jeremy McWilliams had been flown in at the last minute. When Team Roberts decided they needed a commitment from KTM for the rest of the season, not just for one race, the Austrians decided to remove all their equipment from the Roberts garage, the Kurtis Roberts stickers were peeled off the V5, McWilliams went to sign on at race control and Shakey looked just a little crestfallen.

The Repsol Honda pit didn't know what to think – again. Biaggi had suffered his now customary inability to use his Michelin qualifying tyres, yet he rode through the field to the rostrum in an astonishing display of consistency. Max made eight overtakes in the race yet his lap times were all in a narrow band within the 1m

Opposite Jeremy McWilliams made a surprise one-off return to MotoGP on the Proton V5

Below Kenny Roberts stalks his Suzuki team-mate John Hopkins

59s bracket; he only dropped to a two-minute lap time once, while overtaking his team-mate Nicky Hayden. 'Everyone else slowed down or made mistakes,' was Max's simple explanation.

If you wanted optimism, though, all you had to do was wander down to the Ducati pit where, despite Loris readily admitting that 'my place today was third', the old wolfish grin, absent for the best part of two years, was back. After the depths plumbed at Catalunya Bridgestone had worked tirelessly to claw back the advantage Michelin had enjoyed. The French company had again raised the bar at the start of the year, having been given a severe fright by Bridgestone in the closing stages of the '04 season. The Sachsenring race had given a hint that the Japanese company was at last getting its rear race tyres right; their fronts and qualifiers, and especially their wet-weather rubber, as we saw in China and at Donington, were already a match for the opposition. Capirossi's best finish of the season so far was the start of a comeback that would alter the balance of power in the paddock. Not that all the Bridgestone teams had a good time. Suzuki were still capable of qualifying well, but turning one fast lap into twenty was not proving easy, while the Kawasaki has just never performed at this circuit.

With Valentino Rossi marching on towards his seventh championship title, and the worldwide style icon that is Ducati back on form, everything in the MotoGP garden seemed rosy – until you looked closely. Team Roberts were unlikely to reappear until the final race of the year at Valencia, and the WCM team were not able to unveil their six-cylinder Blata engine, as had been hoped.

TESTING TIMES

Above Max Biaggi approaches the completely revised Honda RCV on the Tuesday after the Czech GP

Opposite above Troy Bayliss trying hard – too hard? – as usual

Opposite below Behind you! Sete Gibernau must expect to see Valentino Rossi every time he glances over his shoulder

Below Team KR's Chuck Aksland and KTM's Kurt Nicholl busy not communicating

Honda's latest weapon in the war against Rossi was due to be unveiled in a two-day test after the GP. The new V5 was more than an update, it was a completely new motorcycle. According to HRC bosses the sprockets might be interchangeable, but that was about it: new chassis, new crankcases, new crank, new everything. The bikes look almost identical until you see them next to each other – the new bike is noticeably smaller.

Only Max Biaggi and Sete Gibernau were due to test the new model, ostensibly for the reason that they have radically different riding styles. If the bike could be made to work for the pair of them then Honda would have a more versatile machine, able to accommodate a wider variety of riding styles. This marks a sea change in Honda's modus operandi. Historically, they have made racing motorcycles that work and work well within a small envelope of adjustability. Mick Doohan used to talk about his NSR wanting to be ridden a certain way, not about how he wanted to ride it.

Many riders, usually new to Honda, have asked HRC to make major set-up changes to their bikes and have been told, 'There's your bike, it works, get on with it.'

Unfortunately, whatever plans Honda had were scuppered by a message from Japan on Monday. Parallel testing back home had turned up an unspecified safety issue, so Max and Sete didn't get to ride the new bike until Tuesday afternoon. The handful of laps they managed between them certainly weren't enough to draw any conclusions, and with the next five races being 'flyaway' events, where the teams live out of their flight cases, any hopes Honda had of stealing a march on Rossi and Yamaha were dashed.

The same session saw WCM rider James Ellison testing some new Dunlop tyres. He took three seconds off his race lap times but then suffered a nasty highside crash while trying out an untested design, injuring his left elbow, which put his participation in the next three races in doubt.

BRNO
CZECH GRAND PRIX

ROUND 11

RACE RESULTS

RACE DATE August 28th
CIRCUIT LENGTH 3.357 miles
NO. OF LAPS 22
RACE DISTANCE 73.854 miles
WEATHER Dry, 20°C
TRACK TEMPERATURE 23°C
WINNER Valentino Rossi
FASTEST LAP 1m 58.787s,
101.522mph, Valentino Rossi (record)
PREVIOUS LAP RECORD 1m 59.302s,
101.312mph, Alex Barros, 2004

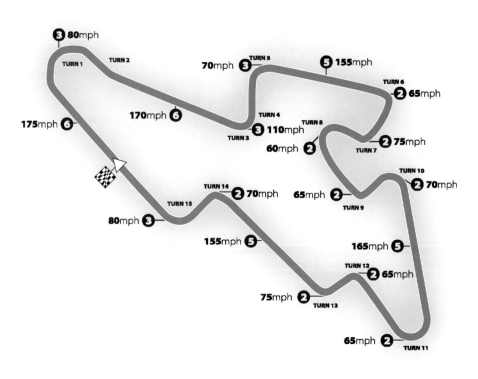

QUALIFYING

	Rider	Nationality	Team	Qualifying	Pole +	Gap
1	Gibernau	SPA	Movistar Honda MotoGP	1m 57.504s		
2	Hayden	USA	Repsol Honda Team	1m 57.551s	0.047s	0.047s
3	Capirossi	ITA	Ducati Marlboro Team	1m 57.685s	0.181s	0.134s
4	Rossi	ITA	Gauloises Yamaha Team	1m 57.875s	0.371s	0.190s
5	Melandri	ITA	Movistar Honda MotoGP	1m 57.999s	0.495s	0.124s
6	Checa C.	SPA	Ducati Marlboro Team	1m 58.185s	0.681s	0.186s
7	Barros	BRA	Camel Honda	1m 58.223s	0.719s	0.038s
8	Hopkins	USA	Team Suzuki MotoGP	1m 58.277s	0.773s	0.054s
9	Edwards	USA	Gauloises Yamaha Team	1m 58.323s	0.819s	0.046s
10	Biaggi	ITA	Repsol Honda Team	1m 58.337s	0.833s	0.014s
11	Nakano	JPN	Kawasaki Racing Team	1m 58.490s	0.986s	0.153s
12	Tamada	JPN	Konica Minolta Honda	1m 58.610s	1.106s	0.120s
13	Bayliss	AUS	Camel Honda	1m 58.662s	1.158s	0.052s
14	Hofmann	GER	Kawasaki Racing Team	1m 58.793s	1.289s	0.131s
15	Elias	SPA	Fortuna Yamaha Team	1m 58.815s	1.311s	0.022s
16	Aoki	JPN	Team Suzuki MotoGP	1m 59.495s	1.991s	0.680s
17	Roberts	USA	Team Suzuki MotoGP	1m 59.734s	2.230s	0.239s
18	Ellison	GBR	Blata WCM	2m 00.529s	3.025s	0.795s
19	Rolfo	ITA	Team D'Antin – Pramac	2m 00.879s	3.375s	0.350s
20	Xaus	SPA	Fortuna Yamaha Team	2m 01.535s	4.031s	0.656s
21	Battaini	ITA	Blata WCM	2m 02.585s	5.081s	1.050s
22	McWilliams	GBR	Team Roberts	2m 04.663s	7.159s	2.078s

FINISHERS

1 VALENTINO ROSSI Had it won before Gibernau broke down, but it was the hardest work he'd done all year. Much of the praise for making him competitive after a horrible first day's qualifying must go to Jerry Burgess and his team – they even managed to respond to Rossi's request for changes after warm-up.

2 LORIS CAPIROSSI Looked like his old self, on and off the track: the big grin was back and so was the race pace. Fastest in the three practice sessions and, thanks to vastly improved Bridgestones, able to stalk Barros in the closing stages and pass him for third. That, said Loris, was 'my place today', but he looked pretty happy to take second.

3 MAX BIAGGI Another disastrous qualifying followed by a sublime race that took him to second in the championship. Every lap bar one was in the mid-1m 59s bracket despite eight overtakes, dropping to 2m 0s only on the penultimate round when he passed Hayden. Max's major problem is mega-chatter with the super-sticky qualifying tyre, which inevitably means a lowly grid position.

4 ALEX BARROS Had the bad luck to be behind Gibernau when the Spaniard's bike cut out, which he believes cost him his chance of the podium. Unlike the previous race in Germany he didn't use up his tyres early in the race; in fact he reckoned 'Both the Michelins and the bike are perfect.'

5 NICKY HAYDEN Fifth, but only 4.3s behind the winner, so not sure whether to laugh or cry. Involved in a great battle with Melandri for third place at the start but, like the Italian, asked too much of his tyres early on and couldn't counter the experience of Barros and Biaggi in the closing laps.

6 MARCO MELANDRI A good start saw him right up with the leading pair of Rossi and Gibernau, then involved in a frantic dice with Hayden. That was enough to, as he put it, 'punish' the front tyre and then it was a matter of getting home for some useful points. Lost second place in the championship table, though.

7 COLIN EDWARDS Never in the hunt all weekend, and in trouble with lack of edge grip from his rear tyre just five laps into the

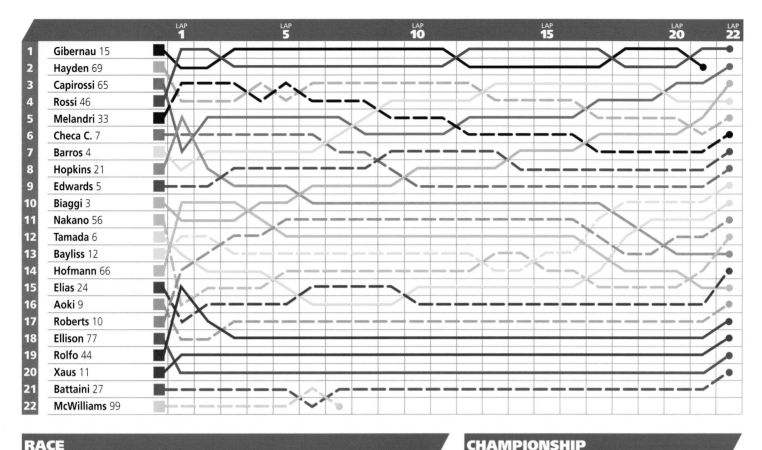

		LAP 1	LAP 5	LAP 10	LAP 15	LAP 20	LAP 22
1	Gibernau 15						
2	Hayden 69						
3	Capirossi 65						
4	Rossi 46						
5	Melandri 33						
6	Checa C. 7						
7	Barros 4						
8	Hopkins 21						
9	Edwards 5						
10	Biaggi 3						
11	Nakano 56						
12	Tamada 6						
13	Bayliss 12						
14	Hofmann 66						
15	Elias 24						
16	Aoki 9						
17	Roberts 10						
18	Ellison 77						
19	Rolfo 44						
20	Xaus 11						
21	Battaini 27						
22	McWilliams 99						

RACE

	Rider	Motorcycle	Race Time	Time +	Fastest Lap	Average Speed
1	Rossi	Yamaha	43m 56.539s		1m 58.787s	186.854mph
2	Capirossi	Ducati	43m 58.376s	1.837s	1m 58.856s	187.476mph
3	Biaggi	Honda	43m 59.983s	3.444s	1m 59.269s	189.961mph
4	Barros	Honda	44m 00.687s	4.148s	1m 58.827s	187.289mph
5	Hayden	Honda	44m 00.902s	4.363s	1m 59.100s	187.476mph
6	Melandri	Honda	44m 07.689s	11.150s	1m 59.044s	188.035mph
7	Edwards	Yamaha	44m 10.071s	13.532s	1m 58.974s	186.792mph
8	Checa C.	Ducati	44m 15.870s	19.331s	1m 58.897s	187.973mph
9	Bayliss	Honda	44m 23.664s	27.125s	2m 00.103s	186.544mph
10	Tamada	Honda	44m 23.787s	27.248s	2m 00.103s	187.787mph
11	Roberts	Suzuki	44m 24.223s	27.684s	1m 59.420s	181.324mph
12	Nakano	Kawasaki	44m 24.342s	27.803s	1m 59.529s	184.928mph
13	Hopkins	Suzuki	44m 24.817s	28.278s	1m 59.847s	184.493mph
14	Elias	Yamaha	44m 25.110s	28.571s	1m 59.669s	186.420mph
15	Hofmann	Kawasaki	44m 26.307s	29.768s	1m 59.863s	181.510mph
16	Aoki	Suzuki	44m 38.317s	41.778s	2m 00.362s	183.437mph
17	Rolfo	Ducati	44m 54.339s	57.800s	2m 01.491s	184.307mph
18	Xaus	Yamaha	45m 04.621s	1m 08.082s	2m 02.040s	182.008mph
19	Ellison	Blata	45m 38.708s	1m 42.169s	2m 02.377s	173.619mph
20	Battaini	Blata	45m 51.323s	1m 54.784s	2m 03.847s	173.805mph
	Gibernau	Honda	41m 57.460s	1 lap	1m 58.819s	
	McWilliams	Proton KR	14m 45.932s	15 laps	2m 03.332s	

CHAMPIONSHIP

	Rider	Team	Points
1	Rossi	Gauloises Yamaha Team	261
2	Biaggi	Repsol Honda Team	129
3	Melandri	Movistar Honda MotoGP	126
4	Edwards	Gauloises Yamaha Team	123
5	Gibernau	Movistar Honda MotoGP	115
6	Barros	Camel Honda	114
7	Hayden	Repsol Honda Team	112
8	Capirossi	Ducati Marlboro Team	92
9	Nakano	Kawasaki Racing Team	69
10	Checa C.	Ducati Marlboro Team	59
11	Bayliss	Camel Honda	54
12	Tamada	JIR Konica Minolta Honda	48
13	Roberts	Team Suzuki MotoGP	41
14	Xaus	Fortuna Yamaha Team	36
15	Hopkins	Team Suzuki MotoGP	35
16	Elias	Fortuna Yamaha Team	31
17	Jacque	Kawasaki Racing Team	25
18	Hofmann	Kawasaki Racing Team	22
19	Rolfo	Team D'Antin – Pramac	15
20	Goorbergh	JIR Konica Minolta Honda	12
21	Checa D.	Fortuna Yamaha Team	4
22	Ellison	Blata WCM	4
23	Battaini	Blata WCM	1
24	Byrne	Team Roberts	1

race. Caught out by the track warming up much more than he and his crew expected. Was the last finisher of the six-man pack battling for second in the championship.

8 CARLOS CHECA Best qualifying since his front row in Portugal, but the race was spoiled by choosing a different rear tyre from team-mate Capirossi. Went with slightly softer rubber and, despite a good start, paid the price before half-distance.

9 TROY BAYLISS No-one can say the guy doesn't try. He wrestled his Honda home for the first time since Laguna Seca and beat Tamada, from which the Aussie drew a little satisfaction.

10 MAKOTO TAMADA Late changes to set-up failed to solve the problems he has braking and turning in – shades of Biaggi.

Immediately after the race had another operation on the wrist he injured at the start of the year.

11 KENNY ROBERTS So ill in qualifying that he only did five laps before being put on a drip in the Clinica Mobile, yet on Sunday he raced with Bayliss, Tamada and Nakano and was the first of the three Suzukis home.

12 SHINYA NAKANO Kawasakis have never got on with Brno, and this year was no exception. However, he recovered from a bad start and, despite lacking traction, made up three places in the last three laps.

13 JOHN HOPKINS Definitely the unhappiest man at the track: 'Still suffering with a lack of acceleration and we are having to ride it on the edge.'

14 TONI ELIAS Not a bad ride – a couple of laps in the 1m 59s bracket, and he finished less than a second behind Hopkins. The man himself was most pleased with the rhythm he established.

15 ALEX HOFMANN A storming first three laps put him tenth and in front of Biaggi. Then he lost rear grip and watched first Max and then the Bayliss group blast past. 'Perhaps the riders in that group did not go 100% at the beginning?'

16 NOBUATSU AOKI Suzuki's test rider had his first wild-card outing of the year, but it was a lonely race. Felt that his bike lost a bit of top end early on.

17 ROBERTO ROLFO His Dunlops didn't last long and Roby was not happy to finish out of the points.

18 RUBEN XAUS Said he didn't arrive at Brno in the best shape, and it looked like it. His lowest finish of the season by four whole places.

19 JAMES ELLISON Another heroic qualifying followed by a race severely limited by Dunlops that chattered going into corners and wouldn't grip coming out.

20 FRANCO BATTAINI Suffered in the same way as team-mate Ellison.

NON-STARTERS

SETE GIBERNAU Deserved second place at the very least after pushing Rossi as hard as anyone has done all year. Stopped on the last lap

when his bike ran out of fuel due to a malfunction in the electronics of the fuel-injection system.

JEREMY MCWILLIAMS The Ulsterman's return to MotoGP was the result of terminal fallout between Team Roberts and their engine supplier, KTM. His race on the old V5 Proton was curtailed when a wheel speed sensor failed and started telling lies to the engine management system resulting in surging on a constant throttle.

NON-FINISHERS

SHANE BYRNE His contract is with KTM, so when they decided not to continue the relationship with Team Roberts Shakey didn't ride.

DEFERRED GRATIFICATION

Rossi had to wait to retain his crown, but Ducati's long-delayed second MotoGP victory also came with pole and fastest lap, plus fourth place, their best-ever result in the class

Valentino Rossi said he didn't really want to retain his title at Motegi because it wasn't the best place for a party. His wish was granted, but not in the circumstances he imagined. After Brno it was obvious that Loris Capirossi and the Bridgestone-shod Ducati would be a threat in Japan. The Japanese tyre company had done many miles of testing at the venue with Ducati's test team and rider Shinichi Itoh, and the previous year Tamada (then a Bridgestone user) had run away with the race. However, all Rossi had to do was finish second to become a seven-times champion, no matter what anyone else did; if neither Biaggi nor Melandri won then fourth would be enough. There were many other permutations, but they were all rendered irrelevant by one incident.

For once that incident was not at the first corner,

Opposite Loris Capirossi on his way to Ducati's first MotoGP win since Catalunya 2003

Above Naoki Matsudo had a wild card ride on the Honda-powered Moriwaki

Below Marco Melandri is stretchered away with a nasty gash to his right foot

the site of mass pile-ups in the two previous years. The organisers had taken the precaution of moving the grid back down the track, towards the last corner, by the best part of a hundred metres. That meant the field would now have to change down a gear and brake whereas previously they'd just slammed the throttle shut in second gear and pitched into the bend. The extra time allowed everyone to sort themselves out and the whole field got to the second corner, although wild-card Naoki Matsudo on the Moriwaki didn't make it round the first lap.

Marco Melandri was having a race that, as in Brno,

began with good qualifying followed by a great start. This time, though, he was on the front row of the grid and took an early lead, holding off Biaggi and Capirossi for the first eleven laps. Then, as in Brno, he started to fade rapidly, losing two places in one lap and running wide in corners. That put Marco within range of Rossi. The Doctor had had a terrible qualifying session and started the race in eleventh place, but he took just two laps to get up to fifth and another two to get past Tamada and into fourth.

To comprehend what happened next you must understand the nature of the 90-degree, off-camber right-hander at the end of the downhill back straight. Go down the outside of the track on entry and cut across to the apex, or run up the inside and take a wider line on the exit: there were plenty of examples of either option in both practice and the race, including several Biaggi–Capirossi pass and repass moves going into and out of the corner. Rossi, closing rapidly on Melandri, decided to run up the inside line. Marco took the other option, sweeping across to the apex, and ran into Valentino. Both men went down. Rossi said he wasn't even trying to attempt a pass at the time – but if anyone made a mistake, it was him. Melandri refused to criticise Rossi, which was pretty magnanimous given that the footrest had sliced through his right boot and inflicted a deep and messy laceration. The wound was bound up and Marco helicoptered to hospital amid fears he could be out for at least two races.

Motegi is a circuit where overtaking is difficult, owing to its lack of long corners out of which riders can get a good drive, so outbraking is the only way to

pass. When there is no distinct machinery advantage this is doubly difficult, and it wasn't only Rossi who misjudged a braking effort. Alex Hofmann took out Roby Rolfo in another bad day for Kawasaki. The new engine they'd tested after Brno proved too peaky for the stop/go nature of the track so Nakano reverted to the old design: he blew that up in practice, then blew up another motor in the race. Shinya walked away from the bike, letting it topple over in the gravel trap: what a contrast to his rostrum finish in 2004. Sete Gibernau didn't fare much better, crashing out of seventh place unaided and further denting any hopes of second place in the championship.

The crashfest left Capirossi and Biaggi clear of Tamada to battle for the win. The Ducati rider was able to dial in throttle at some astonishing lean angles, just as Tamada had done twelve months previously, and once he'd carved inside Biaggi Loris was able to win despite the Roman's dogged pursuit. Despite his troubled season Max not only consolidated his second place in the points standings, he left Japan as the only man with even a mathematical chance of preventing Rossi making it five titles in a row. Tamada took the final rostrum place after a lonely ride, his best result of a difficult season.

Ducati, on the other hand, were able to celebrate their best-ever day in MotoGP. Not only did Loris win from pole, setting a record-breaking fastest lap of the day, the first time he'd got the full set in the top class, but Checa took fourth place (making it the best two-man finish for the team). Capirossi also announced that he'd be a Ducati rider again in 2006. Honda's discomfort in their own back yard was amplified by the fact that this was the first time a non-Japanese bike had won a

premier-class GP held on a Japanese circuit. Bridgestone did uphold Japanese honour with the first two grid positions, again just like the previous year, and first, fourth and fifth places at the flag. That fifth place went to Suzuki's John Hopkins, a career best.

HRC then scored a spectacular own goal by lodging an official protest against Rossi on behalf of all the Honda teams. Valentino was duly summoned to appear before Race Direction but, after lengthy deliberation, the protest was rejected by a unanimous vote of the four-man committee. The decision to protest was forced on the Honda teams by Japanese management, although it was impossible to find anyone in the paddock who thought it was (a) a good idea, or (b) had the slightest chance of success. And that included Marco Melandri.

Unhappily, the Rossi/Melandri crash and its aftermath tended to overshadow the achievements of Loris Capirossi and Ducati. Motegi was always going to be the race where Bridgestone had their best chance to avenge some of the season's earlier humiliations; the question now was could they maintain some momentum through to the end of the season?

Opposite above Rossi in the immediate aftermath of his coming together with Melandri

Opposite below Makoto Tamada restored some respectablility to his season with a fine third place

Right Capirossi and Biaggi on the brakes during their duel for the lead

SMALL FRY

Above Dani Pedrosa didn't win at Motegi but he wrapped up his second consecutive 250cc Championship in Australia three races later

The Motor Sports Manufacturers Association (MSMA) met on the Thursday before the Japanese GP and subsequently unveiled their blueprint for the future of the 125 and 250cc classes as far ahead as 2015.

Technical regulations for the 125cc class will remain unchanged at least until then, as will the rules for 250s up until 2012. Then, for the next two years, 400cc four-stroke twins will be introduced and will race with the 250cc two-strokes. After two years of cohabitation the strokers will be phased out and in 2015 the class will be four-stroke bikes only. These regulations will have to go before the Grand Prix Commission to be ratified in 2008.

As in the MotoGP class, the new four-stroke twins will have to be prototypes. MotoGP itself changes to an 800cc upper-capacity limit in

2007 and that rule will stay for at least five years. As 400cc is half of 800cc, any factory running a four-cylinder MotoGP engine should have done the expensive cylinder head development work already. The decision hopefully gives the smaller members of the MSMA, notably the Piaggio-owned Derbi, Gilera and Aprilia marques, and also KTM, the stability they need to maintain their involvement in the 125 and 250cc classes.

Incidentally, the support class at Motegi was called GP-Mono and featured 250cc four-stroke singles limited to 12,000rpm and 4.25-inch rear rims. Motocross-based engines are mounted in frames off 125cc racers and performance is reckoned to be just below that of two-stroke 125 racers. GP-Mono will be a class in the All-Japan Championship from 2006 onwards, and the Motegi support race featured bikes from each of the big four factories. Is this the shape of things to come?

MOTEGI
JAPANESE GRAND PRIX

ROUND 12

RACE RESULTS

RACE DATE September 18th
CIRCUIT LENGTH 2.983 miles
NO. OF LAPS 24
RACE DISTANCE 71.592 miles
WEATHER Dry, 31°C
TRACK TEMPERATURE 40°C
WINNER Loris Capirossi
FASTEST LAP 1m 46.363s,
100.747mph, Loris Capirossi (record)
PREVIOUS LAP RECORD 1m 48.524s,
98.964mph, Makoto Tamada, 2004

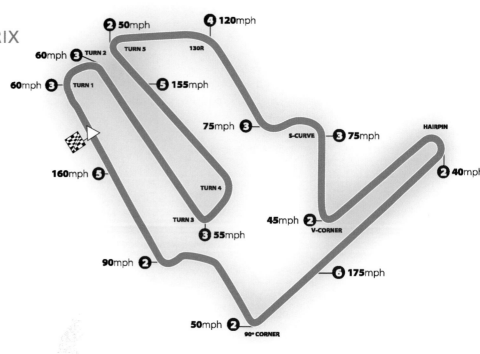

QUALIFYING

	Rider	Nationality	Team	Qualifying	Pole +	Gap
1	Capirossi	ITA	Ducati Marlboro Team	1m 46.363s		
2	Hopkins	USA	Team Suzuki MotoGP	1m 46.861s	0.498s	0.498s
3	Melandri	ITA	Movistar Honda MotoGP	1m 46.867s	0.504s	0.006s
4	Tamada	JPN	Konica Minolta Honda	1m 47.043s	0.680s	0.176s
5	Biaggi	ITA	Repsol Honda Team	1m 47.089s	0.726s	0.046s
6	Hayden	USA	Repsol Honda Team	1m 47.166s	0.803s	0.077s
7	Gibernau	SPA	Movistar Honda MotoGP	1m 47.168s	0.805s	0.002s
8	Roberts	USA	Team Suzuki MotoGP	1m 47.257s	0.894s	0.089s
9	Checa C.	SPA	Ducati Marlboro Team	1m 47.323s	0.960s	0.066s
10	Barros	BRA	Camel Honda	1m 47.562s	1.199s	0.239s
11	Rossi	ITA	Gauloises Yamaha Team	1m 47.563s	1.200s	0.001s
12	Hofmann	GER	Kawasaki Racing Team	1m 47.594s	1.231s	0.031s
13	Edwards	USA	Gauloises Yamaha Team	1m 47.678s	1.315s	0.084s
14	Nakano	JPN	Kawasaki Racing Team	1m 47.787s	1.424s	0.109s
15	Ukawa	JPN	Camel Honda	1m 48.194s	1.831s	0.407s
16	Rolfo	ITA	Team D'Antin – Pramac	1m 48.733s	2.370s	0.539s
17	Elias	SPA	Fortuna Yamaha Team	1m 48.861s	2.498s	0.128s
18	Matsudo	JPN	Moriwaki Racing	1m 49.734s	3.371s	0.873s
19	Xaus	SPA	Fortuna Yamaha Team	1m 49.969s	3.606s	0.235s
20	Battaini	ITA	Blata WCM	1m 51.902s	5.539s	1.933s
21	Ellison	GBR	Blata WCM	1m 51.972s	5.609s	0.070s

FINISHERS

1 LORIS CAPIROSSI A season-redeeming race for both team and rider: Loris announced his decision to stay with Ducati on Thursday, set pole on Saturday and won on Sunday, taking a record-breaking fastest lap. The perfect weekend, with the added bonus of it all happening in Honda's back yard.

2 MAX BIAGGI For once he qualified well, then ran a tough, competitive race at a track where he's won in the past. Heaped praise on Michelin and never mentioned chatter. Strengthened his grip on second place in the championship and was now the only man with even a mathematical chance of stopping Rossi retaining his title.

3 MAKOTO TAMADA His first podium of a troubled year at a track where he won in 2004. Once Rossi and Melandri had gone down in front of him Makoto decided to bring it home safely, wearing a Michelin cap on the rostrum for the first time.

4 CARLOS CHECA Happier with his performance than the result. Ninth in qualifying didn't help his race, but some aggressive riding saw him pass Hayden, Gibernau and Hopkins in the early laps. Reckoned the weekend was a real leap forward for him, the team and their tyres.

5 JOHN HOPKINS Got past the first corner, for the first time in three years, and took his first-ever top-five finish. Brilliant in qualifying and pushed as hard as the bike would allow in

the race. As his team manager said afterwards, he couldn't have done any more – probably made the Suzuki look better than it was.

6 COLIN EDWARDS Suffered from front-end problems and was never going to challenge the leaders. Nevertheless, got it home again and moved to third in the championship.

7 NICKY HAYDEN In his own words, things never clicked from the moment he got off the plane. Ran off track while battling with Barros, lost a few places and then just dug in for some points.

8 KENNY ROBERTS Reckoned it was the worst result possible this side of crashing. Front-end slides early on, maybe due to higher than expected track temperatures, meant he couldn't brake hard; then got

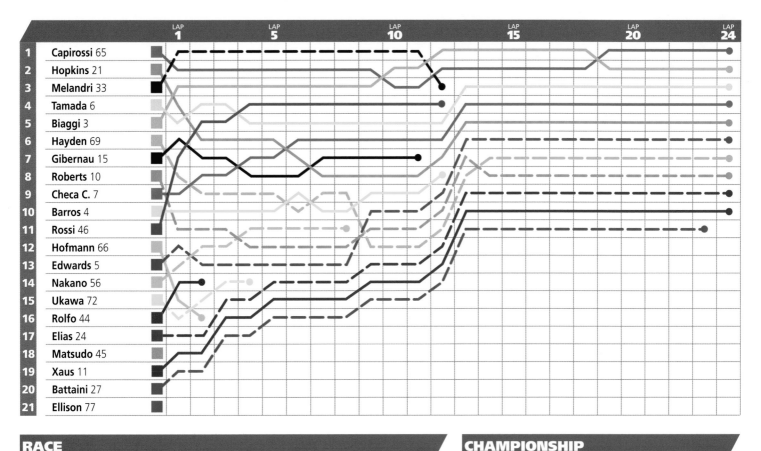

		LAP 1	LAP 5	LAP 10	LAP 15	LAP 20	LAP 24
1	Capirossi 65						
2	Hopkins 21						
3	Melandri 33						
4	Tamada 6						
5	Biaggi 3						
6	Hayden 69						
7	Gibernau 15						
8	Roberts 10						
9	Checa C. 7						
10	Barros 4						
11	Rossi 46						
12	Hofmann 66						
13	Edwards 5						
14	Nakano 56						
15	Ukawa 72						
16	Rolfo 44						
17	Elias 24						
18	Matsudo 45						
19	Xaus 11						
20	Battaini 27						
21	Ellison 77						

RACE

	Rider	Motorcycle	Race Time	Time +	Fastest Lap	Average Speed
1	Capirossi	Ducati	43m 30.499s		1m 47.968s	180.392mph
2	Biaggi	Honda	43m 31.978s	1.479s	1m 47.985s	180.454mph
3	Tamada	Honda	43m 46.726s	16.227s	1m 48.207s	176.539mph
4	Checa C.	Ducati	43m 52.647s	22.148s	1m 48.489s	178.279mph
5	Hopkins	Suzuki	44m 03.711s	33.212s	1m 48.561s	176.850mph
6	Edwards	Yamaha	44m 05.414s	34.915s	1m 48.945s	177.854mph
7	Hayden	Honda	44m 16.393s	45.894s	1m 48.883s	177.906mph
8	Roberts	Suzuki	44m 26.997s	56.498s	1m 48.985s	169.145mph
9	Elias	Yamaha	44m 42.536s	1m 12.037s	1m 50.748s	183.070mph
10	Xaus	Yamaha	45m 05.426s	1m 34.927s	1m 51.585s	173.867mph
11	Battaini	Blata	44m 38.510s	1 lap	1m 53.274s	166.100mph
	Melandri	Honda	21m 49.319s	12 laps	1m 48.186s	179.771mph
	Rossi	Yamaha	21m 50.273s	12 laps	1m 48.014s	177.968mph
	Barros	Honda	21m 59.118s	12 laps	1m 48.731s	175.483mph
	Gibernau	Honda	20m 08.260s	13 laps	1m 48.592s	178.652mph
	Nakano	Kawasaki	14m 43.191s	16 laps	1m 48.841s	171.257mph
	Ukawa	Honda	7m 29.419s	20 laps	1m 49.477s	170.947mph
	Rolfo	Ducati	3m 49.595s	22 laps	1m 50.635s	167.405mph
	Hofmann	Kawasaki	3m 49.960s	22 laps	1m 50.864s	168.585mph

CHAMPIONSHIP

	Rider	Team	Points
1	Rossi	Gauloises Yamaha Team	261
2	Biaggi	Repsol Honda Team	149
3	Edwards	Gauloises Yamaha Team	133
4	Melandri	Movistar Honda MotoGP	126
5	Hayden	Repsol Honda Team	121
6	Capirossi	Ducati Marlboro Team	117
7	Gibernau	Movistar Honda MotoGP	115
8	Barros	Camel Honda	114
9	Checa C.	Ducati Marlboro Team	72
10	Nakano	Kawasaki Racing Team	69
11	Tamada	JIR Konica Minolta Honda	64
12	Bayliss	Camel Honda	54
13	Roberts	Team Suzuki MotoGP	49
14	Hopkins	Team Suzuki MotoGP	46
15	Xaus	Fortuna Yamaha Team	42
16	Elias	Fortuna Yamaha Team	38
17	Jacque	Kawasaki Racing Team	25
18	Hofmann	Kawasaki Racing Team	22
19	Rolfo	Team D'Antin – Pramac	15
20	Goorbergh	JIR Konica Minolta Honda	12
21	Battaini	Blata WCM	6
22	Checa D.	Fortuna Yamaha Team	4
23	Ellison	Blata WCM	4
24	Byrne	Team Roberts	1

frustrated and overshot corners. In the end, he said, he was 'riding round lost'.

9 TONI ELIAS Suffering more pain in the arm he broke after Le Mans, following an operation to remove the pins. Under the circumstances did another professional job and collected useful points, despite never finding a good set-up.

10 RUBEN XAUS Saw all the crashes happening around him and decided that discretion was the better part of valour. Reported that the rise in track temperature made things even more complicated than usual.

11 FRANCO BATTAINI The WCM team's best finish of the year so far came from the usual dogged persistence plus an unusually large number of crashes and a mechanical failure from a Honda V5.

NON-FINISHERS

MARCO MELANDRI Taken down by Rossi at the right-hander at the end of the back straight: helicoptered away with a nasty laceration to his right heel that required thirty stitches. Initial doubts about his ability to ride until at least Phillip Island were thankfully proved overly pessimistic.

VALENTINO ROSSI Collided with Melandri at the end of the fast back straight and both men crashed. Distraught that Marco received a nasty injury. Honda protested his riding but Race Direction found there was no case to answer. Would have retained his title with a fourth-place finish.

ALEX BARROS Blazing mad after crashing on oil from Nakano's blown motor; didn't know why he'd crashed until told by Edwards, who'd been behind the Kawasaki. Reported front-fork and tyre problems but managed to get past a few riders, then crashed in a straight line, losing valuable points and dropping two places in the table.

SETE GIBERNAU Crashed while running behind Checa and totally honest about the situation, blaming no-one but himself.

SHINYA NAKANO A terrible weekend for Shinya and the Kawasaki team at the circuit where he scored a rostrum finish in 2004. Tried the new motor is qualifying but it didn't suit the circuit. Blew up an engine in qualifying and another in the race.

TOHRU UKAWA Returned to the Camel Honda team he'd ridden for in 2003 as a replacement for the injured Troy Bayliss. Suffered that most unusual of circumstances, an RC211V engine problem in the race, which forced him to pull in.

ROBERTO ROLFO The innocent victim of Hofmann's crash. Unlike the German, Roby escaped without injury.

ALEX HOFMANN Tried to overtake Ukawa on the third lap but collided with Rolfo at the hairpin at the top of the circuit. The incident left Alex with a broken ankle and out for at least the next two races.

NAOKI MATSUDO His first MotoGP ride as a wild card on the Moriwaki. Did not even last a lap before he ran off the track.

NON-STARTERS

JAMES ELLISON An elbow injury sustained while tyre testing the day after the Czech GP left the Brit without any strength in his left arm. He qualified but decided it would be unsafe to race.

TROY BAYLISS A motocross training accident the Monday before the race left Troy with a badly broken left wrist and doubtful for the rest of the season.

SEVEN UP

Valentino clinched his seventh word title and his fifth consecutive crown in the top class, but again it was Ducati who had the best weekend

Just about everyone who turned up to Valentino Rossi's latest celebration party had reasons to be cheerful. The man himself equalled Mick Doohan's run of five top-class titles, Loris Capirossi and Ducati won two in a row for the first time, Bridgestone set their first consecutive poles, Marco Melandri was able to race despite the injury he'd received in Japan, Shakey Byrne got to ride a Honda V5, Nicky Hayden set another lap record and nearly 50,000 people filled the giant grandstand along the front straight. Suzuki and Kawasaki should have

been cheerful but events conspired against them. The non-cheerful minority consisted of Honda and Sete Gibernau.

Anyone who thought Bridgestone's familiarity with the Motegi tarmac was the only thing that helped Capirossi and Ducati to the win on them last time out were quickly disabused of that notion. Loris's lupine grin was, if that were possible, even wider than at Motegi. Everything went as well as it possibly could: lengthy high-speed runs on race tyres in practice, another storming pole in qualifying, then a coolly calculating race in which he first saw off the early charge of Nicky Hayden and then dealt with Rossi's inevitable attack. True to form, the Bridgestones took a little longer than the Michelins to work at their best, with Hayden setting his record on the fourth lap but then losing the final rostrum slot to a delighted Carlos Checa on the second Ducati in the closing stages. It looked for a while, in fact, as if Checa was going to snatch second place from Rossi, but the Doctor clinically blocked him at the last corner. That sent three happy men to the rostrum, and they all seemed pleased to see each other there.

Capirossi was leading at half-distance when Rossi attacked on the brakes at the first corner. Three laps later Capirossi retook the lead and piled on the pressure. 'It took me three corners to understand,' Rossi reported. 'He was playing with me like a cat plays with a mouse.' Maybe so, but there was that giveaway sign of Valentino's left foot flapping off the rest on the way into corners on the brakes. We'd seen it early in the race in the fight with Hayden, and it surfaced again as he tried to match the Ducati's pace. Hayden, meanwhile, was in

a frantic outbraking duel with Checa. Three times they went wide together at the last turn before the Spaniard got the upper hand. Nicky had been running wide in corners since the early laps and he did well to put up the fight he did towards the end of the race, delaying Carlos just enough to prevent a Ducati one–two.

The man doing better than anyone had any right to expect was Melandri. He'd been pushed into his hotel in a wheelchair, with more than thirty stitches in his right foot, and wasn't expected even to try and ride – but ride he did, and in every session, although he reported that the effort of using the rear-brake pedal pulled his stitches painfully. Marco's team-mate, Sete Gibernau, had an even worse time, though. He was the instigator of the barging in the first corner, and then he tried diving up the inside of Shinya Nakano, losing the front and scooping up the luckless Kawasaki rider. Sete waved an apology, sinking to his knees in what looked like prayer; the crowd saw it all on the big screens and let out a collective sigh of sympathy. Very understanding people, Malaysians.

It is doubtful if Shinya felt as sympathetic. He'd qualified on the front of the second row, avoided the bumping and barging, was running with the leaders and had the same tyres as the winner. After a couple of seriously depressing races it looked as if Kawasaki were in with a shout, in dry conditions. Hopkins had a similar tale of woe. He'd qualified on the front row in consecutive races for the first time, but was then the principal victim of the first-lap fairing bashing. John got shuffled back down the top ten and never recovered. When a rider relies on carrying corner speed for lap

Opposite Shakey Byrne prepares to discover the delights of a Honda V5 for the first time

Above The MotoGP field dives into the first corner in front of the biggest crowd ever to attend a Malaysian GP

Above It was Ducati's best ever day in their GP history, never before had they put two riders on the rostrum

Below Shinya Nakano looked good all weekend – until he was torpedoed by Sete Gibernau

times it's difficult to pass on a circuit where outbraking is the primary weapon.

Shane Byrne couldn't work out whether he was having a good time or not. He'd taken over Troy Bayliss's Camel Honda, so it should have been a good weekend: a Honda V5 on Michelins is what every rider wants (whether he'll admit it or not). However, taking it over with no test time and not having the usual thumb-operated rear brake while all the rest have had nine months to sort themselves out is almost the definition of the phrase 'on a hiding to nothing'. Shakey himself admitted that he was the first to think that all the factory riders had to do was turn up and twist the throttle. He found himself working a lot harder than he'd expected just to be in the sort of position he used to be in on the Team Roberts bike. Damp conditions in one of the three practice sessions didn't help much either. Byrne treated the bike as if it were a newborn baby through Friday and Saturday and only really enjoyed his dice with Ruben Xaus in the last laps of the race. That scary little cameo involved approximately five changes of position on the final lap.

It was hard to work out who was happiest, Rossi and his team or Ducati's red brigade. The Italian factory's race triumph was tempered, however, by their sympathy for team-manager Livio Suppo: he'd flown home to be with his wife, whose mother had died in an accident. Loris and Carlos dedicated their races to Livio and his family.

Over at Yamaha joy was truly unconfined. Rossi joined Mick Doohan and Giacomo Agostini as the only racers to have won five or more world titles in the premier class, and Yamaha celebrated the first of its planned objectives for marking the factory's fiftieth anniversary. True to form, the Rossi fan club had a photo opportunity planned to celebrate the seventh title. Snow White and the Seven Dwarfs duly appeared, with each dwarf bearing the date of a championship win. 'Was that your mother in the Snow White costume?' Rossi was asked. 'No; but my mother is the real Snow White!' Well, his life is a fairy tale.

LOCAL HERO

Top Rossi celebrates his
seventh world title with
an appropriate number of
members of his fan club

Above Indonesian teenager
Doni Pradata, a wild card in
the 125cc class and a name
to remember

There was a new name in the 125cc
class in Malaysia, a 15-year-old
Indonesian racer called Doni Tata
Pradita. There's nothing out of the
ordinary about teenage riders in
the 125s, but this kid is already a
champion and although he was
racing with the backing of his local
importer it was very noticeable
that all his publicity material came
direct from Yamaha's corporate PR
department in Japan.

Doni won the 2005 Asian
Championship, contested in
Malaysia, Indonesia and China on
'underbones', that's stripped down
stepthrough chassis housing 115cc
engines. This was the first time
Doni had ridden a 125cc GP bike yet
he qualified and finished the race
without being lapped on a bike that
was well down on power.

His minders from Yamaha
Indonesia were talking about getting
Doni into GPs as quickly as possible.
There is no doubt that the Rossi
effect is being felt in South East Asia
– there were stepthroughs with Rossi

replica paint highly visible on the
roads on race day.

The market for powered two-
wheelers in this part of the world
is massive; manufacturers talk in
markets of tens of millions, so if
the object of going racing is to sell
motorcycles it makes sense to race
here and of course to try and find a
rider from the area to bring on.

Malaysian Sharol Yuzi rode a
Yamaha sponsored by the giant state
petroleum company Petronas from
2000 to 2002 scoring a dozen top-ten
finishes, but much to the disgust of
the local press no successor has
been found.

The popularity of racing with
spectators is growing too. The
regular midweek underbone races
at the Shah Alam circuit pull big
crowds, but it is more difficult
– and expensive – to get out of
Kuala Lumpur to the Sepang track.
Nevertheless, the pit lane grandstand
was full on race day and the stand
along the back straight had a good
sprinkling of spectators as well.

SEPANG
MALAYSIAN GRAND PRIX

ROUND 13

RACE RESULTS

RACE DATE September 25th
CIRCUIT LENGTH 3.447 miles
NO. OF LAPS 21
RACE DISTANCE 72.387 miles
WEATHER Dry, 40°C
TRACK TEMPERATURE 50°C
WINNER Loris Capirossi
FASTEST LAP 2m 01.731s,
101.725mph, Loris Capirossi (record)
PREVIOUS LAP RECORD 2m 03.253s,
100.696mph, Valentino Rossi, 2004

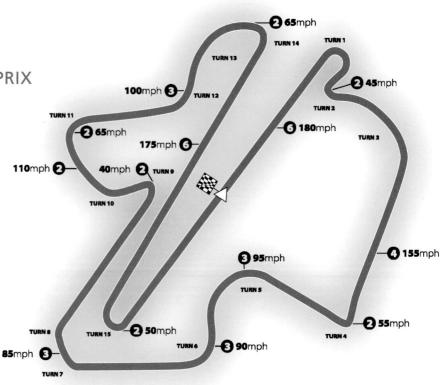

QUALIFYING

	Rider	Nationality	Team	Qualifying	Pole +	Gap
1	Capirossi	ITA	Ducati Marlboro Team	2m 01.731s		
2	Gibernau	SPA	Movistar Honda MotoGP	2m 01.867s	0.136s	0.136s
3	Hopkins	USA	Team Suzuki MotoGP	2m 02.017s	0.286s	0.150s
4	Nakano	JPN	Kawasaki Racing Team	2m 02.178s	0.447s	0.161s
5	Roberts	USA	Team Suzuki MotoGP	2m 02.215s	0.484s	0.037s
6	Hayden	USA	Repsol Honda Team	2m 02.377s	0.646s	0.162s
7	Rossi	ITA	Gauloises Yamaha Team	2m 02.412s	0.681s	0.035s
8	Checa C.	SPA	Ducati Marlboro Team	2m 02.419s	0.688s	0.007s
9	Melandri	ITA	Movistar Honda MotoGP	2m 02.660s	0.929s	0.241s
10	Edwards	USA	Gauloises Yamaha Team	2m 02.805s	1.074s	0.145s
11	Barros	BRA	Camel Honda	2m 03.013s	1.282s	0.208s
12	Biaggi	ITA	Repsol Honda Team	2m 03.210s	1.479s	0.197s
13	Jacque	FRA	Kawasaki Racing Team	2m 03.364s	1.633s	0.154s
14	Elias	SPA	Fortuna Yamaha Team	2m 03.397s	1.666s	0.033s
15	Tamada	JPN	Konica Minolta Honda	2m 03.974s	2.243s	0.577s
16	Xaus	SPA	Fortuna Yamaha Team	2m 04.010s	2.279s	0.036s
17	Rolfo	ITA	Team D'Antin – Pramac	2m 05.092s	3.361s	1.082s
18	Byrne	GBR	Camel Honda	2m 06.493s	4.762s	1.401s
19	Battaini	ITA	Blata WCM	2m 07.492s	5.761s	0.999s
20	Ellison	GBR	Blata WCM	2m 08.352s	6.621s	0.860s

FINISHERS

1 LORIS CAPIROSSI The first time he'd set pole position in successive races in the top class; the first time he, Ducati and Bridgestone have won consecutive races in MotoGP; and the first time a non-Japanese motorcycle has taken successive wins since the days of MV Agusta. It was also Loris's 25th win in all classes of GP racing, and it shot him up to third in the championship.

2 VALENTINO ROSSI Second was enough to retain his world title, his seventh in all classes, but he had to work hard in the closing stages to hold off the rapidly closing Ducati of Checa.

3 CARLOS CHECA His first rostrum as a Ducati rider, and he was so close to making it a one–two for the team. One of the victims of the bunching in the first couple of turns but fought back from eighth place and was the fastest man on the track for lengthy periods of the race.

4 NICKY HAYDEN Took a couple of knocks from Gibernau and then lost a strip of rubber from the centre of his rear tyre. Involved in a frantic braking duel with Checa for third place. Set the fastest lap of the race and now has a lap record to go with his two poles and that win in Laguna Seca.

5 MARCO MELANDRI Amazingly, he raced with his right foot full of stitches from the incident at Motegi. Suffering with heat from his motor and 'pulling' of the stitches

when he used the rear brake. Under the circumstances, fifth was not only his best result since Assen but also a return to form.

6 MAX BIAGGI This time there was no charge upfield from his fourth-row start. Instead, Max was left to lament the contrast between this performance and the pre-season test: 'It is not the same machine it was at the start of the year.'

7 KENNY ROBERTS His best dry-race finish of the year, and he beat his team-mate for the second time in three races. Just when you think the 2000 World Champion is a spent force he reminds you how good he can be.

8 ALEX BARROS Unhappy with his lowest finish of the year (apart from China, where he got a stop/go penalty). Blamed a lack of front-

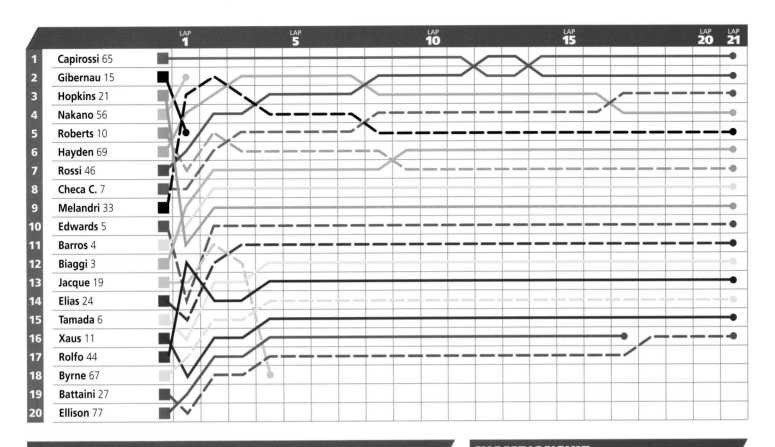

		LAP 1	LAP 5	LAP 10	LAP 15	LAP 20	LAP 21
1	Capirossi 65						
2	Gibernau 15						
3	Hopkins 21						
4	Nakano 56						
5	Roberts 10						
6	Hayden 69						
7	Rossi 46						
8	Checa C. 7						
9	Melandri 33						
10	Edwards 5						
11	Barros 4						
12	Biaggi 3						
13	Jacque 19						
14	Elias 24						
15	Tamada 6						
16	Xaus 11						
17	Rolfo 44						
18	Byrne 67						
19	Battaini 27						
20	Ellison 77						

RACE

	Rider	Motorcycle	Race Time	Time +	Fastest Lap	Average Speed
1	Capirossi	Ducati	43m 27.523s		2m 03.435s	190.645mph
2	Rossi	Yamaha	43m 29.522s	1.999s	2m 03.328s	191.453mph
3	Checa C.	Ducati	43m 29.592s	2.069s	2m 03.527s	190.272mph
4	Hayden	Honda	43m 36.750s	9.227s	2m 02.993s	190.148mph
5	Melandri	Honda	43m 43.409s	15.886s	2m 03.699s	190.396mph
6	Biaggi	Honda	43m 44.349s	16.826s	2m 03.817s	191.577mph
7	Roberts	Suzuki	43m 44.772s	17.249s	2m 03.686s	185.860mph
8	Barros	Honda	43m 45.744s	18.221s	2m 03.854s	188.222mph
9	Hopkins	Suzuki	43m 47.648s	20.125s	2m 03.681s	188.284mph
10	Edwards	Yamaha	43m 49.798s	22.275s	2m 04.131s	190.459mph
11	Elias	Yamaha	43m 57.379s	29.856s	2m 04.471s	189.837mph
12	Tamada	Honda	44m 19.195s	51.672s	2m 05.051s	189.651mph
13	Rolfo	Ducati	44m 32.888s	1m 05.365s	2m 06.070s	188.159mph
14	Byrne	Honda	44m 46.629s	1m 19.106s	2m 06.743s	186.606mph
15	Xaus	Yamaha	44m 46.879s	1m 19.356s	2m 07.014s	185.487mph
16	Battaini	Blata	45m 23.405s	1m 55.882s	2m 08.652s	176.291mph
	Ellison	Blata	36m 38.849s	4 laps	2m 07.378s	171.941mph
	Jacque	Kawasaki	8m 47.858s	17 laps	2m 05.089s	180.081mph
	Nakano	Kawasaki	2m 09.640s	20 laps	2m 09.640s	183.623mph
	Gibernau	Honda	2m 10.100s	20 laps	2m 10.100s	177.285mph

CHAMPIONSHIP

	Rider	Team	Points
1	Rossi	Gauloises Yamaha Team	281
2	Biaggi	Repsol Honda Team	159
3	Capirossi	Ducati Marlboro Team	142
4	Edwards	Gauloises Yamaha Team	139
5	Melandri	Movistar Honda MotoGP	137
6	Hayden	Repsol Honda Team	134
7	Barros	Camel Honda	122
8	Gibernau	Movistar Honda MotoGP	115
9	Checa C.	Ducati Marlboro Team	88
10	Nakano	Kawasaki Racing Team	69
11	Tamada	JIR Konica Minolta Honda	68
12	Roberts	Team Suzuki MotoGP	58
13	Bayliss	Camel Honda	54
14	Hopkins	Team Suzuki MotoGP	53
15	Elias	Fortuna Yamaha Team	43
16	Xaus	Fortuna Yamaha Team	43
17	Jacque	Kawasaki Racing Team	25
18	Hofmann	Kawasaki Racing Team	22
19	Rolfo	Team D'Antin – Pramac	18
20	Goorbergh	JIR Konica Minolta Honda	12
21	Battaini	Blata WCM	6
22	Checa D.	Fortuna Yamaha Team	4
23	Ellison	Blata WCM	4
24	Byrne	Team Roberts/Camel Honda	3

end grip which meant he couldn't outbrake anyone: he tried it once to get past Roberts, but ran wide. After that it was a matter of survival.

9 JOHN HOPKINS The main victim of the barging in the first turn, which negated any advantage his front-row start might have given. Got on the back of the four-man dice with his team-mate, Barros and Biaggi but couldn't make any move stick.

10 COLIN EDWARDS Never got the set-up he was happy with, going to a different construction of front tyre in warm-up which fixed one problem but created another. Raced with the back of the bike set too low and hit problems early in the race.

11 TONI ELIAS Quite happy in practice and qualifying but had a problem with front-end

grip during the race. Not keen on the painkilling injections he still needs before each race, either.

12 MAKOTO TAMADA Doubly disappointed given the momentum generated by Motegi and his speed here in pre-season testing. Crashes in practice and qualifying, both on the same corner, did nothing for his confidence or the set-up of the bike, and relegated him to the back of the fifth row of the grid. Lacked any feel for the bike in the race.

13 ROBERTO ROLFO Happy with his start, if nothing else, but did acknowledge the improvements in his Dunlop tyres. Both consistency and useful life are much improved though there is still a way to go to catch the opposition.

14 SHANE BYRNE Called in as a replacement for Bayliss. Didn't get a chance to test the Honda, but at least he'd tested the Aprilia here. One damp practice session didn't help him and he found the going a lot harder than he expected. Concentrated on his riding and got the bike home for a couple of points.

15 RUBEN XAUS Didn't feel well on Saturday and didn't get much sleep before the race – and yet again he didn't feel at home with the bike.

16 FRANCO BATTAINI Outgunned on the big straights but did get the WCM home.

LOSAIL
QATARI GRAND PRIX

ROUND **14**

DESERT SONG

Rossi took his revenge at the track where he felt seriously slighted last year, but he had to fight off a magnificent Marco Melandri to do it

There's no getting away from the fact that Qatar is a strange place for a motorcycle race – there are more bikes in pit lane than there are in the car parks – but once again the desert track gave us superb entertainment. Last year much of the interest centred on paddock politicking which saw Rossi and Biaggi demoted to the back of the grid, leading to an astonishing charge by Valentino in the early laps followed by a crash as he closed on the front runners. That gave rise to what one incorrigible press-room wit called 'The Curse of Qatar'. Rossi blamed Gibernau for all his ills and declared that one of

Above Sete leads early on, before Capirossi faded and he ran off track

Opposite Toni Elias was back to his old, spectacular self as his injured arm grew stronger

Below Once he'd had his off-track excursions, Sete had a lonely ride to fifth place

his major motivations was to ensure that Sete didn't win another race in 2004. The Curse worked well, and it was still working when MotoGP came to Qatar for the second time. Would its strength ebb once past its first birthday?

After qualifying it looked that way. Gibernau was second, only bested by another astonishing Capirossi charge to pole, making it a hat-trick for Loris, Ducati and Bridgestone. However, Sete seemed to have the best set-up judging by the number of lengthy runs he put in on race tyres. It looked that way on race day, too. Once he'd banged fairings with Hayden (again) in the first corner and seen the quick-starting Capirossi slide backwards with a dearth of grip from the rear

tyre on corner entry, Gibernau set the pace and pulled out what looked like a significant lead. By lap 6 he had the best part of a second's advantage over Rossi, who was having to contend with a spirited challenge from Melandri. Only Hayden, who set a new lap record early on, and, for a while, Edwards could stay in touch.

At the other end of the field Shakey Byrne, in his second replacement ride on the Camel Honda, was enjoying himself more than he'd done in Malaysia. He'd started to think about the bike, as opposed to his riding, and was a lot closer to the other factory riders than the previous week. On paper his results do not look that dissimilar, but the reality was quite different. Another

Above Rossi came under
serious pressure from
Melandri in the closing stages

Below Roby Rolfo had his
most competitive race of the
season so far on the Dunlop-
shoed D'Antin Ducati

underdog having a good day was Roby Rolfo. He'd
charged up to eighth place at the first corner on the
Dunlop-shod D'Antin Ducati and, thanks to good work
in Birmingham, his tyres stayed with him for a lot longer
than has usually been the case; again, his eventual
finishing place of twelfth does not look that much of
an improvement on the norm, but his lap times only
dropped off in the last few laps.

Rossi wasn't the only man with revenge on his mind.
Michelin's runners were putting Bridgestone firmly in
their place. Hopkins had to come in and change his rear
tyre, Capirossi was losing the back end when he flicked
the bike into corners, even when he didn't have the

throttle open, leaving Checa and Nakano running round
in sixth and seventh as the top Bridgestone men.

Gibernau was looking very solid at the front as the
race wore on. The lead occasionally came down to half
a second or so, but Sete seemed to be able to cover any
moves. In any case, Rossi and Melandri appeared a little
too involved in their own fight. When Melandri did get
in front Rossi seemed to have the power to ride past him
as he pleased down the front straight. Then, with eight
laps to go, the gap seemed to dematerialise. Two laps
later, Melandri went inside Rossi at the first of the pair
of right-handers that make up Turns 4 and 5. Valentino
immediately moved to repay the compliment, only to
have to stand his bike up to avoid Marco sweeping
back to the second apex off a wide line: twice in three
weekends would have been too much to explain. That
looked to have ended the Doctor's interest in the race
win; indeed, he only just fended off Hayden at the
hairpin that followed. Next, Melandri made an optimistic
charge up the inside at the hairpin and took the lead
momentarily from Gibernau. The only effect of that move
was to allow Rossi to close the gap between himself and
Marco from 1.25 seconds to virtually nothing.

Marco had another go at the first of the trio of high-
speed right-handers that make up the most challenging
part of the Losail track. Again, Sete came straight back
up the inside – this time, though, he was carrying far
too much speed, couldn't make the next apex and ran
into the enormous gravel trap, extricating himself to
rejoin down in fifth place.

The only question left was could Melandri hold off
Rossi. Valentino piled the pressure on for two laps and
then made an astonishing pass at Turn 1 with two laps to

ELECTRICAL PROBLEMS

Above Makoto Tamada was one of the victims of Honda's electrical problems in Qatar

Below All-Italian celebrations in parc fermé

Two Honda V5s broke down in Qatar, Biaggi's and Tamada's. One of HRC's products stopping is a remarkable enough event in itself, but two at the same time is almost unheard of. Before this season the last mechanical malfunction to stop an RCV happened to Nicky Hayden at Jerez in 2003 (the same rider suffered a holed radiator at Catalunya last year, but that doesn't really count as a mechanical problem). But when you add in Sete Gibernau's breakdown in Brno and Tohru Ukawa's engine blow up in Motegi you have what looks like a rash of problems. Were HRC really pushing the limits to try and catch Rossi?

The most spectacular failure, Ukawa's, was traced to impurities in the oil. It is thought debris, possibly from a sight glass, was introduced during pressurization of the oiling system and found its way to a big end bearing. Both the Qatar failures were traced to nothing more complex than faults with the

wiring loom. According to HRC, no-one made a mistake and the faults didn't occur in service parts that are scheduled for replacement at set intervals. Both failures were down to the proverbial 50p component and, HRC are keen to emphasise, couldn't have been predicted. Tamada said his bike just stopped while Biaggi's motor could be heard misfiring badly, lending credence to the claim of an electrical problem.

That only leaves Gibernau's Czech problem, and that is the one that Honda have not found an explanation for. They know what happened, the electronics of the fuel injection system said one thing and did another. As Brno is not a track where fuel consumption is critical, most people believed HRC's explanation. However, they aren't all that comfortable everywhere because there were strong indications that in Japan RCV riders had their rev limit reduced by 500rpm, and Motegi is a track where fuel consumption is critical.

go. Getting good drive out of the final corner, Rossi went to Melandri's left and then was supernaturally late on the brakes; effectively, it was a round-the-outside pass at the end of a kilometre-long straight. Even that move didn't discourage Marco, or the tell-tale sight of Rossi's left boot flicking off the footrest on the penultimate lap, which only happens when he's trying, and trying hard. On the last lap Melandri wound himself up for an all-or-nothing effort, diving up the inside at the first of the three rights. As he would later admit, he never thought it was going to work but he had to make the attempt. Sure enough, the young Italian went wide and ran off the edge of the track: dust was coming off his tyres a metre before he went from the tarmac and onto the Astroturf that lines the track. Thankfully some justice was done, as Marco didn't lose enough time for Nicky Hayden to get him, and they finished second and third.

This was Rossi's tenth win of the year, a new record for Yamaha riders in the 500cc/MotoGP class. It was his 78th premier-class podium, putting him third equal in the all-time rostrum list with Eddie Lawson, behind only the inevitable Mick Doohan and Giacomo Agostini. The victory also made him the only rider ever to have won ten or more races in a season on two different makers' bikes (he clocked up eleven wins with Honda in 2002).

Amid yet another blizzard of record-breaking Rossi stats it's worth remembering that it was less than two weeks since Melandri had suffered that nasty foot injury in Japan and he was far from fully recovered. It was just as good, if not better a performance than his Assen assault on Fortress Rossi. Valentino himself was moved to call it the best race of the year. And he used to say he didn't like the Losail track.

RACE RESULTS

RACE DATE October 1st
CIRCUIT LENGTH 3.343 miles
NO. OF LAPS 22
RACE DISTANCE 73.546 miles
WEATHER Dry, 34°C
TRACK TEMPERATURE 48°C
WINNER Valentino Rossi
FASTEST LAP 1m 56.917s,
102.706mph, Loris Capirossi (record)
PREVIOUS LAP RECORD 1m 59.293s,
100.888mph, Colin Edwards, 2004

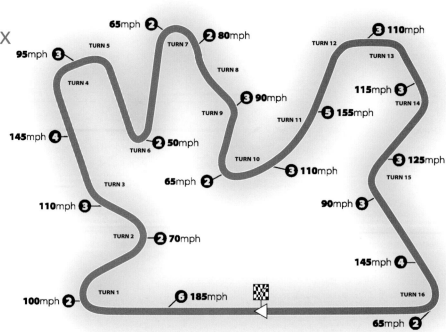

QUALIFYING

	Rider	Nationality	Team	Qualifying	Pole +	Gap
1	Capirossi	ITA	Ducati Marlboro Team	1m 56.917s		
2	Gibernau	SPA	Movistar Honda MotoGP	1m 56.994s	0.077s	0.077s
3	Rossi	ITA	Gauloises Yamaha Team	1m 57.360s	0.443s	0.366s
4	Edwards	USA	Gauloises Yamaha Team	1m 57.447s	0.530s	0.087s
5	Melandri	ITA	Movistar Honda MotoGP	1m 57.468s	0.551s	0.021s
6	Checa C.	SPA	Ducati Marlboro Team	1m 57.481s	0.564s	0.013s
7	Nakano	JPN	Kawasaki Racing Team	1m 57.697s	0.780s	0.216s
8	Hayden	USA	Repsol Honda Team	1m 57.872s	0.955s	0.175s
9	Elias	SPA	Fortuna Yamaha Team	1m 57.902s	0.985s	0.030s
10	Tamada	JPN	Konica Minolta Honda	1m 58.317s	1.400s	0.415s
11	Roberts	USA	Team Suzuki MotoGP	1m 58.329s	1.412s	0.012s
12	Hopkins	USA	Team Suzuki MotoGP	1m 58.527s	1.610s	0.198s
13	Biaggi	ITA	Repsol Honda Team	1m 58.622s	1.705s	0.095s
14	Barros	BRA	Camel Honda	1m 59.084s	2.167s	0.462s
15	Rolfo	ITA	Team D'Antin – Pramac	1m 59.392s	2.475s	0.308s
16	Xaus	SPA	Fortuna Yamaha Team	1m 59.482s	2.565s	0.090s
17	Byrne	GBR	Camel Honda	2m 00.097s	3.180s	0.615s
18	Ellison	GBR	Blata WCM	2m 00.909s	3.992s	0.812s
19	Battaini	ITA	Blata WCM	2m 01.678s	4.761s	0.769s
20	Jacque	FRA	Kawasaki Racing Team			

FINISHERS

1 VALENTINO ROSSI The man himself said it was his best win of the year, and no-one was arguing. Also became the first Yamaha rider ever to win ten races in a year in the top class. Along with team-mate Edwards's fourth place, the result clinched the Teams' World Championship for the Gauloises Yamaha squad.

2 MARCO MELANDRI A brilliant comeback after his foot injury, and his best result since the Dutch TT back in June. Doubly impressive as he didn't have a front-row start and had to get past Hayden and Edwards to reach the leaders. Jumped from fifth to third in the championship and right back in the fight for second place overall.

3 NICKY HAYDEN Rescued what looked like being as bad a weekend as Motegi thanks to changes his crew made after warm-up. Set a new lap record for the second race running and was able to mix it with the leaders, only dropping off their pace in the last couple of laps.

4 COLIN EDWARDS Disappointed he couldn't fight for the win as he'd done in '04, but happy to help clinch the teams' championship. Used the same front tyre as most of the Michelin runners but found he was pushing the front a lot in corners.

5 SETE GIBERNAU A better result than the non-finishes of the three previous rounds, but only just. Top Michelin qualifier and race leader until four laps from the flag when he ran off track following a challenge from team-mate Melandri.

6 CARLOS CHECA Chose a harder compound rear Bridgestone tyre after warm-up so couldn't push hard early on, then had a pretty uneventful ride to sixth place. Held off Nakano to be top Bridgestone finisher.

7 SHINYA NAKANO After a hectic first couple of laps settled in behind Checa's Ducati – they had the same tyres and could run similar lap times but there wasn't a chance to pass. Another consistent, error-free race for his ninth top-ten finish of the year, and a relief after the troubles of the last three races.

8 TONI ELIAS His best finish in MotoGP on a weekend that showed he was regaining his pre-wrist-injury form. Still not happy with his race, mainly because he finds it difficult to press hard early on with a full tank of petrol.

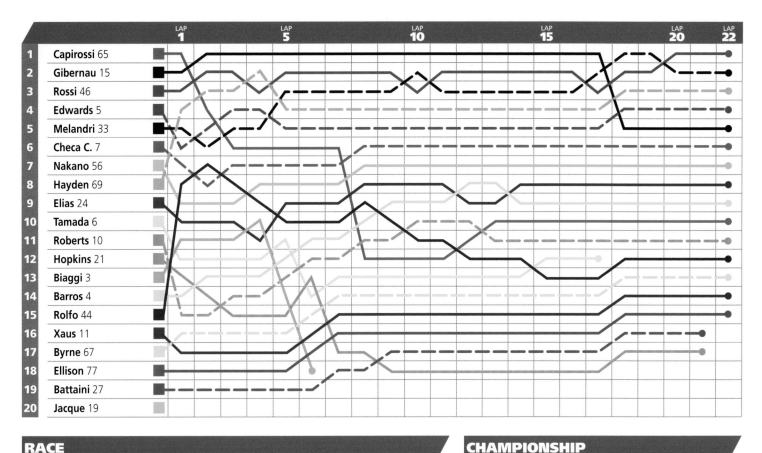

		LAP 1	LAP 5	LAP 10	LAP 15	LAP 20	LAP 22
1	Capirossi 65						
2	Gibernau 15						
3	Rossi 46						
4	Edwards 5						
5	Melandri 33						
6	Checa C. 7						
7	Nakano 56						
8	Hayden 69						
9	Elias 24						
10	Tamada 6						
11	Roberts 10						
12	Hopkins 21						
13	Biaggi 3						
14	Barros 4						
15	Rolfo 44						
16	Xaus 11						
17	Byrne 67						
18	Ellison 77						
19	Battaini 27						
20	Jacque 19						

RACE

	Rider	Motorcycle	Race Time	Time +	Fastest Lap	Average Speed
1	Rossi	Yamaha	43m 33.759s		1m 57.910s	192.634mph
2	Melandri	Honda	43m 35.429s	1.670s	1m 57.939s	195.492mph
3	Hayden	Honda	43m39.295s	5.536s	1m 57.903s	193.938mph
4	Edwards	Yamaha	43m 48.496s	14.737s	1m 58.345s	194.125mph
5	Gibernau	Honda	43m 54.190s	20.431s	1m 58.079s	189.029mph
6	Checa C.	Ducati	44m 05.191s	31.432s	1m 59.177s	195.741mph
7	Nakano	Kawasaki	44m 06.742s	32.983s	1m 58.939s	192.509mph
8	Elias	Yamaha	44m 13.647s	39.888s	1m 59.316s	191.018mph
9	Barros	Honda	44m 15.551s	41.792s	1m 59.434s	191.577mph
10	Capirossi	Ducati	44m 18.011s	44.252s	1m 58.904s	193.876mph
11	Roberts	Suzuki	44m 22.504s	48.745s	1m 59.488s	187.538mph
12	Rolfo	Ducati	44m 35.750s	1m 01.991s	1m 59.951s	194.373mph
13	Byrne	Honda	44m 38.564s	1m 04.805s	2m 00.526s	190.210mph
14	Xaus	Yamaha	44m 47.583s	1m 13.824s	2m 01.194s	187.600mph
15	Ellison	Blata	45m 42.401s	2m 08.642s	2m 02.387s	170.450mph
16	Battaini	Blata	43m 59.063s	1 lap	2m 04.663s	169.020mph
17	Hopkins	Suzuki	44m 38.818s	1 lap	1m 59.724s	190.148mph
	Tamada	Honda	34m 21.723	5 laps	1m 59.764s	192.634mph
	Biaggi	Honda	12m 32.752	16 laps	1m 59.285s	192.385mph

CHAMPIONSHIP

	Rider	Team	Points
1	Rossi	Gauloises Yamaha Team	306
2	Biaggi	Repsol Honda Team	159
3	Melandri	Movistar Honda MotoGP	157
4	Edwards	Gauloises Yamaha Team	152
5	Hayden	Repsol Honda Team	150
6	Capirossi	Ducati Marlboro Team	148
7	Barros	Camel Honda	129
8	Gibernau	Movistar Honda MotoGP	126
9	Checa C.	Ducati Marlboro Team	98
10	Nakano	Kawasaki Racing Team	78
11	Tamada	JIR Konica Minolta Honda	68
12	Roberts	Team Suzuki MotoGP	63
13	Bayliss	Camel Honda	54
14	Hopkins	Team Suzuki MotoGP	53
15	Elias	Fortuna Yamaha Team	51
16	Xaus	Fortuna Yamaha Team	45
17	Jacque	Kawasaki Racing Team	25
18	Hofmann	Kawasaki Racing Team	22
19	Rolfo	Team D'Antin – Pramac	22
20	Goorbergh	JIR Konica Minolta Honda	12
21	Battaini	Blata WCM	6
22	Byrne	Team Roberts/Camel Honda	6
23	Ellison	Blata WCM	5
24	Checa D.	Fortuna Yamaha Team	4

9 ALEX BARROS Much as in Malaysia, never found a front tyre in which he had confidence. Bike and set-up were good, but the conditions and temperature stopped him getting any feel for the front. It made for what he described as his worst weekend of the year, though he did manage to overtake a few people.

10 LORIS CAPIROSSI The first hat-trick of pole positions for a non-Japanese bike since John Kocinski on the Cagiva in 1993–4 but, despite getting the holeshot, Loris rapidly slipped down the order. Lack of grip at the rear was the problem (not under power but on turn in) – if flicked in like normal the rear end just came round on him.

11 KENNY ROBERTS Out-qualified his team-mate and beat him again in the race.

Looked like catching Capirossi towards the end, but nearly crashed when he got within a second of the Ducati.

12 ROBERT ROLFO A great start saw him eighth early on and able to run with the men around him. Much credit goes to new Dunlop tyres which lasted better than earlier in the season. A front-end slide saw Roby run wide in mid-race and then take a few laps to get his rhythm back.

13 SHANE BYRNE The result doesn't look much better than the previous week, but he was much nearer the pace than in Malaysia. Worked more on the bike than his riding and improved with every session. Raced with some pain from his left hand after a coming-together with Checa during warm-up.

14 RUBEN XAUS This time it was the front tyre that was the limiting factor. Went with a harder compound but found if he pushed hard the bike moved around too much and his lap times didn't improve. Settled for a few more points.

15 JAMES ELLISON Raced with a painkilling injection in his injured elbow and was rewarded with a point for the first time since China – and he wasn't lapped.

16 FRANCO BATTAINI Another solid ride and another finish.

17 JOHN HOPKINS Suffered the same tyre problems as Capirossi and ran off track trying to catch Barros and team-mate Roberts. Came in for new rubber, a tyre the team had only

tried once in practice but that Kenny was using, which immediately saw him turning competitive lap times.

NON-FINISHERS

MAKOTO TAMADA Another bad weekend chasing front-end set-up, followed by a breakdown in the race: he felt a vibration and then the bike just stopped.

MAX BIAGGI Dreadful qualifying followed by electrical problems in the race. Max was as depressed as he's been all season, saying the bike had been uncompetitive since Motegi. 'It's impossible to turn into a corner, this is not just the set-up of the machine, it's something bigger

than that. With the set-up you can improve. It's more than just an engine-braking problem.'

NON-STARTERS

OLIVIER JACQUE Kawasaki's replacement crashed in the first practice session but got on his spare bike. Later felt some discomfort in his lower back and went for treatment but seized up completely on the Clinica Mobile massage table. An X-ray revealed nothing but the team suspected some rib damage.

ALEX HOFMANN Replaced by Jacque due to a broken ankle sustained at Motegi.

TROY BAYLISS Replaced by Byrne due to injuries sustained before Motegi.

PHILLIP ISLAND
AUSTRALIAN GRAND PRIX

ROUND 15

FULL HOUSE

Rossi won again but Hayden made him work for it all the way. The victory also gave Yamaha the constructors' title they so wanted, in their 50th year, to go with their rider and team titles

With the possible exception of his win at Laguna Seca, this was the best race of Nicky Hayden's MotoGP career. Anyone who gives Valentino Rossi something to think about around one of his favourite tracks is doing something right, and Nicky made the Doctor think for the whole weekend. Hayden used to have trouble using his qualifying tyres; not any more. His pole-position lap was, to use one of his own favourite words, awesome. And he pressured Rossi for the entire race, the first time that has happened. It took a masterful piece of trackcraft from Valentino to make the difference in the race, prompting the World

Champion to say that Nicky had been at the same level as him 'and I am at the maximum'. In a pointed remark, given the prevailing paddock debate about young riders getting a break in MotoGP, he then said that Nicky was the future of MotoGP. Marco Melandri could have been included in that remark as well: he followed up his fine ride in Qatar with a combative display and his first-ever fastest lap of a MotoGP race, and was only deprived of a rostrum finish when crafty old Carlos Checa used Ducati power to mug him on the line.

Two of the old guard did not make it past the first session. Kenny Roberts and Loris Capirossi suffered similar crashes at the fearsomely fast first turn. Initially both men thought they'd suffered mechanical failures, but investigation ruled that possibility out. The only other common factor was their use of Bridgestones, and it could be that the right side of the dual-compound tyres didn't get up to working temperature in what were decidedly cool conditions. Whatever the cause, the crashes put both men out of racing for the immediate future. Roberts broke his wrist and wasn't allowed to fly home until Sunday, just to make sure the bang on his head and general beating-up he'd taken in the 120mph highside weren't masking further injury. Immediately paddock gossip turned to whether Kenny had ridden his last MotoGP race. Capirossi had no broken bones, but the beating he'd suffered started bleeding into one lung and he was helicoptered to Melbourne where a drain was inserted. He too was allowed to fly back home, although a doctor from the Clinica Mobile had to accompany him. Not surprisingly, Loris described it as the worst crash of his long career.

Just to give the old hands more to worry about, a media frenzy surrounded the first MotoGP appearance of young Aussie Chris Vermeulen as replacement for Troy Bayliss on the Camel Honda. Chris had just finished second in the World Superbike Championship for Ten Kate Honda and was widely regarded as the best young talent in the class and a sure-fire MotoGP prospect in the near future. British fans first saw the remarkably

Opposite Makoto Tamada having fun

Above Chris Vermeulen getting acquainted with a MotoGP Honda

Below The awesome 200mph downhill charge into Turn 1 – Doohan's Corner

self-assured 17-year-old rider after Barry Sheene advised him to go to the UK to further his career. Now, at 23, with a World Supersport title and that second place in World Superbike under his belt he was making his MotoGP debut at home in Australia. If he felt any extra pressure he didn't show it; in fact he did nothing wrong despite intense scrutiny from the local media. The rest of us were busy comparing his performance, session by session, with that of Shakey Byrne. Come the race Vermeulen made a tentative start, unsure of how the carbon brakes would react early on. He then passed Jacque, Xaus and Hopkins, only to be stalked by the Suzuki man and retaken on the last lap. Everyone was impressed except Chris, who called it 'an okay race, nothing more'.

Up front, a fascinating duel was unfolding. Rossi took the lead on the third lap and tried two or three times to break away: Hayden went with him each time. At half-distance Valentino changed tactics. If, he reasoned, an opponent has a better rhythm than you then that rhythm must be disrupted. Rossi set his fastest lap of the race, 1m 30.505s, on lap 13, then slowed the pace by nearly two seconds over the next three laps. Nicky accepted the invitation and went to the front but could only run high 1m 31s laps, which allowed Melandri and Checa to close in – so Rossi went back to the front. Sure enough, Melandri got past the young American, was quickly repassed, then went by again. When Hayden finally regained second place, with a breathtaking pass going up to Lukey Heights, he was a second adrift of the Doctor.

There was a disturbing episode when Alex Barros crashed towards the end of the race. At first it looked

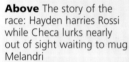

Above The story of the race: Hayden harries Rossi while Checa lurks nearly out of sight waiting to mug Melandri

Below Nicky at speed and ever so slightly sideways

Opposite The last we will see of Kenny Roberts in Suzuki colours; his season ended when he broke a wrist in practice

as if he would just slide at speed across the grass but, when he reached the edge of a gravel trap, he was flipped in the air and tumbled over several sickening times. The Brazilian veteran escaped serious injury but the debate on gravel traps versus tarmac or grass run-off was reignited. Despite what TV pictures suggested, there was no raised lip on the trap. What to do? Grass over the traps or look for a standard size of gravel that won't cause a sliding rider to be tossed into the air?

Rossi described that one-second gap as 'gold'. He was right. Hayden closed on the last lap but couldn't get near enough to attempt a pass. As Nicky said later, you just can't give Rossi a second round here – or anywhere really – with a few laps to go. Valentino had no time for any sort of celebration as he went over the line, save for a frenzied shake of the head, and he was unstinting in his praise of Hayden and the circuit: 'It is an old-style track like Assen and Donington, not designed with a computer.' The victory gave Yamaha the coveted constructors' title but the main reason for Rossi's joy was reaching a total of 11 wins for the season, a feat he had previously achieved with both Aprilia (in 1997) and Honda (in 2002). There was also the extra motivation of most of his pit crew being Australian.

Before the race Jerry Burgess said that the combination he most feared was Checa, the rapid Ducati and its Bridgestone tyres. Sure enough, Carlos was able to run low 1m 31s laps all race, and last time round he attacked Melandri. They swapped positions twice before Checa got a good run out of the final turn and drafted past to take third place. What, everyone including Rossi wondered, would have happened if Loris Capirossi had been fit to race?

Above Mike Hailwood aboard the four-cylinder Honda at the 1966 Isle of Man TT, then also the race that counted as the British round of the World Championship

REASONS TO BE CHEERFUL

Despite Rossi and Yamaha stealing all the headlines, Honda had reason to celebrate at Phillip Island. When Dani Pedrosa won the 250 race they notched up 600 wins in all GP classes, confirming their status as the most successful manufacturer in racing history.

Their first win came in 1961, courtesy of Aussie Tom Phillis, at the Spanish 125 GP held in Barcelona's Monjuich Park; he was riding an RC142 twin and beat second-placed Ernst Degner's two-stroke MZ by over 20 seconds.

Honda's most successful rider is another Aussie, Mick Doohan. He won 54 races, all in the 500cc class, and also scored more points (2298) and set more pole positions (58) than any other Honda rider. Not surprisingly, given Mick's prowess, the NSR500 that he rode to five consecutive world titles is Honda's most successful machine with 132 victories (although the NSR250 is only a few races behind and still going strong). As well as Mick, Wayne

Gardner, Freddie Spencer and Eddie Lawson all became World Champions on the ultimate two-stroke.

Above all, Honda prides itself on being an engineering company, one reason why losing the constructors' title this year hurts so much. One of their proudest achievements came in 1966 when they won the constructors' title in every solo class, as Honda's four-strokes struggled to stem the rising two-stroke tide. That was the year Luigi Taveri won the 125 riders' title on the astounding five-cylinder RC149, Mike Hailwood took 250 victory on the most famous Honda of them all, the six-cylinder RC166, backing that up with the 350 title, and only just failing to wrest the 500cc crown away from MV and Agostini at the first attempt. He was thwarted at the last race by a broken exhaust valve.

PHILLIP ISLAND
AUSTRALIAN GRAND PRIX

ROUND 15

RACE RESULTS

RACE DATE October 16th
CIRCUIT LENGTH 2.764 miles
NO. OF LAPS 27
RACE DISTANCE 74.628 miles
WEATHER Dry, 17°C
TRACK TEMPERATURE 23°C
WINNER Valentino Rossi
FASTEST LAP 1m 29.337s,
111.129mph, Nicky Hayden (record)
PREVIOUS LAP RECORD 1m 31.421s,
108.841mph, Valentino Rossi, 2003

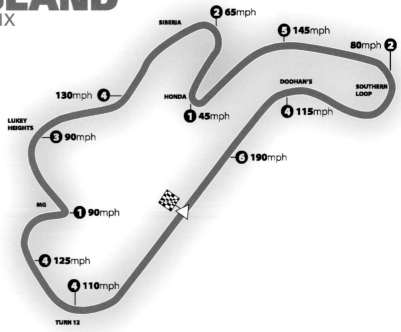

Track map labels: SIBERIA — ❷ 65mph; ❺ 145mph; ❷ 80mph; 130mph ❹; HONDA; DOOHAN'S; SOUTHERN LOOP; ❶ 45mph; ❹ 115mph; LUKEY HEIGHTS; ❸ 90mph; ❻ 190mph; MG; ❶ 90mph; ❹ 125mph; ❹ 110mph; TURN 12

QUALIFYING

	Rider	Nationality	Team	Qualifying	Pole +	Gap
1	Hayden	USA	Repsol Honda Team	1m 29.337s		
2	Rossi	ITA	Gauloises Yamaha Team	1m 29.443s	0.106s	0.106s
3	Gibernau	SPA	Movistar Honda MotoGP	1m 29.729s	0.392s	0.286s
4	Checa C.	SPA	Ducati Marlboro Team	1m 29.775s	0.438s	0.046s
5	Edwards	USA	Gauloises Yamaha Team	1m 29.943s	0.606s	0.168s
6	Biaggi	ITA	Repsol Honda Team	1m 30.070s	0.733s	0.127s
7	Elias	SPA	Fortuna Yamaha Team	1m 30.094s	0.757s	0.024s
8	Melandri	ITA	Movistar Honda MotoGP	1m 30.322s	0.985s	0.228s
9	Tamada	JPN	Konica Minolta Honda	1m 30.624s	1.287s	0.302s
10	Nakano	JPN	Kawasaki Racing Team	1m 30.628s	1.291s	0.004s
11	Hopkins	USA	Team Suzuki MotoGP	1m 30.667s	1.330s	0.039s
12	Barros	BRA	Camel Honda	1m 30.757s	1.420s	0.090s
13	Jacque	FRA	Kawasaki Racing Team	1m 31.079s	1.742s	0.322s
14	Vermeulen	AUS	Camel Honda	1m 31.654s	2.317s	0.575s
15	Xaus	SPA	Fortuna Yamaha Team	1m 31.728s	2.391s	0.074s
16	Rolfo	ITA	Team D'Antin – Pramac	1m 33.495s	4.158s	1.767s
17	Ellison	GBR	Blata WCM	1m 33.673s	4.336s	0.178s
18	Battaini	ITA	Blata WCM	1m 35.933s	6.596s	2.260s
19	Roberts	USA	Team Suzuki MotoGP			
20	Capirossi	ITA	Ducati Marlboro Team			

FINISHERS

1 VALENTINO ROSSI Had to work for his 11th win of the year and was clearly delighted with the victory, which equalled his personal season's best tally of wins and brought Yamaha the constructors' title in their 50th anniversary year. But what seemed to give him most pleasure was winning at a track he loves.

2 NICKY HAYDEN The first time he has gone head to head with Rossi for a whole race; definitely his best showing of the season so far with the possible exception of the win at home in Laguna Seca. The pole-position lap was exceptional, as was his crew's work on Saturday night in getting a race set-up.

3 CARLOS CHECA Used the longevity of his Bridgestones to take third place on the last lap after being dropped by the leaders in the early stages. So pleased with his rostrum finish, which he dedicated to injured team-mate Capirossi, that he declared it 'tasted like a victory'.

4 MARCO MELANDRI In the hunt immediately, despite starting from the third row. Looked to be heading into traction troubles again but, now fully recovered from his Motegi injuries, was able to ride through any problems. Gave Hayden a hard time, enabling Rossi to escape, but outpowered by Checa on the final straight.

5 SETE GIBERNAU His front-row start was a reflection of how well he uses a qualifying tyre, nothing else. Struggled all weekend to find a set-up, challenged Melandri and Checa early on, but eventually finished 10 seconds behind his team-mate.

6 COLIN EDWARDS Never found the pace he'd shown here in pre-season testing. Used Rossi's settings, in desperation, after running out of time and ideas. That gave him too much wheelspin under power even when the front wheel was off the ground which, as he said, wasn't normal.

7 SHINYA NAKANO Had problems after missing a gear early on, which compromised any efforts to pass on the brakes, so forced to follow Tamada and Elias. A wonderfully spirited final lap: overtook Tamada on the fast sweeper out of Siberia and then got enough

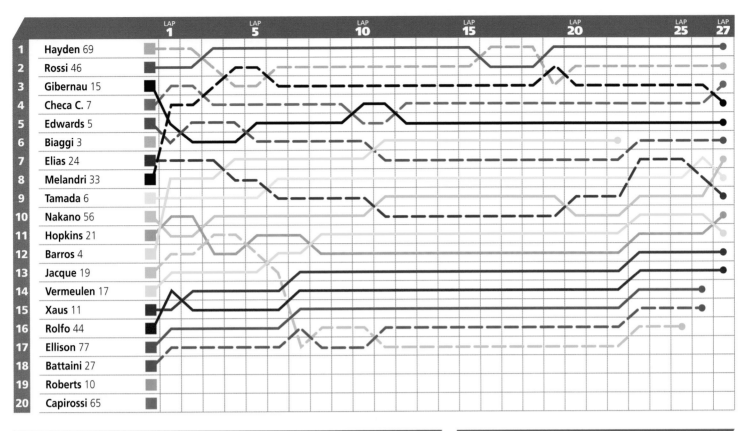

	LAP 1	LAP 5	LAP 10	LAP 15	LAP 20	LAP 25	LAP 27
1 Hayden 69							
2 Rossi 46							
3 Gibernau 15							
4 Checa C. 7							
5 Edwards 5							
6 Biaggi 3							
7 Elias 24							
8 Melandri 33							
9 Tamada 6							
10 Nakano 56							
11 Hopkins 21							
12 Barros 4							
13 Jacque 19							
14 Vermeulen 17							
15 Xaus 11							
16 Rolfo 44							
17 Ellison 77							
18 Battaini 27							
19 Roberts 10							
20 Capirossi 65							

RACE

	Rider	Motorcycle	Race Time	Time +	Fastest Lap	Average Speed
1	Rossi	Yamaha	41m 08.542s		1m 30.505s	196.424mph
2	Hayden	Honda	41m 09.549s	1.007s	1m 30.438s	197.108mph
3	Checa C.	Ducati	41m 12.757s	4.215s	1m 30.837s	203.943mph
4	Melandri	Honda	41m 12.774s	4.232s	1m 30.332s	198.972mph
5	Gibernau	Honda	41m 22.630s	14.088s	1m 30.657s	198.599mph
6	Edwards	Yamaha	41m 41.742s	33.200s	1m 30.827s	198.102mph
7	Nakano	Kawasaki	41m 53.597s	45.055s	1m 31.892s	194.249mph
8	Tamada	Honda	41m 53.645s	45.103s	1m 31.644s	195.865mph
9	Elias	Yamaha	41m 53.646s	45.104s	1m 31.618s	196.113mph
10	Hopkins	Suzuki	41m 58.802s	50.260s	1m 32.170s	195.119mph
11	Vermeulen	Honda	41m 59.239s	50.697s	1m 32.350s	197.170mph
12	Xaus	Yamaha	42m 16.866s	1m 08.324s	1m 32.895s	191.950mph
13	Rolfo	Ducati	42m 40.279s	1m 31.737s	1m 33.841s	191.701mph
14	Ellison	Blata	41m 43.184s	1 lap	1m 34.145s	182.443mph
15	Battaini	Blata	42m 15.829s	1 lap	1m 36.195s	180.019mph
16	Jacque	Kawasaki	41m 56.837s	2 laps	1m 32.282s	195.554mph
	Barros	Honda	33m 47.165s	5 laps	1m 31.119s	198.785mph
	Biaggi	Honda				

CHAMPIONSHIP

	Rider	Team	Points
1	Rossi	Gauloises Yamaha Team	331
2	Hayden	Repsol Honda Team	170
3	Melandri	Movistar Honda MotoGP	170
4	Edwards	Gauloises Yamaha Team	162
5	Biaggi	Repsol Honda Team	159
6	Capirossi	Ducati Marlboro Team	148
7	Gibernau	Movistar Honda MotoGP	137
8	Barros	Camel Honda	129
9	Checa C.	Ducati Marlboro Team	114
10	Nakano	Kawasaki Racing Team	87
11	Tamada	JIR Konica Minolta Honda	76
12	Roberts	Team Suzuki MotoGP	63
13	Hopkins	Team Suzuki MotoGP	59
14	Elias	Fortuna Yamaha Team	58
15	Bayliss	Camel Honda	54
16	Xaus	Fortuna Yamaha Team	49
17	Jacque	Kawasaki Racing Team	25
18	Rolfo	Team D'Antin – Pramac	25
19	Hofmann	Kawasaki Racing Team	22
20	Goorbergh	JIR Konica Minolta Honda	12
21	Battaini	Blata WCM	7
22	Ellison	Blata WCM	7
23	Bryne	Team Roberts/Camel Honda	6
24	Vermeulen	Camel Honda	5

drive off the last corner to pass Elias on the run to the flag.

8 MAKOTO TAMADA Lost feel and confidence in his front tyre, especially in left-hand corners, but dropped out of his 1m 31s rhythm after seven laps. Had an entertaining dice with Elias, whom he beat in a photo finish.

9 TONI ELIAS Lost two places on the last lap, which did not please him at all, but in practice, qualifying and the race showed that the old aggression and speed were coming back.

10 JOHN HOPKINS Got bumped by Nakano on the second lap and passed by both Kawasakis. The Suzuki's lack of acceleration made it difficult to close the gap with no slipstream to use. Followed Vermeulen when he came past and then mugged him on the last lap.

11 CHRIS VERMEULEN Slow off the start and cautious on the first lap because of lack of experience with carbon brakes. Raced well, making a couple of overtakes, and enjoyed himself. Learnt a lot, especially about making tyres last in longer races – and impressed team boss, Sito Pons.

12 RUBEN XAUS Lost a lot of ground in the early laps when he couldn't keep the bike on line. The team reckoned it was his best race of the year, though, and that he might even be starting to enjoy riding the M1.

13 ROBERTO ROLFO Another great start, but his Dunlops didn't like the cold track which severely limited Roby's options. Unable to hold a line early on when the tank was full.

14 JAMES ELLISON After a fraught qualifying, which included a couple of uncharacteristic crashes, James was more than happy to pick up a couple of points.

15 FRANCO BATTAINI Didn't quite make the qualifying cut-off time but included in the line-up at Race Direction's discretion. Finished over 30 seconds behind his team-mate but still scored a point.

16 OLIVIER JACQUE Had so many problems with stability on the brakes that he ran straight on at the Honda hairpin twice in practice, once in warm-up and twice in the race. Pitted to change the rear tyre, then rejoined the race, going past Hopkins and Vermeulen to prove a point.

NON-FINISHERS

ALEX BARROS Another bad qualifying, but a brutal first lap promoted him from twelfth to eighth, and he got up to sixth before losing the front end in the fast right at Hayshed. It looked to be a harmless, if very fast, slide across the grass until he hit a gravel trap and was flung in the air. Spleen damage was feared but the tests were negative.

MAX BIAGGI Very fast in warm-up after another disappointing qualifying, but fell on the brakes first time round, going into the right-hand hairpin of Honda corner.

NON-STARTERS

KENNY ROBERTS Crashed at Turn 1 on Friday morning and broke his left wrist. Back home in the States, further damage was discovered that put him out of the final two races of the year.

LORIS CAPIROSSI Crashed in a near-identical manner to, and in the same session as, Roberts. Was found to have bleeding on a lung and had a drain inserted. Flown home to Italy with a doctor from the Clinica Mobile a few days later, but certainly unfit for Turkey and probably Valencia too.

ALEX HOFMANN Broke an ankle in Japan.

TROY BAYLISS Broke his wrist in training before Japan.

MAIDEN VOYAGE

New track, new winner: Marco Melandri was fast from the first session and went on to dominate the race. Rossi had a terrible weekend, by his standards, but still came second

The second brand-new circuit of the year provided a few surprises, not least for the riders who found themselves confronted with a fresh contender for the title of season's fastest corner. The right-hand kink in the back straight is taken flat out in fifth gear, although Valentino Rossi reported that late in the race, with a light fuel load, he attacked it in sixth. The previous title-holder, Turn 1 at Le Mans, is taken on a closed throttle as riders prepare to brake for the Dunlop chicane, whereas the Turkish corner is attacked with the twistgrip well and truly open. Both Olivier Jacque and Colin Edwards ran wide on the exit and pronounced themselves shaken and stirred.

In contrast with Shanghai, this year's other new venue, Istanbul Park features complex multi-apex corners and more changes of elevation than any circuit

Above Valentino Rossi prepares to lay rubber out of the fastest corner in the calendar

Below Shinichi Ito replaced Capirossi for Ducati but had a very short GP

Opposite Barros and Tamada's dice livened up the closing stages

this side of Spa or Oulton P. The riders loved it, with the possible exception of the flip/flop chicane that ends the lap. Turkish motorcycle racing fans have only ever seen one-day meetings, so there weren't many people in the stands on Friday and Saturday. However, race day saw a steady stream of spectators coming in, many of them on motorcycles, despite what were considered high ticket prices. The circuit has been built with government money for two reasons. First, Turkey's desire to join the EU, and secondly to encourage people to visit the country. Tourism is a major plank of the economy.

All three tyre companies found it a challenge, too. Michelin arrived with dual-compound tyres using soft rubber on the right and hard on the left, only to find that all the right-hand corners loaded the rear tyre so much they actually needed the harder rubber on the right side. Bridgestone thought that, as no-one had tested here, they'd be at least as competitive as they'd been in Brno; they were wrong as well. Dunlop's runners also had problems. The unusually large time gaps between riders in the practice sessions spoke eloquently of crews tussling with a complex circuit for which they had no data.

Whatever the problems most people – and especially the Yamaha teams – were having, Fausto Gresini's Movistar Honda riders hit the ground running. Marco Melandri and Sete Gibernau dominated practice, with the Italian's form slightly more impressive due to the number of fast laps he was able to string together. It looked for a time as if Marco would secure his first MotoGP pole position, but Sete again demonstrated his mastery of the qualifying tyre. Unfortunately, he also reacquainted himself with the little devil that was sitting on his shoulder in Germany and Qatar.

Gibernau was leading the race , just like at the Sachsenring, and leading his team-mate too, as at Losail, when he ran off the track at the second left-hander and dropped to sixth place. That put Melandri in front, tailed by Hayden, with only Rossi looking as if he could mount a challenge. Valentino tried very, very hard but the Honda was visibly more agile in the slow corners and Marco's lead was never seriously challenged. The young Italian even had enough in hand to set the fastest lap five laps from the flag.

The fact that Rossi was anywhere near Melandri was a tribute to his own determination and his team's

work ethic. After Saturday morning practice, which Valentino declared the worst session of his entire career, he was ready to go home. The team had been moving from his normal settings back towards those used by Elias and Edwards. In simple terms, Rossi puts a lot of weight on the front and the other two use set-ups that place more weight on the rear. His team started unloading the front, but after they'd run through Ohlins's entire range of spring rates they were still well off the pace. In Sunday morning warm-up, therefore, they found they needed to go in the other direction, working back to their usual setting and on to an extreme version of it. The bike was far from perfect, tyre choice was hurried, yet Valentino found the motivation to race hard despite professing himself tired and still on Melbourne time after the Australian GP the previous weekend. He certainly looked shattered after qualifying. Yamaha have made giant strides with the M1 this year but here was proof that the Honda remains a much easier bike to set up and a more forgiving machine to ride. Valentino was of the opinion that the track did not like Yamahas, and watching Colin Edwards in practice you certainly saw a bike misbehaving seriously in corners. The World Champion looked as smooth as ever, though; only a stopwatch would indicate he was off the pace.

Melandri wasn't the only young gun to make an impression in Turkey. Toni Elias, still recovering from his arm injuries, put in his best-ever qualifying and backed it up with his best race in MotoGP. He'd been making a habit of latching onto fast guys at the end of qualifying (it was Toni who distracted Rossi in Australia; the Doctor slowed, then Xaus got past and messed up his final qualifying lap). This time Elias got a tow from Edwards, and when he saw the Texan in the paddock minutes later he flashed a toothy grin, waved and shouted 'Thank you, Colin!' On Sunday Toni added injury to insult by overtaking Colin on the run to the flag to take sixth place. Mind you, he had to overtake the same group twice to do it, as he ran off track at the same place as Gibernau. He told Tech 3 team manager Hervé Poncharal that he was glad about the off-track excursion because it made the race much more fun.

Marco Melandri's win opened up clear blue water between himself and Nicky Hayden in the fight for second place in the championship. The Italian was obviously pleased about that, but considerably more excited by his first win in MotoGP. He said it was a totally different experience from his 125 and 250 victories. Marco hadn't known it was Valentino pressuring him because he'd asked his crew not to put any names on his pit board, just time gaps. However, he had a little difficulty in communicating these feelings as his voice had all but gone: he'd spent most of the slow-down lap screaming with joy inside his crash helmet.

Top Right Nicky Hayden talked the talk and then he walked the walk: three podiums in a row for the first time in his career

Left An ecstatic Marco Melandri shouting himself hoarse on the slowdown lap

DECISIONS, DECISIONS

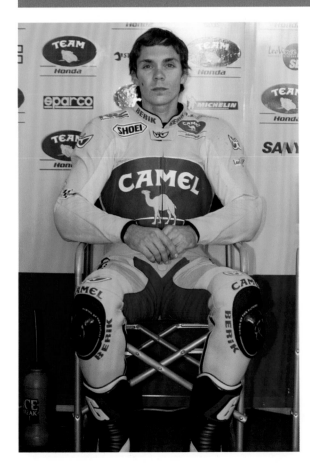

In his second ride for the Honda Pons team, Chris Vermeulen continued to impress. It wasn't just his very respectable pace but the way he went about his work. He got faster with every session, didn't make any mistakes, and impressed the Pons team more than a little with his feeling for the bike.

The only problem on Chris's personal radar was that HRC wanted him to stay in the World Superbike Championship for another year. But, as one Italian member of the Pons squad put it, 'He has tasted the chocolate and honey; he wants to stay here!'

Chris faced a choice that may determine the course of his whole career. When UK fans first saw him as a 17-year-old, over here on Barry Sheene's advice, we thought we were lookng at a future World Champion. If he were to stay in Superbike, as Honda wanted, he would surely be a favourite for the 2006 world title, but could he afford to wait another year before going

to MotoGP? He had a factory Honda at the Suzuka 8 Hours on Michelins and took a while to adapt.

Sito Pons won his world titles on Hondas and has always run Hondas in his team, so it would be highly unlikely that they would go against the wishes of HRC and sign a rider the factory wanted to deploy elsewhere.

And of course there's the question of whether there would be a vacancy in a Honda team in 12 months' time. So Chris decided to sign for Suzuki.

It cannot have been easy to go against the wishes of Honda – a rider rarely gets a second chance with HRC. However, Chris calculated that joining a factory, as opposed to satellite, team would give him greater input into the bike being designed for the 800cc class limit that arrives in 2007. It's undoubtedly a high-risk strategy, especially for a young rider, but the taste of that chocolate and honey is obviously pretty special.

ISTANBUL
TURKISH GRAND PRIX

ROUND 16

RACE RESULTS

RACE DATE October 23rd
CIRCUIT LENGTH 3.311 miles
NO. OF LAPS 22
RACE DISTANCE 72.838 miles
WEATHER Dry, 19°C
TRACK TEMPERATURE 25°C
WINNER Marco Melandri
FASTEST LAP 1m 53.111s,
105.373mph, Marco Melandri (record)

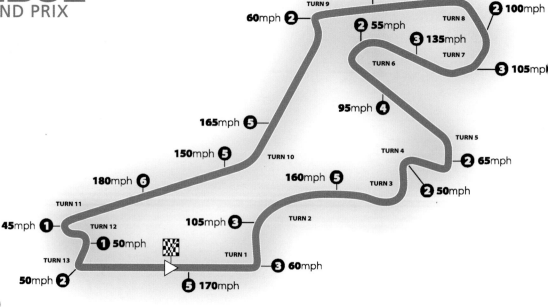

QUALIFYING

	Rider	Nationality	Team	Qualifying	Pole +	Gap
1	Gibernau	SPA	Movistar Honda MotoGP	1m 52.334s		
2	Melandri	ITA	Movistar Honda MotoGP	1m 52.463s	0.129s	0.129s
3	Hayden	USA	Repsol Honda Team	1m 52.976s	0.642s	0.513s
4	Rossi	ITA	Gauloises Yamaha Team	1m 53.177s	0.843s	0.201s
5	Edwards	USA	Gauloises Yamaha Team	1m 53.219s	0.885s	0.042s
6	Elias	SPA	Fortuna Yamaha Team	1m 53.230s	0.896s	0.011s
7	Tamada	JPN	Konica Minolta Honda	1m 53.667s	1.333s	0.437s
8	Barros	BRA	Camel Honda	1m 53.719s	1.385s	0.052s
9	Checa C.	SPA	Ducati Marlboro Team	1m 53.836s	1.502s	0.117s
10	Nakano	JPN	Kawasaki Racing Team	1m 54.023s	1.689s	0.187s
11	Vermeulen	AUS	Camel Honda	1m 54.217s	1.883s	0.194s
12	Biaggi	ITA	Repsol Honda Team	1m 54.358s	2.024s	0.141s
13	Jacque	FRA	Kawasaki Racing Team	1m 54.407s	20.73s	0.049s
14	Hopkins	USA	Team Suzuki MotoGP	1m 54.434s	2.100s	0.027s
15	Ito	JPN	Ducati Marlboro Team	1m 54.669s	2.335s	0.235s
16	Xaus	SPA	Fortuna Yamaha Team	1m 55.414s	3.080s	0.745s
17	Rolfo	ITA	Team d'Antin Pramac	1m 55.838s	3.504s	0.424s
18	Ellison	GBR	Blata WCM	1m 56.576s	4.242s	0.738s
19	Battaini	ITA	Blata WCM	1m 58.417s	6.083s	1.841s

FINISHERS

1 MARCO MELANDRI Right from the first session, at a brand-new track, there was never any doubt who'd win. It was his first MotoGP victory (and his first win since the 250 race at Valencia in 2002). A dominating performance in practice was followed by the fastest lap of the race as he controlled Rossi's attack.

2 VALENTINO ROSSI Never gives up: dreadful practice and a bad start meant he was struggling all weekend, yet he was Melandri's only challenger. The fact he was competitive was as much down to the Yamaha pit crew as the rider, but it was Rossi who dug in on Sunday.

3 NICKY HAYDEN Said after qualifying he didn't really have the rhythm to win, yet got on the podium for the third time in a row, for the first time in his GP career. Melandri's victory put him at a serious disadvantage in the fight for second place overall, however.

4 SETE GIBERNAU Like his team-mate was fast from the first session, and his mastery of the qualifying tyres put him on pole, his fourth of the season. All that good work was negated when he ran off track early on while leading – and again it was Melandri pressuring him: shades of Qatar.

5 CARLOS CHECA By far the best Bridgestone runner but suffered from a bad start, then lack of rear grip part way through

the race. Rider and team agreed that it was probably the best result they could have expected with the package they had.

6 TONI ELIAS Aside from Melandri, Elias was the hero of the weekend. Put in his best-ever MotoGP qualifying, then improved on his previous top race result despite running off track and losing three places on lap 14. He'd got them all back by the flag.

7 COLIN EDWARDS Just as lost as Rossi in practice. Tried to adapt his riding for the race but reverted to his Superbike days at the start before segueing into a style more akin to his distant 250 days: 'I set my fastest lap on lap 20, which tells its own story.'

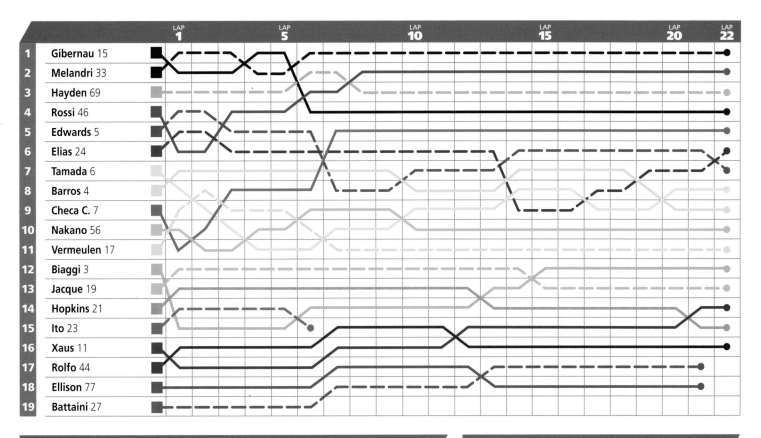

		LAP 1	LAP 5	LAP 10	LAP 15	LAP 20	LAP 22
1	Gibernau 15						
2	Melandri 33						
3	Hayden 69						
4	Rossi 46						
5	Edwards 5						
6	Elias 24						
7	Tamada 6						
8	Barros 4						
9	Checa C. 7						
10	Nakano 56						
11	Vermeulen 17						
12	Biaggi 3						
13	Jacque 19						
14	Hopkins 21						
15	Ito 23						
16	Xaus 11						
17	Rolfo 44						
18	Ellison 77						
19	Battaini 27						

RACE

	Rider	Motorcycle	Race Time	Time +	Fastest Lap	Average Speed
1	Melandri	Honda	41m 44.139s		1m 53.111s	183.375mph
2	Rossi	Yamaha	41m 45.652s	1.513s	1m 53.305s	187.165mph
3	Hayden	Honda	41m 51.012s	6.873s	1m 53.270s	183.561mph
4	Gibernau	Honda	41m 56.559s	12.420s	1m 53.414s	183.561mph
5	Checa C.	Ducati	42m 11.102s	26.963s	1m 53.507s	187.911mph
6	Elias	Yamaha	42m 13.244s	29.105s	1m 53.901s	184.928mph
7	Edwards	Yamaha	42m 13.394s	29.255s	1m 54.327s	184.493mph
8	Tamada	Honda	42m 17.484s	33.345s	1m 54.358s	186.668mph
9	Barros	Honda	42m 17.929s	33.790s	1m 54.376s	184.182mph
10	Nakano	Kawasaki	42m 28.364s	44.225s	1m 54.965s	183.126mph
11	Vermeulen	Honda	42m 30.238s	46.099s	1m 55.136s	183.375mph
12	Biaggi	Honda	42m 34.323s	50.184s	1m 55.383s	183.685mph
13	Jacque	Kawasaki	42m 40.905s	56.766s	1m 55.363s	184.804mph
14	Xaus	Yamaha	42m 45.499s	1m 01.360s	1m 55.948s	180.392mph
15	Hopkins	Suzuki	42m 47.530s	1m 03.391s	1m 55.235s	180.640mph
16	Rolfo	Ducati	43m 01.793s	1m 17.654s	1m 56.012s	185.612mph
17	Battaini	Blata	42m 09.486s	1 lap	1m 59.639s	168.834mph
18	Ellison	Blata	42m 47.811s	1 lap	1m 56.135s	172.562mph
	Ito	Ducati				

CHAMPIONSHIP

	Rider	Team	Points
1	Rossi	Gauloises Yamaha Team	351
2	Melandri	Movistar Honda MotoGP	195
3	Hayden	Repsol Honda Team	186
4	Edwards	Gauloises Yamaha Team	171
5	Biaggi	Repsol Honda Team	163
6	Gibernau	Movistar Honda MotoGP	150
7	Capirossi	Ducati Marlboro Team	148
8	Barros	Camel Honda	136
9	Checa C.	Ducati Marlboro Team	125
10	Nakano	Kawasaki Racing Team	93
11	Tamada	JIR Konica Minolta Honda	84
12	Elias	Fortuna Yamaha Team	68
13	Roberts	Team Suzuki MotoGP	63
14	Hopkins	Team Suzuki MotoGP	60
15	Bayliss	Camel Honda	54
16	Xaus	Fortuna Yamaha Team	51
17	Jacque	Kawasaki Racing Team	28
18	Rolfo	D'Antin MotoGP – Pramac	25
19	Hofmann	Kawasaki Racing Team	22
20	Goorbergh	JIR Konica Minolta Honda	12
21	Vermeulen	Camel Honda	10
22	Battaini	Blata WCM	7
23	Ellison	Blata WCM	7
24	Bryne	Team Roberts/Camel Honda	6

8 MAKOTO TAMADA Lacked confidence in his front tyre early on – just as he has for much of the year. Was able to make progress once the rubber got up to temperature.

9 ALEX BARROS Not 100 per cent fit after his horrific crash at Phillip Island a week previously, but refused to use injury as an excuse for a poor result. Suffered from lack of grip in the second half of the race, probably because he couldn't push hard enough in practice to get his set-up right.

10 SHINYA NAKANO Reported serious wheelspin from lap 10 onwards, which meant he couldn't fight as he wished. From then on it was a lonely race and a battle to hold his concentration.

11 CHRIS VERMEULEN Achieved his ambition of beating one of the other Hondas home, but lost touch with his dice after making a mistake. Didn't seem much happier with this result than the Phillip Island one, but the Pons crew were mightily impressed with him and his ability to communicate and learn.

12 MAX BIAGGI A dreadful, humiliating weekend for the four-times World Champion in what was his 200th consecutive GP start. Has not missed a race since the French GP of 1992, but there's no getting away from the fact that he was miles off the pace throughout.

13 OLIVIER JACQUE Like his team-mate Nakano he suffered from tyre problems, specifically lack of edge grip in some of the long corners. Like Edwards, he altered his riding style to get the bike home.

14 RUBEN XAUS A bad start was followed by a heartening race, but the fact he set his best time on the very last lap of the race tells you all you need to know.

15 JOHN HOPKINS A heavy cold and tyre troubles conspired to produce the most lacklustre weekend of the year: his fastest lap of the very first session was only 0.05s slower than his best race lap. Half way through the race his rear tyre blistered and from then on it was damage limitation.

16 ROBERTO ROLFO Another man handicapped by tyre troubles. Roby reported a good start but after just five laps began to have grip problems with his rear tyre and dropped back from a good dice.

17 FRANCO BATTAINI A workmanlike job, although he also had tyre problems.

18 JAMES ELLISON Came into the pits to change his rear tyre after suffering a serious lack of grip.

NON-FINISHERS

SHINICHI ITO Riding as a replacement for Capirossi but jumped the start, didn't pull into the pits for a ride-through penalty and so was black flagged.

NON-STARTERS

ALEX HOFMANN Replaced by Jacque due to the broken ankle sustained at Motegi. Kawasaki's announcement that Nakano's contract was being renewed meant Alex was out of a job in 2006.

TROY BAYLISS Replaced by Vermeulen due to injuries sustained before Motegi.

LORIS CAPIROSSI Replaced by Ito due to injuries sustained at Phillip Island.

KENNY ROBERTS Out due to injuries sustained at Phillip Island. Suzuki announced during the weekend that Kenny would be leaving the team at the end of the season.

RICARDO TORMO
VALENCIAN GRAND PRIX

ROUND **17**

YOUNG GUNS

Melandri and Hayden showed that they are the future of MotoGP, while the paddock wondered if they'd seen the last of Max Biaggi and Alex Barros

The now traditional end-of-season party had an end-of-era feel about it. The established stars (or dead wood, depending on your point of view) were well and truly put in the shade by the youngsters. At 26, Valentino Rossi gets upset if you refer to him as old. On track, Marco Melandri backed up his maiden win in Turkey with a faultless display and set the best lap of the race for the third consecutive GP. Nicky Hayden was nearly as impressive, racking up his fourth consecutive rostrum and harrying Melandri all the way. Off track, interest was centred on the intentions of 250cc championship runner-up Casey Stoner. At the start of the weekend he was reckoned to have a Yamaha MotoGP seat on offer; by Sunday night that had morphed into a three-year Honda deal, starting with a Honda Pons ride in 2006.

The issue was complicated by a falling-out between Honda and the team's sponsor, Camel, over Biaggi: Camel wanted him, Honda didn't. That dispute was spiced up by reports that Max had said some extremely uncomplimentary things about Honda in a TV interview after Turkey. HRC went as far as to get the item translated and sent to Japan. It transpired that it was the interviewer who was trying to inflame the issue and that Max's answers had, in the words of HRC MD Horiike-san, been 'very correct'. He did mention that he was very disappointed with Max's results, though, and after the race Camel, who wanted to retain Max, announced that they'd been unable to reach an agreement with Honda.

There was so much going on it was almost possible to overlook the fact that Valentino Rossi was going to start the race from 15th place on the grid. A big crash halfway round his first flying lap on a qualifying tyre destroyed his Yamaha and caused him to swallow 'about a kilo of gravel'. The stage finally seemed set for pole-man Sete Gibernau to lift the Curse of Qatar and win in front of his home crowd, before announcing his move to Ducati.

It all looked to be going well. The two Movistar Honda riders started from the first two places on the grid, at the most difficult track of the year for passing. Melandri got away quickest, with Gibernau settling into third behind Hayden. The pattern lasted just three laps: early in the fourth Sete suddenly slowed, his engine smoking. It has sometimes been difficult to sympathise with the Spanish rider when he's in what Rossi has christened his 'Hollywood mode', but not this time. He

parked the bike and sunk to his knees before marching away without making any comment. A couple of hours later Ducati announced that Gibernau would be riding in red in 2006. The Spanish media immediately latched gleefully on to any passing conspiracy theory to explain that rarest of motorcycle racing events – the sight of a works Honda blowing up.

HRC could comfort themselves with the fact that two more of their bikes were running five seconds in front of the field. Remarkably, the man in third place was Valentino Rossi, looking slightly unfamiliar in the retro red and white corporate Yamaha livery to celebrate the company's 50th birthday. On Saturday night he'd said he was racing for a top-five finish, but he was into fifth place by lap four. A first lap of superbly controlled aggression raised him to eighth. On lap three he got past Barros. Next time round it was Capirossi – and then Gibernau's demise put him fifth. Biaggi was the victim on lap five, Checa on lap six; Rossi was then looking at five seconds' worth of empty tarmac between himself and the leaders, too much even for the Doctor. Valentino was the fastest man on track for a good part of the second half of the race but could still only take fractions of a second out of the leaders each lap. He was three seconds behind at the flag.

Melandri later said that he'd contemplated letting Hayden through so he could study his strengths and weaknesses, but then decided that it might be a bit too difficult to get back to the front. His instinct was correct. The American probed and experimented with different lines in an effort to find a way past, but it was apparent that it would take a mistake from Melandri for

Opposite Colin Edwards in Yamaha's 50th anniversary livery wheelying his way to eighth place

Below Biaggi, Capirossi and Barros entertain the 124,000 raceday crowd

Above Hayden pressured him all the way, but Melandri simply didn't make a mistake

Below Kenny Roberts Snr contemplates life after Proton and KTM. Will he be back?

him to get by. Two equally matched riders on the same machines at this track will always produce this sort of race. In the final couple of laps Nicky tried a radical deep entry to a tight right-hander to try and get a run on his rival. 'Just like a good dirt-tracker going up high and cutting back,' said the spectating Randy Mamola, but Marco didn't fall for it.

Once Rossi had beaten off a persistent Checa, the best action on track was the Biaggi/Barros/Capirossi dice. Loris reckoned he was 80 per cent fit after his Australian crash but, judging from the way he looked, that was a highly optimistic over-estimate. He'd had to drive to Valencia as the airlines didn't yet consider him

fit enough to fly, then to add financial insult to injury his motorhome caught fire just outside St Tropez and burnt down to its axles. Alex Hofmann also returned from long-term injury to ride his last race for Kawasaki. He was fortunate to escape the first-turn melee that sent Roby Rolfo's Ducati cartwheeling down the track. Shinya Nakano, on the other Kawasaki, was also held up. The Japanese had suffered two crashes in practice and his left hand had taken a hard knock; he raced with the help of painkilling injections but went home straight after the race, missing the testing scheduled for the next day. Who said the season was over?

Two familiar faces were participating in their first MotoGP races for a while: Ryuichi Kiyonari took over Troy Bayliss's Camel Honda and Kurtis Roberts rode his dad's Proton V5, as Team KR raced for the first time since Brno. 'Kiyo' was on the Honda because of Chris Vermeulen's decision to sign for Suzuki, and looked the part: he'd had the best part of a season on an RCV after the death of Daijiro Kato in 2003 (his previous experience had been limited to the Supersport class). Now, after two years on a factory bike in the British Superbike Championship and a win in the Suzuka 8 Hours he looked very much at home on a MotoGP bike. Kurtis struggled throughout on the Banbury-built V5, out-qualifying only Battaini's WCM, then racing with James Ellison and Ruben Xaus before being stopped by a mechanical problem. With the absence of big brother Kenny and the parlous state of his father's team it was impossible not to wonder if there would be a Roberts in the paddock in 2006. That really would mark the end of an era.

SMELLS LIKE TEAM SPIRIT

Anyone who thought that the World Champion would take it easy for the last race as he looked forward to some time off in Ibiza should have been around him after qualifying for the race. He wasn't desperately happy with the way he and the team had worked and said that they must do better: 'In future we have to make sure we work better in practice.'

A bit harsh you might feel, given no-one got more pole positions than Rossi over the season. His crew chief Jerry Burgess was unflustered. They had gone wrong, he suggested after the race, on their front fork settings and hadn't understood the problem until Sunday morning. Burgess offered an interesting insight into the way the team works. He did admit that as the championship was wrapped up they might have tried some ideas that wouldn't have been countenanced under normal circumstances. In one session, Sete Gibernau was the fastest man doing lap times of, say,

1min 33.0sec while Rossi was 0.6sec slower. Examination of the data didn't reveal any of the problems Valentino was complaining about, which meant the team were making educated guesses about their next move.

The situation was that Valentino, having run into a problem that didn't let him ride the bike as he wanted to, had adjusted some element of his riding style to cope, thereby effectively rendering it invisible on the data. Jerry and the team realised that they had to go back to slower laps, say in the 1min 33.9sec area, to see what Valentino was complaining about and work out what to do about it.

The story illustrates just what an inexact science setting up a racing motorcycle still is, even in the MotoGP era. It also underlines the value of an experienced and clear-thinking crew chief and the trust a rider must have in him. That's one lesson that certainly hasn't been lost on Valentino.

Below The final rostrum of 2005 could very well bear a strong resemblance to the first few in 2006. Rossi versus the fast youngsters was the pattern for the end of '05 and there's no reason to suppose it'll be different next time round

RICARDO TORMO
VALENCIAN GRAND PRIX

ROUND 17

RACE RESULTS

RACE DATE November 6th
CIRCUIT LENGTH 2.483 miles
NO. OF LAPS 30
RACE DISTANCE 74.493 miles
WEATHER Dry, 21°C
TRACK TEMPERATURE 32°C
WINNER Marco Melandri
FASTEST LAP 1m 33.043s,
96.075mph, Marco Melandri (record)
PREVIOUS LAP RECORD 1m 33.317s,
95.793mph, Valentino Rossi, 2003

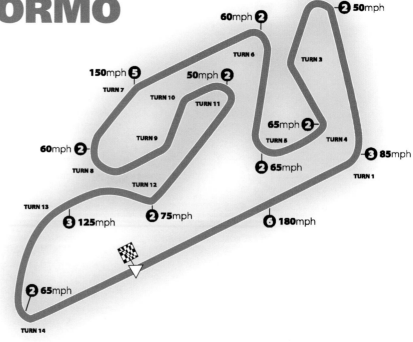

QUALIFYING

	Rider	Nationality	Team	Qualifying	Pole +	Gap
1	Gibernau	SPA	Movistar Honda MotoGP	1m 31.874s		
2	Melandri	ITA	Movistar Honda MotoGP	1m 32.111s	0.237s	0.237s
3	Hayden	USA	Repsol Honda Team	1m 32.217s	0.343s	0.106s
4	Checa C.	SPA	Ducati Marlboro Team	1m 32.374s	0.500s	0.157s
5	Biaggi	ITA	Repsol Honda Team	1m 32.384s	0.510s	0.010s
6	Edwards	USA	Gauloises Yamaha Team	1m 32.456s	0.582s	0.072s
7	Capirossi	ITA	Ducati Marlboro Team	1m 32.482s	0.608s	0.026s
8	Barros	BRA	Camel Honda	1m 32.518s	0.644s	0.036s
9	Nakano	JPN	Kawasaki Racing Team	1m 32.663s	0.789s	0.145s
10	Tamada	JPN	Konica Minolta Honda	1m 32.682s	0.808s	0.019s
11	Hopkins	USA	Team Suzuki MotoGP	1m 32.785s	0.911s	0.103s
12	Hofmann	GER	Kawasaki Racing Team	1m 32.966s	1.092s	0.181s
13	Elias	SPA	Fortuna Yamaha Team	1m 33.005s	1.131s	0.039s
14	Aoki	JPN	Team Suzuki MotoGP	1m 33.393s	1.519s	0.388s
15	Rossi	ITA	Gauloises Yamaha Team	1m 33.503s	1.629s	0.110s
16	Kiyonari	JPN	Camel Honda	1m 33.846s	1.972s	0.343s
17	Xaus	SPA	Fortuna Yamaha Team	1m 34.874s	3.000s	1.028s
18	Rolfo	ITA	Team d'Antin Pramac	1m 34.978s	3.104s	0.104s
19	Ellison	GBR	Blata WCM	1m 35.158s	3.284s	0.180s
20	Roberts	USA	Team Roberts	1m 35.374s	3.500s	0.216s
21	Battaini	ITA	Blata WCM	1m 35.712s	3.838s	0.338s

FINISHERS

1 MARCO MELANDRI First man to open his account with back-to-back victories since Kenny Roberts at the start of 1999: this time it was a flag-to-flag win under sustained, race-long pressure from Hayden. Secured the runner-up spot in the championship but, just as important, his final four races marked him out as the fastest of the young pretenders to Rossi's crown, and most likely to challenge the Doctor's domination in 2006.

2 NICKY HAYDEN Got over the disappointment of not winning pretty quickly. Attacked Melandri incessantly and cleverly but never given a chance to pass. Finished with 89 more points than in 2004, a matter for

some satisfaction (even though there was one more race), as was his run of four rostrums to finish the year.

3 VALENTINO ROSSI Just another run-of-the-mill miracle: from 15th on the grid to fifth on lap four and third at the end, plus fastest man on track for most of the second half of the race. Actually looked displeased with the result and gave a short lecture on how 'we have to make sure we work better in practice'. Anyone still doubting his motivation?

4 CARLOS CHECA Desperately wanted to finish his year with Ducati by getting on the rostrum, but hit some chatter when his Bridgestones came good and he started to push. Stayed with Rossi for a while but the chatter got bad towards the end and he had to slow.

5 ALEX BARROS Came out on top of a hectic three-man dice, but when he finally got past Biaggi it was too late to attack Checa. A great comeback from his nasty Australian crash – and maybe his last hurrah in the top class of bike racing?

6 MAX BIAGGI A sad end to a sad year, not helped by a crash in morning warm-up. Never matched his lap times from Saturday and finished 21s down on the winner, compared to 0.4s 12 months before. As with most of the races, complained of serious patter at the front.

7 LORIS CAPIROSSI For a man not fit to travel by air, this was an heroic ride. Started the weekend with a crash, then involved in a hectic three-way fight in the race, only easing

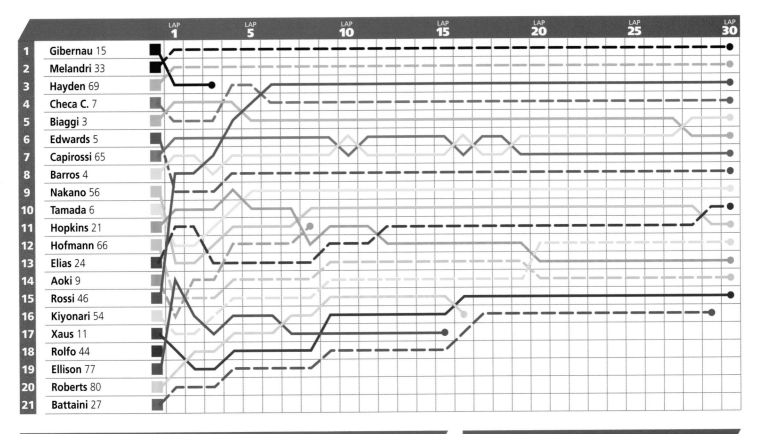

		LAP 1	LAP 5	LAP 10	LAP 15	LAP 20	LAP 25	LAP 30
1	Gibernau 15							
2	Melandri 33							
3	Hayden 69							
4	Checa C. 7							
5	Biaggi 3							
6	Edwards 5							
7	Capirossi 65							
8	Barros 4							
9	Nakano 56							
10	Tamada 6							
11	Hopkins 21							
12	Hofmann 66							
13	Elias 24							
14	Aoki 9							
15	Rossi 46							
16	Kiyonari 54							
17	Xaus 11							
18	Rolfo 44							
19	Ellison 77							
20	Roberts 80							
21	Battaini 27							

RACE

	Rider	Motorcycle	Race Time	Time +	Fastest Lap	Average Speed
1	Melandri	Honda	46m 58.152s		1m 33.043s	191.456mph
2	Hayden	Honda	46m 58.249s	0.097s	1m 33.106s	192.634mph
3	Rossi	Yamaha	47m 01.111s	2.959s	1m 33.199s	193.750mph
4	Checa C.	Ducati	47m 16.870s	18.718s	1m 33.622s	194.866mph
5	Barros	Honda	47m 18.858s	20.706s	1m 33.896s	192.510mph
6	Biaggi	Honda	47m 19.406s	21.254s	1m 34.008s	194.804mph
7	Capirossi	Ducati	47m 21.294s	23.142s	1m 33.845s	195.362mph
8	Edwards	Yamaha	47m 23.830s	25.678s	1m 33.880s	192.014mph
9	Tamada	Honda	47m 34.862s	36.710s	1m 33.962s	194.184mph
10	Elias	Yamaha	47m 37.268s	39.116s	1m 34.393s	192.758mph
11	Nakano	Kawasaki	47m 39.288s	41.136s	1m 33.981s	192.076mph
12	Kiyonari	Honda	47m 43.843s	45.691s	1m 34.272s	192.324mph
13	Hopkins	Suzuki	47m 44.659s	46.507s	1m 34.391s	188.418mph
14	Hofmann	Kawasaki	47m 48.008s	49.856	1m 34.553s	188.976mph
15	Xaus	Yamaha	48m 17.595s	1m 19.443s	1m 35.790s	188.79mph
16	Battaini	Blata	47m 35.920s	1 lap	1m 36.839s	178.002mph
	Roberts	Proton KR	26m 11.135s	14 laps	1m 35.599s	184.76mph
	Ellison	Blata	24m 15.926s	15 laps	1m 36.030s	179.800mph
	Aoki	Suzuki	12m 47.346s	22 laps	1m 34.159s	190.650mph
	Gibernau	Honda	4m 47.317s	27 laps	1m 33.476s	192.138mph
	Rolfo	Ducati				

CHAMPIONSHIP

	Rider	Team	Points
1	Rossi	Gauloises Yamaha Team	367
2	Melandri	Movistar Honda MotoGP	220
3	Hayden	Repsol Honda Team	206
4	Edwards	Gauloises Yamaha Team	179
5	Biaggi	Repsol Honda Team	173
6	Capirossi	Ducati Marlboro Team	157
7	Gibernau	Movistar Honda MotoGP	150
8	Barros	Camel Honda	147
9	Checa C.	Ducati Marlboro Team	138
10	Nakano	Kawasaki Racing Team	98
11	Tamada	JIR Konica Minolta Honda	91
12	Elias	Fortuna Yamaha Team	74
13	Roberts	Team Suzuki MotoGP	63
14	Hopkins	Team Suzuki MotoGP	63
15	Bayliss	Camel Honda	54
16	Xaus	Fortuna Yamaha Team	52
17	Jacque	Kawasaki Racing Team	28
18	Rolfo	D'Antin MotoGP – Pramac	25
19	Hofmann	Kawasaki Racing Team	24
20	Goorbergh	JIR Konica Minolta Honda	12
21	Vermeulen	Camel Honda	10
22	Battaini	Blata WCM	7
23	Ellison	Blata WCM	7
24	Bryne	Team Roberts/Camel Honda	6

up in the last two laps. Delighted to have finished sixth in the championship: 'If I hadn't come here I would have finished eighth.' That's a real racer talking.

8 COLIN EDWARDS By his own admission, not a stellar end to the season. Started to push hard in the middle of the race but abused his tyres too much catching the men in front. As in Turkey, was trying to ride the bike like a 250 or a Superbike. Already looking forward to next year.

9 MAKOTO TAMADA Made early progress after a bad start. Got to within a second of Edwards by lap 10, then his rear tyre started to spin and he lost the confidence to push at 100%.

10 TONI ELIAS Started the weekend badly, never finding solutions to the problems that

dogged him on Friday. A disappointing end to the season, especially after his heroics in Istanbul.

11 SHINYA NAKANO Two falls on Friday resulted in a painful left hand. Add in a motor whose characteristics don't suit the tight track and that's a recipe for a tough weekend, which is exactly what Shinya had. Not helped by the first-turn melee that ended in Rolfo's crash.

12 RYUICHI KIYONARI Replaced Troy Bayliss at Camel Honda and impressed everyone except himself: 'We could have done a lot better.'

13 JOHN HOPKINS Pushed hard in the first few laps, elbowed his way into the top ten, then hit grip problems with his rear tyre.

Changed his style to cope and, once he'd worked out what to do, was running at a good pace in the closing stages.

14 ALEX HOFMANN Had to avoid Rolfo's tumbling Ducati in Turn 1, then latched on to the back of the midfield group. His leg, broken only seven weeks ago, wouldn't allow him to press so decided an overtaking attempt would be too dangerous. Achieved his objective of scoring points on his last Kawasaki ride and declared it was the maximum his body would let him do.

15 RUBEN XAUS A difficult end to a difficult year. Didn't enjoy himself on the bike very much, but at least got in the points.

16 FRANCO BATTAINI Another workmanlike ride to bring the WCM home.

NON-FINISHERS

KURTIS ROBERTS Back on the Proton V5 as Team Roberts returned to MotoGP for the first time since Brno. Got past Ellison to take 16th place on lap seven only to have his gearbox pack up.

JAMES ELLISON Held off Roberts and Xaus in the early laps and was enjoying the dice when the WCM engine broke a valve at half-distance.

NOBUATSU AOKI Suzuki's test rider stood in as replacement for the injured Kenny Roberts. Was outracing team-mate Hopkins when the bike stopped: the team reported an electrical malfunction. Not a just reward for his riding.

SETE GIBERNAU Started from pole and looking good in third when his motor let go on the fourth lap. Proof that when your luck is out it's really out. He walked straight out of the track: next stop Ducati.

ROBERTO ROLFO Came together with Nakano on the first lap and was sent flying. It was a nasty-looking crash and Roby was lucky to escape injury.

NON-STARTERS

TROY BAYLISS Absent due to injuries sustained before the Japanese GP.

KENNY ROBERTS Absent due to injuries sustained in practice for the Australian GP.

WORLD CHAMPIONSHIP CLASSIFICATIONS

MOTOGP

	Rider	Nation	Motorcycle	SPA	POR	CHN	FRA	ITA	CAT	NED	USA	GBR	GER	CZE	JPN	MAL	QAT	AUS	TUR	VAL	Points
1	Rossi	ITA	Yamaha	25	20	25	25	25	25	25	16	25	25	25	-	20	25	25	20	16	367
2	Melandri	ITA	Honda	16	13	16	13	13	16	20	-	9	10	-	11	20	13	25	25		220
3	Hayden	USA	Honda	-	9	7	10	10	11	13	25	-	16	11	9	13	16	20	16	20	206
4	Edwards	USA	Yamaha	7	10	8	16	7	9	16	20	13	8	9	10	6	13	10	9	8	179
5	Biaggi	ITA	Honda	9	16	11	11	20	10	10	13	-	13	16	20	10	-	-	4	10	173
6	Capirossi	ITA	Ducati	3	7	4	9	16	4	6	6	10	7	20	25	25	6	-	-	9	157
7	Gibernau	SPA	Honda	20	-	13	20	-	20	11	11	-	20	-	-	11	11	13	-		150
8	Barros	BRA	Honda	13	25	5	-	9	13	9	-	16	11	13	-	8	7	-	7	11	147
9	Checa C.	SPA	Ducati	6	11	-	-	11	5	7	-	11	-	8	13	16	10	16	11	13	138
10	Nakano	JPN	Kawasaki	11	8	-	8	6	7	8	7	-	10	4	-	-	9	9	6	5	98
11	Tamada	JPN	Honda	8	-	-	-	8	-	2	9	9	6	6	16	4	-	8	8	7	91
12	Elias	SPA	Yamaha	4	2	2	7	-	-	-	3	7	4	2	7	5	8	7	10	6	74
13	Roberts	USA	Suzuki	-	4	-	3	1	1	-	2	20	5	5	8	9	5	-	-	-	63
14	Hopkins	USA	Suzuki	2	-	9	-	5	-	3	8	5	-	3	11	7	-	6	1	3	63
15	Bayliss	AUS	Honda	10	5	-	6	3	8	5	10	-	-	7	-	-	-	-	-	-	54
16	Xaus	SPA	Yamaha	-	6	6	4	2	6	4	5	-	3	-	6	1	2	4	2	1	52
17	Jacque	FRA	Kawasaki	-	-	20	5	-	-	-	-	-	-	-	-	-	-	-	3	-	28
18	Rolfo	ITA	Ducati	1	3	-	1	-	2	-	-	6	2	-	-	3	4	3	-	-	25
19	Hofmann	GER	Kawasaki	5	-	-	-	4	-	-	4	8	-	1	-	-	-	-	-	2	24
20	Goorbergh	NED	Honda	-	-	10	2	-	-	-	-	-	-	-	-	-	-	-	-	-	12
21	Vermeulen	AUS	Honda	-	-	-	-	-	-	-	-	-	-	-	-	-	-	5	5	-	10
22	Battaini	ITA	Blata	-	-	-	-	-	-	-	-	-	1	-	5	-	1	-	-	-	7
23	Ellison	GBR	Blata	-	1	3	-	-	-	-	-	-	-	-	-	-	1	2	-	-	7
24	Byrne	GBR	Proton/Honda*	-	-	-	-	-	-	-	1	-	-	-	-	2*	3*	-	-	-	6
25	Kiyonari	JPN	Honda	-	-	-	-	-	-	-	-	-	-	-	-	-	-	-	4		4
26	Checa D.	SPA	Yamaha	-	-	-	-	-	3	1	-	-	-	-	-	-	-	-	-	-	4
27	Ukawa	JPN	Moriwaki	-	-	1	-	-	-	-	-	-	-	-	-	-	-	-	-	-	1

CONSTRUCTOR

	Motorcycle	SPA	POR	CHN	FRA	ITA	CAT	NED	USA	GBR	GER	CZE	JPN	MAL	QAT	AUS	TUR	VAL	Points
1	Yamaha	25	20	25	25	25	25	25	20	25	25	25	10	20	25	25	20	16	381
2	Honda	20	25	16	20	20	20	20	25	16	20	16	20	13	20	20	25	25	341
3	Ducati	6	11	4	9	16	5	7	6	11	7	20	25	25	10	16	11	13	202
4	Kawasaki	11	8	20	8	6	7	8	7	8	10	4	-	-	9	9	6	5	126
5	Suzuki	2	4	9	3	5	1	3	8	20	5	5	11	9	5	6	1	3	100
6	Blata	-	1	3	-	-	-	-	-	-	1	-	5	-	1	2	-	-	13
7	Proton KR	-	-	-	-	-	-	-	1	-	-	-	-	-	-	-	-	-	1
8	Moriwaki	-	-	1	-	-	-	-	-	-	-	-	-	-	-	-	-	-	1

TEAM

	Team	SPA	POR	CHN	FRA	ITA	CAT	NED	USA	GBR	GER	CZE	JPN	MAL	QAT	AUS	TUR	VAL	Points
1	Gauloises Yamaha Team	32	30	33	41	32	34	41	36	38	33	34	10	26	38	35	29	24	546
2	Repsol Honda Team	9	25	18	21	30	21	23	38	-	29	27	29	23	16	20	20	30	379
3	Movistar Honda MotoGP	36	13	29	33	13	36	31	11	-	29	10	-	11	31	24	38	25	370
4	Ducati Marlboro Team	9	18	4	9	27	9	13	6	21	7	28	38	41	16	16	11	22	295
5	Camel Honda	23	30	5	6	12	21	14	10	16	11	20	-	10	10	5	12	15	220
6	Kawasaki Racing Team	16	8	20	13	10	7	8	11	8	10	5	-	-	9	9	9	7	150
7	Fortuna Yamaha Team	4	8	8	11	2	9	5	8	7	7	2	13	6	10	11	12	7	130
8	Team Suzuki MotoGP	2	4	9	3	6	1	3	10	25	5	8	19	16	5	6	1	3	126
9	Konica Minolta Honda	8	-	10	2	8	-	2	9	9	6	6	16	4	-	8	8	7	103
10	Team D'Antin – Pramac	1	3	-	1	-	2	-	-	6	2	-	-	3	4	3	-	-	25
11	Blata WCM	-	1	3	-	-	-	-	-	-	1	-	5	-	1	3	-	-	14
12	Team Roberts	-	-	-	-	-	-	-	1	-	-	-	-	-	-	-	-	-	1

125cc

	Rider	Nation	Points
1	Thomas Luthi	SWI	242
2	Mika Kallio	FIN	237
3	Gabor Talmacsi	HUN	198
4	Mattia Pasini	ITA	183
5	Marco Simoncelli	ITA	177
6	Fabrizio Lai	ITA	141
7	Julian Simon	SPA	123
8	Tomoyoshi Koyama	JPN	119
9	Hector Faubel	SPA	113
10	Manuel Poggiali	RSM	107
11	Mike Di Meglio	FRA	104
12	Sergio Gadea	SPA	68
13	Pablo Nieto	SPA	64
14	Joan Olive	SPA	60
15	Alvaro Bautista	SPA	47

250cc

	Rider	Nation	Points
1	Daniel Pedrosa	SPA	309
2	Casey Stoner	AUS	254
3	Andrea Dovizioso	ITA	189
4	Aoyama Hiroshi	JPN	180
5	Jorge Lorenzo	SPA	167
6	Sebastian Porto	ARG	152
7	Alex De Angelis	RSM	151
8	Randy De Puniet	FRA	138
9	Hector Barbera	SPA	120
10	Sylvain Guintoli	FRA	84
11	Yuki Takahashi	JPN	77
12	Alex Debon	SPA	67
13	Roberto Locatelli	ITA	61
14	Simone Corsi	ITA	59
15	Mirko Giansanti	ITA	36

Gregorio Lavilla
BSB Champion

WINNING RIDERS KNOW
www.driversknow.co.uk

Thomas Luthi
125cc World Champion

Dani Pedrosa
250cc World Champion

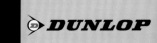

WIN TWO GOLD & SILVER PASSES TO A 2006 MotoGP RACE OF YOUR CHOICE. WORTH UP TO £1000. TO ENTER, VISIT:

www.haynes.co.uk

Just visit the Haynes website and follow the instructions there on how to enter our free prize draw. No purchase is necessary. The draw closes on 1 March 2006.

The fabulous prize will allow you to experience the excitement of a MotoGP race from the most exclusive location in the finest style.

A Gold Pass gives you access on Sunday/Race Day and a Silver Pass on Saturday/Qualifying practice day.

Our lucky prize winner will receive a full Gold & Silver package for two people for any race on the 2006 MotoGP calendar.

Subject to availability – no travel or hotel costs or other expenses are included.

Best Location and Exclusive Privileges

Situated at the heart of the action, either directly above the Pit Lane or in a smart village area, VIP Village puts you as close as you can get to the world's top motorcycle racers.

Privileged Parking, excellent views, race coverage on closed-circuit TV, Pit Lane Walk, Paddock Tour, Service Road Tour and complimentary Official Programme on Sunday.

The VIP Village Game will offer all guests the chance to win the possibility to view races from the pit wall, a service road tour and one of the many licensed MotoGP products.

Best Service and Excellent Cuisine

Hospitality is of the highest quality, from the buffet breakfast in the morning to gourmet lunch and afternoon petit fours, with a complimentary bar all day.

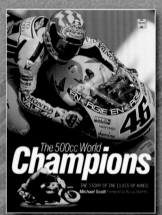
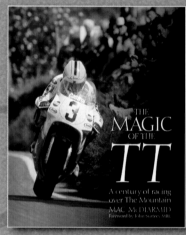
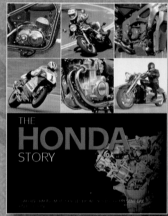
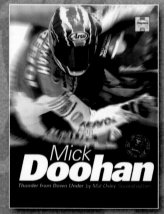
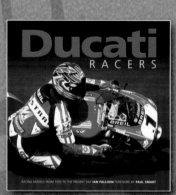
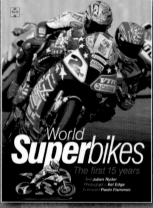
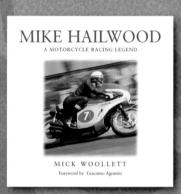

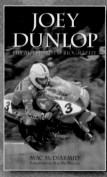

RIDERS FOR HEALTH 2004–5

by Barry Coleman

Co-founder & joint CEO, Operations – Riders for Health

It seems a long time now since the boy Mamola and I stepped off that Boeing 707 in Mogadishu, Somalia. It was in 1988, and the beginning of the idea for Riders (now MotoGP's official charity) was born. It has taken all that time – or, you could say, that little time – to establish our non-governmental organisation as a serious player in the field of global development.

And however you look at it, we have only just begun. Saving the world, or even just its biggest continent, has always been known to be a bit of a struggle. It's a struggle for Mohale, AJ and the teams in Africa, and it's a struggle for Andrea and her glamorous assistant Jeanette in the paddock.

In some ways, 2005 was the year in which Riders went global, and a lot of that's thanks to you all – the people in the MotoGP paddock and its supporters and fans. Your support has helped us make such a recognisable difference in Africa that early in 2005 the management was summoned to Washington to receive a 'global' award. We were declared by the Global Health Council to have shown the rest of the world the way to work in best practice in health anywhere on the planet – something for us all to be pretty proud of. But before we review the year in Riders, it might be helpful to remember why we do it and why it started.

Some people think we decided it might be a good

AT A GLANCE
Riders in 2005

Number of motorcycles in
Riders-managed fleets
770

People reached by health
workers using Riders-
managed fleets
6,500,000

People trained at
Riders' Academy
370

Countries in which Riders
operates (Gambia, Nigeria,
Zimbabwe and Kenya)
4

Number of organisations in
health using Riders' services
(tackling HIV/AIDS, malaria,
tuberculosis, polio, maternal
and infant mortality, etc.)
38

Number of people
employed in UK
14

Number of people
employed in Africa
128

Below Gambian
health worker Manyo
Gibba on her rounds

idea to help the process of delivering health care in Africa by buying and sending motorcycles for health workers to ride. And some people know that we just don't do that. In fact, that's where and why we came in. All sorts of presumably well-intentioned people had already had that thought and, because there's so little connection between a thought and reality, they have sent motorcycles to Africa by the million. What they didn't think of was that it might be good idea to look after them. Or, more to the point, to train someone, somewhere in the 'system', to make sure that they would run for a few years without adding to the Great Junkpile of Africa. Riders, however, have made sure that now, when motorcycles and other vehicles are donated to the areas of Africa in which we work, they're kept running day in, day out, for years and years. If we didn't do this, millions more people would continue to die of easily preventable or treatable diseases.

That's the problem we work on and we know how to solve it. But that doesn't mean to say it's actually solved. It takes about a year to set up one of our programmes – and that's working flat out with everything going to plan. So our job has become twofold. One is explaining morning, noon and night that humankind hasn't yet invented a vehicle that runs itself, or one that doesn't wear out its vital parts in the course of its natural mechanical life. The other is putting in place vehicle management systems invented and developed by us that allow motorcycles (or anything else) to run for years in precisely the way God and the Japanese intended.

That's the point of Riders. We preach and do the godly thing of clearing the way for vehicles to work normally, however harsh the conditions, and we train

their riders and drivers to allow them to do it by not T-boning baobab trees or driving over Victoria Falls.

We can do this because we're motorcyclists and we come from the great worldwide community of motorcyclists. All motorcycles used for sport operate in harsh conditions. Being ridden at the limit by Valentino Rossi or routinely projected at a snarling rock face by Dougie Lampkin asks a lot of a motorcycle. And yet we don't expect them to break down. So out there in the wilds of rural Africa, motorcycles run by Riders and ridden by riders trained by Riders simply don't break down. This is one of the most important unsung developments in Africa over the past 15 years. Because it means that all the other vital, life-saving things developed in those 15 years can, at last, be delivered. And who did that? We did. We motorcycle fans.

So, to the year 2005. In some ways, it was the year in which we became an overnight success. At the same time as the world was focusing on 'making poverty history', the key people in development were realising that it can't be done without managed transport. Riders' submission was included in Blair's Africa commission report, where it says unequivocally that health systems in Africa need an integrated fleet of vehicles (eg motorcycles, trucks, sidecar ambulances) and proper maintenance training for health workers.

Then there was the Global Health Council award and also another kind of useful recognition. At precisely the moment the season came to an end with Valentino's victory parade and another *Dia de los Campeones* at Valencia, Riders was starring in a movie in America – in fact, more than a movie. *Time* magazine and a major US Public Broadcasting System station, WGBH, conspired with others to bring the question of global health (or lack of it) to a worldwide audience in a pretty big way. There was a three-day conference in New York attended by a relatively select group of global development bigwigs and Bono and us. And there was a networked six-hour marathonashow narrated by Brad Pitt and screened over three days which showed, with music and rather fetching costume drama, the pioneering work of everyone ever concerned with global health from Louis Pasteur to Bono – and us!

Recognition means a lot in the humanitarian field. It's recognition inside the motorcycle community that has enabled the FIM, Dorna, Donington Park and the fans themselves to become such staunch supporters of Riders. In the first place, no-one knew what we did or why we did it. But, gradually, the Day of Champions became a major event in itself (we have done 12 now and this year's was the biggest success yet, raising over £170,000 – thank you all, so much) and people have

begun to trust not just Riders but Riders' events.

That's probably why Enduro Africa sold out almost as soon as it was announced from the stage at DoC. In this amazing event, which will take place in November 2006, 100 motorcyclists, including celebrities, will tour the breathtaking bits of South Africa and Lesotho and end up delivering their off-road bikes to health workers in the Riders' programme in Zimbabwe (to add, among others, to the 75 XL125s donated by Honda). We hope this will be the first of many. If it is, by 2010 Zimbabwe will be the first country in Africa to have every public health worker completely and reliably mobile forever.

That's what you have done. That's what coming to Day of Champions means. And, don't forget, one mobile motorcycling health worker can reach 20,000 people on a regular basis to prevent everything from HIV/AIDS to bubonic plague. In fact, when you do the maths it works out at only nine euros to reach 100 people with regular health care for a whole year. That's a bargain.

You may remember that *MCN*'s Motorcyclist of the Year a couple of years back was Jenifer Mutede, an environmental health technician from Makoni district in Zimbabwe. Jenifer's life is amazing. She travels tirelessly from village to village, barely seeing a normal road, criss-crossing her terrain like a slow-motion enduro rider. She knows her villages – now – because she has been able to visit them. In the old days, she could never reach them by walking. She couldn't even look at them on the map. There's no map. One day, perhaps there will be.

In Zimbabwe, there's a problem with inflation, now running at about 400 per cent. There are fuel shortages and the traditional poverty endured by rural and urban communities has got very much worse. But the great Riders' Zimbabwe fleet, Ngwarati Mashonga presiding, continues to grow and continues to deliver the goods. Not least because HRC, encouraged by what they had seen Andrea and Jeanette bringing about in the MotoGP paddock, persuaded Honda back home to donate 75 motorcycles to the programme. They're all now at work, saving lives in a big way in the districts of Chegutu and Gutu. The health workers using them have reported dramatic decreases in outbreaks of disease in their areas, simply because they've been able to reach all their communities more regularly. Thank you, Honda.

The Riders IAVM in Zimbabwe (our International Academy of Vehicle Management) continues to have fantastic results in its dedicated training of anyone working with transport in harsh conditions. The school, run by Alfred Gonga, takes in a wide range of delegates, from the manager of one tiny mission hospital to the fleet manager for a ministry of health.

In Nigeria we now service all the UN vehicles based in and around the capital, Abuja, as well as keeping the polio-eradication fleet on the road in spite of its alarming age. With a bit of luck, we may be on the way to adding a very serious motorcycle fleet to our existing programme. Can't do without them. Segun Adeyemo is now in charge in that fair country.

In the Gambia Therese Drammeh presides over an innovative and fast-growing programme. As well as looking after all the ministry of health's needs, we run motorcycles for a lot of valuable NGOs, including Sight Savers, one of our favourite partners. This means, simply, that people who would otherwise be blind have their sight restored because Sight Savers know what they're doing and we change motorcycle filters on time. One

important step forward in the Gambia this year was the introduction of the amazing 'Uhuru' sidecar into the programme, supported by Rotary clubs both in the UK and the Gambia. This follows a similar initiative in Zimbabwe, where the Uhuru (designed by an old sidecar racer, of course) is actually manufactured.

The MotoGP paddock played a very direct part in the Gambia programme during the year. From the Kawasaki team came engineer Hamish Jamieson, who spent 12 months thinking not about how to get another second a lap for Shinya Nakano, but about how to get still better performances out of the Riders' technicians who look after nine-horsepower motorcycles. Hamish had a very hot little workshop in one corner of the compound and two very dedicated disciples learning all the things you have to know to keep a whole fleet of bikes working at optimum performance. Hamish was the perfect trainer. He inspired his team and gave them a new kind of confidence. We are hoping he will consider another spell with us soon.

So, another year and another significant step forward. The message is getting through: if people want to save the continent of Africa and stop people dying of pointless medieval diseases, there will have to be very large fleets of very well-managed motorcycles taking public health workers out into every corner. Change those air filters or go blind or die from bubonic plague. Now which is it going to be?

Thank you all for getting us this far and helping us to get Africa on track – now let's keep it going!

Above With the help of Suzi Perry, the top price at the DoC auction was realised by Makoto Tamada's 'Batman Returns' leathers: £5,100

Below Developed by Riders for Health, the Uhuru sidecar being filmed for the WGBH/PBS series on global health

WIN

A FABULOUS RIDE WITH RANDY MAMOLA ON THE DUCATI TWO-SEAT MotoGP BIKE

IN ASSOCIATION WITH **RIDERS FOR HEALTH**

What's the most frequently asked question in the MotoGP paddock? It's 'How do I get a ride with Randy Mamola on the two-seat Ducati?' Team members ask it, journalists ask it, spectators ask it and VIP visitors ask it.

The simple answer is that you can't buy one from anywhere in the world (the privilege is normally reserved for celebrities, VIPs and famous sports people) except through the amazing African development charity Riders for Health – the official charity of MotoGP. Even then, because the spectacular rides are in such high demand, you have to be able to make a sizeable donation to Riders (about £2,500). Randy is co-founder of Riders and knows just how much of a difference can be made in Africa with the money someone is willing to pay to ride with him at GP speeds on a GP circuit.

Riders for Health will be able to offer more of these rides in 2006. Look out for the chance to bid for them at upcoming auctions or, if you don't fancy risking it in a bidding war, just give Riders a call on 01327 300047 to book one of the limited places. As very few people, however, can afford the kind of donation necessary, we at Haynes Publishing have made it possible for one lucky purchaser of this book to win one of these amazing rides – for free!

All you have to do is answer the simple question below, clip the little triangular coupon off the bottom corner of the rear inner flap of the dustjacket, and send it with your answer to the address below. Then wait to hear when during the weekend of the British GP (29 June to 2 July 2006) you'll be getting on the back of the only two-seat MotoGP machine in existence and blasting down towards Redgate and the Craner Curves, behind a man who won 13 GPs on three different makes of motorcycle. Three laps later... well, look at the picture...

This is a one-off opportunity to win one of these once-in-a-lifetime rides. If you want to experience what a MotoGP motorcycle feels like, enter this fantastic competition.

To enter this fabulous competition, all you have to do is answer this question:

In which year did Randy Mamola win his first Grand Prix?

Write your answer on a postcard (or the back of a sealed envelope), stick on the coupon from the back flap of this book's dustjacket, add your name and address, and send to:

Ducati Two-Seater MotoGP Competition, Haynes Publishing (Books Division), Sparkford, Yeovil, Somerset BA22 7JJ

riders

To find out more about Riders for Health and what is being achieved with motorcycles for healthcare delivery in Africa, read the article by CEO Barry Coleman (page 205) and visit

www.riders.org